CHRISTIANS
in the
HOUSE

CHRISTIANS
in the house

NIGEL BOVEY

EGON
Egon Publishers Limited

First published in 1998 by
Egon Publishers Ltd, Royston Road, Baldock, Herts SG7 6NW

Copyright © 1998 The General of The Salvation Army

ISBN 1 899998 39 X

Origination and Reprographics by Climacs Imagin, Baldock, SG7 6NW
Cover design by Stephen Pearson
Printed in England by
Woolnough Bookbinding Ltd, Irthlingborough, NN9 5SE
Cover printed by
Streets Printers, Royston Road, Baldock, Herts SG7 6NW

Contents

The Interviews

Acknowledgments

THE Wild West prospectors of old had quite a life. They hunted out a plot. Staked a claim. Dug around. Sifted their findings. Threw out the dross and jumped for joy when they struck gold! They then handed over the newly found nuggets for polishing and setting before the gems were ready for public view.

As one who has worked the wilds of Westminster and Belfast in the course of unearthing the pearls of wisdom for this series, I'm beginning to appreciate how those old timers must have felt.

I also appreciate the efforts of the team of craftsmen and women who refine and set my discoveries in *The War Cry* week by week.

My thanks go, then, to: Charles King, who as editor continually supports and occasionally battles on my behalf;

Stephen Pearson, production editor, for his professional insight, constructive criticism and dependable opinion. And for his cover design of this book;

Gill Cox, designer, for using her artistic gifts in bringing the interviews to life in the paper;

Joanne Camplin, secretary, for cheerfully transcribing interviews, organising the paperwork and generally making sure I don't miss appointments;

Jenty Fairbank, Trevor Howes, Ray Caddy for checking proofs, Rossia Mockett, for typing interviews and Colin Potter for technical trickery.

My thanks too to: the featured Members of Parliament for their courtesy and generosity in giving me so much of their time – and to their secretaries for making sure they turned up!;

Rt Hon Derek Foster and Canon Donald Gray for their enthusiastic involvement and efforts on my behalf;

Annabel Robson of Hodders for recognising the book's potential and John Street of Egon Publishers for realising it;

Don and Heather Luke for their professional guidance and encouragement;

Ken and Jo Bovey, my parents, and Reg and Stella Poyzer, my in-laws, for their continual love and encouragement;

Janine and Andrew Bovey, for coping with a dad who has had his mind on other things. Now we can play cricket, kids!

Lastly to my wife Maggie, for transcribing interviews and reading proofs, for understanding what's important to me, for being my inspiration. And for having this crazy idea in the first place!

The Speaker

Speaker's House Westminster London SW1A 0AA

It is fairly widely known that each day's proceedings of the House of Commons open with prayers. What is not always appreciated is that these prayers are an official part of the day's business and take place in the Chamber of the House.

These prayers are private. The doors of the chamber close behind the Speaker's Procession and only open again after prayers are over; no TV cameras or microphones are switched on during that time. Yet the fact remains that every parliamentary day I kneel side by side with my chaplain in front of the Speaker's chair, always accompanied by a representative number of MPs from all parties, for four minutes of prayer. The privacy is maintained because it is no concern of anyone, only the Members themselves, who, or who does not, join in this short act of Christian worship.

In this book a number of Members have chosen to put their heads above the parapet and talk about their Christian faith. By doing so they are not suggesting that they are the only believers, or indeed that they are something special because they have made a contribution.

I am sure the contributors would be the first to accept that they are representative of MPs of varying degrees of belief and religious commitment. By taking part they make a witness not only to the faith that is in them, but also to the profound seriousness that all Members bring to the practical political decisions which are their parliamentary responsibility.

Denis Boothroyd

Speaker

Preface

ON the afternoon of 4 May 1979 Margaret Thatcher returned to Downing Street following an invitation from the Queen to form the next government. Crowds of well-wishers had gathered outside Number 10. The new Prime Minister acknowledged the cheers before turning to the television cameras. For her first public words as premier Mrs Thatcher quoted the Franciscan prayer for peace. 'Where there is discord,' she began 'may we bring harmony.' It was not the first time the political and spiritual worlds have overlapped. Nor would it be the last. During her 11-and-a-half years in office Mrs Thatcher faced criticism of government policy from church leaders (notably Dr David Jenkins, Bishop of Durham) and, in typical style, riposted in kind.

During the Major years media (and public) interest in the private lives of MPs verged at times on the obsessive. Barely a week would pass without allegations of conduct unbecoming. But it was not all bad news. In 1992 John Smith, a Christian devoted to the aims of Christian Socialism, succeeded Neil Kinnock as Leader of the Opposition. He was followed in 1994 by Tony Blair, whose *Sunday Telegraph* article of Easter Day 1996 put the fact that MPs can have private spiritual convictions squarely into the public domain.

Interviews with Christian MPs in a BBC TV *Everyman* programme at a time when 'back to basics' and 'the morality debate' were everyday expressions reinforced the idea that, contrary to other media opinion, there *were* many people of principle in the Houses of Parliament.

While the initial novelty value might have rubbed off with the next tabloid Westminster scandal, the fact that people in power are motivated by Christian values and commitment is not without fascination – as public interest in Anglican Prime Minister Tony Blair attending mass in a Roman Catholic church in 1997 demonstrated.

The build-up to the 1997 election campaign was characterised by a scramble for the moral high ground. We were pounded with stories of sleaze and scandal. Conservatives warned us of Tony Blair's 'demon' eyes.

A reborn Labour became New Labour. Things, they told us in the words of their election theme song, could only get better.

On 1 May 1997 the people gave their answer. A Labour majority of 179 – a landslide. We said morality policy is as important as monetary policy. We wanted the man in the white suit not the man with a chequered past.

We elected more women MPs than ever before and there are more declared Christian MPs than in many previous parliaments.

Within the Government there is strong adherence to the principles of Christian Socialism, even from those who are not members of the burgeoning Christian Socialist Movement. As the Government continues to make its mark we will judge its performance not just on whether it keeps its election promises but on whether it stays true to its Christian influence.

Introduction

'Look at them! Grown men shouting at each other like a bunch of school kids. And to think we pay for them! They ought to know better.'

Since 1989 television clips of Prime Minister's Questions have shown the confrontational side of politics. Cut-and-thrust duels from the dispatch boxes (two sword's length apart as the lines on the floor of the chamber remind us) make compulsive viewing. Quick wit, mocking, baying, point-scoring yah boo makes the governance of the nation look interesting. But it also suggests MPs of opposite parties (and occasional irritants from their own) are always at each other's throats.

To then witness the Prime Minister and the Leader of the Opposition, who the day before might have been going hammer and tongs at each other, chat amiably as they make their annual televised saunter into the House of Lords to hear the Queen formally open Parliament seems to add to the increasingly cynical public view that politics is just a game and that politicians are little better than hypocrites.

Sleaze and scandal fuel the cynic's fire. MPs' misdemeanours are headline news. Stories of honourable members acting less than honourably – taking another man's money or another man's wife – arouse more public interest than the happenings of yesterday in parliament. It's only a matter of time before more of us give in to the conclusion that MPs are only in it for themselves.

But who's really to blame? Democracy, after all, is the governing of the people by the people. 'We get the MPs we deserve' is one of Westminster's mantras. MPs are MPs because we, the public, chose them. MPs are very sensitive to public opinion – after all they live and die by it. The cross that brings political life to one delivers political death to another.

A favourite view expressed by MPs is that they are a cross-section of society. If there's the occasional rogue in Westminster, they argue, that's only because there are rogues in society at large. 'Representing people is about being ordinary,' as one of their number puts it.

The job does not appear ordinary however. Most people do not work in one of the nation's most splendid and most photographed buildings, guided by custom and guarded by constables. We do not regularly appear on television. We do not hold press conferences or charity receptions hoping our every utterance will be latched onto with the enthusiasm of a parent hearing junior's first word. We do not get the privileges of access to state and sporting occasions (and restaurants) because of our jobs. We are not people's last resort – holders of the keys that can unlock bureaucracy and get drains fixed or a by-pass rerouted.

We do not live apart from our families for days at a time only to spend most of the weekend looking after other people's concerns. We don't live in an air of confined detachment which leads us to think people are at our beck and call. And most of us don't live with the knowledge that we have to go door to door looking for a job every five years.

One of the ironies of our democracy is that we entrust the nation's security into the hands of those whose own careers are less than secure. No MP is guaranteed a job for life. As one interviewee remarked, 'Every political career ends in failure – you either retire or you are defeated.'

Another insecurity is an MP's standing with his or her colleagues. Anyone who thinks the Commons is no more than a glorified old-pals act might take note of one MP's observation: 'Many of us don't trust our personal feelings to colleagues because we are, to some extent, nervous lest some piece of information be used against us.'

The final insecurity is with oneself. MPs want to be liked. They need to be liked. They survive on being popular – if not overwhelmingly so then sufficient to be (and stay) elected.

Against such a background perhaps it's not so surprising that grown men occasionally act like small boys.

THE WAR CRY SERIES

In January 1996 The Salvation Army newspaper *The War Cry* launched a series of exclusive interviews with Christian MPs – Christians in the House. This volume, with minor editing, is the book of the series. While the interviews are exclusive, the series title does not make the same claim. Those who took part are not the only Christians in the House.

The idea for the *War Cry* series was born against a widespread perception – fuelled, if not in some instances ignited, by some sections of the tabloid press – that MPs are self-seeking, untrustworthy, immoral individuals who are either on the make or on the take.

While the passage of time might have revealed an element of truth in individual cases, it never was the whole truth for the entire breed known as MPs. In that sense the *War Cry* series started as a backlash, with David Alton, who was interviewed in November 1995, as its first subject. One aim was to tell the public that not all MPs should be tarred with the same brush. And that while none is perfect, as contributors readily admit, there are people of principle – and specifically of Christian conviction – in parliament, at every level and in every party.

The series has never defined 'Christian'. MPs were not required to sign declarations of faith or doctrinal creeds as a precondition to interview. The result is that MPs show Christianity to be a very broad church. There is room for differences of experience and expression. And just because your Christian experience is different to mine doesn't mean I'm right and you're wrong.

Something I suspect which would have been lost if a limited definition of 'Christian' had been adopted. Some readers might be surprised at some of the names included in this book.

Maybe that is a parable in itself!

It was not intended for the series to take the form of a survey. While there was a basic core of questions asked of each member, room was allowed for the conversation to reflect the character of the interviewee. However, having interviewed nearly 50 MPs of Christian conviction (more than seven per cent of all MPs) some broad conclusions can be drawn – and these appear in the concluding chapter.

An overriding principle has been to let MPs speak for themselves and for them to be commended or condemned from their own mouths. This does not imply the granting of carte blanche for party political broadcasts nor that statements were left naively unchallenged. Interview time and newspaper space, however, were both in limited supply and on occasions themes could not be developed as fully as the interviewee or the interviewer might have liked.

Setting aside such frustrations, the reader is invited to let the MPs speak for themselves in this volume – and commend or condemn accordingly.

David Amess

Conservative MP for Southend West since 1997. MP for Basildon, 1983 – 1997. Born in Plaistow in 1952. Before becoming an MP David was a junior school teacher and worked in accountancy. Parliamentary Private Secretary to Minister of State, Department of Transport, 1988 – 1990. Parliamentary Private Secretary to Minister of State, Department of Environment, 1990 – 1992. Parliamentary Private Secretary to Chief Secretary to the Treasury, 1992 – 1994. Parliamentary Private Secretary to Secretary of State for Employment, 1994 – 1995. Parliamentary Private Secretary to Secretary of State for Defence, 1995 – 1997. He is a member of the Broadcasting Select Committee. David is a member of the Roman Catholic Church. Married Julia in 1983. Has one son and four daughters.

The interview was conducted on 13 May 1996.

MANY able people are put off standing for Parliament because of the intrusive nature of the media. So says David Amess, Conservative MP for Basildon since 1983. 'It may mean them sacrificing their families and they're not prepared to do it,' he says. 'Whereas MPs used to be kept at a distance and put on pedestals, now they're considered as being public property.'

David, who earlier this year hosted a House of Commons reception for the National Viewers' and Listeners' Association, the television watchdog organisation, has been concerned about media coverage of politics and politicians for some time.

'I am a dinosaur,' says 44-year-old Amess. 'I understand I must embrace change, but the power of the media is undemocratic. Parliament is now media driven. Press and television commentators clamour to know when we're going to have the next election. Where's it going to end? I love America but we have too many of her bad practices here. Is it going to be like the White House, where you have the television cameras right next door?'

David describes the televising of Parliament as 'an unmitigated disaster'.

'Colleagues stupidly thought that by being seen on television it would make them better loved,' he says. 'In fact, it's resulted in the removal of a Prime Minister and in the trivialising of Parliament. The debating chamber has become diminished. There aren't the great orators there once were and this awful phenomenon of sound bites has become all-important. My critics say, "Well, David, people can stop buying newspapers. People can turn off their televisions." But that's not good enough.

'The media is very, very powerful. There are many wonderful TV programmes and newspaper articles but, my goodness, there's a hell of a lot of trash. There is much shown on television which is seen and copied by vulnerable members of society that has damaged the quality of the British way of life. Our institutions – the monarchy, Parliament, the legal profession – have been damaged by the media.

'Reading about sex morning, noon and night means it's not as interesting as it used to be. There's no mystery. Other than completely taking one's clothes off, what else is there to see? The media, which has an explanation for everything, appeals to a person's baser elements. They give publicity to things which don't warrant any publicity whatsoever, like intruding into personal grief.'

How can Parliament help to reverse that trend?

'I'm totally against all the so-called reforms here. The general public is being fed with the idea that MPs are a lot of rubbish. But MPs are themselves members of the general public. The public can't stand aside and disown us. We are representatives of the general public. So if they don't like the quality of the democracy, it's the responsibility of the general public to change it.'

David, describing himself as a 'victim of the media', has first-hand experience of media intrusion into his personal life.

'My wife and I believe in single-sex education for our children. As Roman Catholics we send our children to local state Catholic schools. That's our choice and we're not prepared to argue it. There are no single-sex secondary schools in Basildon. The nearest school for our son is eight miles from where we live.

'We applied to send our son to a non-grant-maintained, non-selective school in Havering. The night the governing body met to consider his application, I was in America. When I arrived home, I was met by my very upset wife and our five children, whom she'd had to take out of school.

'The night the governing body had approved the application, unanimously except for one Labour councillor, Labour members went to the local press with the story: "Local schools not good enough for MP".

'They blew the whole thing out of proportion. Some of the parents at our children's schools turned nasty. They withdrew party invitations to our five and six-year-olds. It was a nightmare. Whereas some people were absolutely wonderful, others were absolutely disgusting.

'Imagine my outrage when, just weeks later, I discover that the leader of the Labour party, together with his health spokesperson, have been sending their children not only out of their area, but to grant-maintained and selective schools! And justifying it on the basis that it's all right for them if local education isn't good enough! Not one Labour person in my constituency condemned what they did. They just attacked me.

'The local media didn't even wait for me to return home from America. They put it in the papers before we knew our son had been offered the place and, in my judgment, behaved absolutely disgustingly about the whole thing. They thought they were very responsible and tried to justify the whole thing. We took it to the Press Complaints Commission which, under the strict terms of reference, found there was no case to answer. But it made a judgment which amounted to a criticism of the paper. Did an apology appear on the front page? No. Inside, hidden away.'

The treatment dished out to his family made David think hard about standing again for the seat he'd held for 12 years.

'When I was first chosen to stand for election I was a young man and single. When you have a wife and children, it's not just down to you. They have to be considered. I'm not going to be pushed around by the opposition. Told what to do. There's more things in life than politics. There's a life worth living, so I listened to my wife and put my family first.

'When this school business exploded, my wife said, "I've stuck by you for 13 years putting up with all this rubbish, I'm not prepared to put up with it any more. That's it. I don't want you to stand any more." This went on for two weeks. Eventually she gave way and agreed I should stand at the next election – but in Southend.'

How does David describe his faith?

'I'm not fussed what religion anyone is,' he says. 'I was born a Roman

Catholic; it's all I've ever known. I'm pretty sure I will die a Roman Catholic, that's the way it is. I believe in God. How people want to celebrate that fact is a matter for them. I don't spend my life arguing that one faith has more to offer than another.'

An altar server until he was 18, David cannot point to one particular moment when his faith came alive. 'I loved it all,' he says. 'If it was up to me, I'd still have the mass in Latin. I'd still have the May procession. I love that side of things. Even the papacy has an attraction. But there have been occasions when the Catholic Church has disappointed me, over the Family Law Bill for instance.

'I condemn the popularity of transient relationships. The biggest impact on my work is people moving in and out of relationships and expecting the state to pick up the tab for looking after their children. It was barmy for my party to get involved with the Family Law Bill to make divorce easier. I acted as chief whip and by four votes we extended the qualifying period to 18 months. I'm very proud we did that. But I wish the Catholic Church had been a little more forthcoming on that issue.'

Changing the stance of his church is one thing, what would he like to change about the country?

'This is the greatest country in the world,' he says. 'I'm proud to be British. I regret that if the British aren't moaning about the weather, we're moaning about everything under the sun. We should rejoice and celebrate that we are British. When you think that over the centuries we've ruled and civilised so much of the world, what are we ashamed of? Let's celebrate that now!

'The most important thing I want is families back together again. I want community spirit restored. The state can't do it. Political parties can't do it. We can't have this nanny state any more, where you have the baby and the state takes responsibility for it straight away. Where when you get old, the state takes responsibility again.

'I was brought up not to waste food. It sickens me the way food is chucked away these days, whether it's by the EEC or by ourselves, personally. I was taught we should help one another. Parents looked after you. You looked after your parents. You took responsibility for children. You didn't give them money as soon as they came home from school, to spend round the shops. Parents have got to take responsibility.'

For David, the biggest issue facing the next Government is that of sovereignty.

'Literally, it's who governs this country,' he says. 'There's no point in me continuing as an MP if we're going to have more and more power taken away from us – if all that's required of me is to smile at the cameras and give interviews. There's no way I would sign up to a United States of Europe, with one government and a single currency.

'The issue that affects us all is getting an atmosphere whereby people accept responsibility for each other. Now, the first time there's a row at home, the children clear off. We can't house everyone in these circumstances. As soon as kids learn to drive they're not content with an old banger, they want a new car straight away. It goes on and on.

'We've got to look at jobs and work practices. It's no good MPs of different political parties going round schools and saying how wonderful information technology and cable TV is. Jobs are being lost all the time. We've got to look at all these things. I don't understand people being bored. There is so much to do.'

David has not exactly been idle since, at the age of 11, he decided his burning ambition was to become an MP. An East End boy, he joined the Conservative Party when he was 16. In the intervening 28 years, he has been a teacher, a Lloyd's underwriter and chairman of an accountancy recruitment firm. He has also fought one GLC, three London borough and four general elections.

David is now Parliamentary Private Secretary to Defence Secretary Michael Portillo. A job he describes as being 'the eyes and ears of the minister'.

'I'm the buffer between the minister and backbenchers. Part of my job is to keep my own colleagues happy. Some of them feel that, despite *glasnost* and *perestroika* and the world appearing to be more peaceful, everything is more uncertain now. They are concerned about reductions in defence spending. Troop reductions have had a huge impact and colleagues want to keep the armed forces, and their constituents, happy. The other part of my work is to tell Michael Portillo what parliamentary colleagues and military people are thinking.'

For David Amess that's work best done out of the glare of publicity.

David Atkinson

Conservative MP for Bournemouth East since 1977. Born in Westcliff-on-Sea in 1940. Before becoming an MP David was a company director. Parliamentary Private Secretary to Minister for the Civil Service, 1979 – 1981. Parliamentary Private Secretary to Minister for the Arts, 1981 – 1983. Parliamentary Private Secretary to Minister for Trade, 1983 – 1986. Parliamentary Private Secretary to Secretary of State for Trade and Industry, 1986 – 1987. Leader of the British Conservative Delegation to the Council of Europe. Chair of the European Democratic Group on the Council of Europe. David is a member of the Roman Catholic Church. Divorced. Has one son and one daughter.

The interview was conducted on 27 August 1997.

IT was while on a hitch-hiking holiday in the then Soviet Union that David Atkinson stumbled on something that would change the direction of his life. At the time David was studying engineering with plans of entering his father's garage business. It was, however, a form of social engineering that grabbed his attention.

'I was in Leningrad – now St Petersburg,' says the Conservative MP for Bournemouth East. 'I'm interested in architecture and always visit old churches when I'm abroad. Most of the churches in Leningrad were closed under Stalin and had fallen into a terrible state of disrepair. Those that remained open were treated as museums of religion and atheism.

'There was no respect for people who were genuine about their faith. The aim was to ridicule the Church. I was appalled to see how a Communist country treated its Christians. Even though I was a student I was determined to do something about it. This was my first personal commitment to human rights.'

The second came after graduation when David hitch-hiked to Israel and worked on a kibbutz.

'As I stood in the very places where Jesus walked I was completely captivated and enthralled. I had total belief in what the New Testament says about him. It was while visiting the site where Jesus shared the Beatitudes that his words: "Blessed are those who are persecuted for my name's sake, they shall see the Kingdom of Heaven" went ringing round my mind.'

David returned to his Westcliff home renewed and envisioned. He joined the family business and the local Young Conservatives. ('It had the reputation for having the best girls at the time!') Eventually he started his own printing business, rose through the YC ranks and determined to be an MP before his 40th birthday.

'I wanted to serve people, and being an MP seemed to be a most fulfilling job,' he reasons.

But the feeling that he should be doing something for persecuted Christians never went away.

Within months of being elected in November 1979 David was invited to a film screening at the House of Commons, organised by Christian Solidarity International. 'I felt I had to go,' he says. 'Only two MPs turned up. The film – *Beyond the Cross* – showed how Christians were being mistreated in Romania. Again, I was appalled. It brought back memories of Leningrad so I asked the organisers how I could help.'

David joined the group. Within two years he was chairman. His commitment gave him opportunities to see first-hand the plight of fellow believers.

'My first trip was to Romania to meet some of the people in the film. Then I went to Moscow where I met a group of Christians called the Committee for the Defence of Believers' Rights. Some of their leaders were later arrested by the KGB and sent to the gulags.

'Later I went to Czechoslovakia and East Germany to meet persecuted Christians, or "dissidents" as they were called.'

Shortly before she became Prime Minister, Margaret Thatcher appointed David to the British delegation on the Parliamentary Assembly of the

Council of Europe. (This post-war body aims to safeguard European heritage and promote democracy, human rights and freedoms throughout its member states. In 1950 it formulated the European Convention on Human Rights.)

David's membership of the Council's Committee for Relations with Non-Member Countries gave him the opportunity to use what he knew of religious intolerance in the Eastern bloc.

'Over several years I was able to highlight the situation of persecuted Christians. I believe the recommendations passed by the Parliamentary Assembly and later endorsed by member countries in their foreign policies did much to help raise the profile of freedom of religion in Communist countries.

'Much of what I suggested as a definition for freedom of religion was endorsed by the Council of Europe and appeared in the Charter of Paris, signed by heads of states and governments in November 1990 when they met formally to end the Cold War and to commit themselves to democracy, human rights and market economies.'

That same year David was elected chairman of the Committee for Relations with Non-Member Countries. His new responsibility coincided with the throwing off of Communism in eastern Europe.

When countries such as Poland, Hungary, Romania and Russia applied to join the Council of Europe David's definition of religious freedom was, he says, the bench test of them becoming accepted democracies.

'I found myself responsible for dealing with these countries' applications and we were determined to maintain our standards for membership – democracy, human rights, and the rule of law.

'The top of my personal list was to ensure these countries satisfied my definition of freedom of thought, conscience and religion. Only when I was satisfied that they did could I, through my committee, recommend to the Parliamentary Assembly that the country be allowed full membership.

'By the time my period as chairman finished in 1995 most of the countries of eastern Europe had joined the Council of Europe – on my terms.'

Europe dealt with, David turned his attentions further afield, securing the release of imprisoned Christians in Nepal, visiting Christians in Pakistan who faced the death sentence for proselytising, and pleading with government officials in Iran.

'There I met members of the Armenian Church which, while it is relatively free because it is an historic part of Iran, is strictly controlled. I was able to produce a report for Parliament recommending that Iran would be more likely to become a more tolerant, less fundamentalist society if we were to establish a dialogue with it rather than to boycott it, which is the American policy.

'The new Iranian President, although an ayatollah, appears to be much more open-minded than his predecessors. So there is hope that Iran will become a more tolerant society.'

Despite a sense of great personal fulfilment that he has had influence for God on a world stage, David is very aware that the needs of his south-coast constituents come first.

'Even in an apparently affluent place such as Bournemouth there are very grave social and human problems which I have always sought to tackle,' he says. 'Now my party is in opposition I have more time to spend in the constituency.

'I am preparing a programme to visit all those excellent organisations involved in trying to restore the dignity of drug addicts, alcoholics, those with mental health problems and the homeless. I want to see what I can do to help them locally and in Parliament.'

If there were one thing David could change about the country overnight it would be in the area of mental illness.

'A friend of mine committed suicide,' he says. 'I didn't know at the time, but he was schizophrenic. If someone could find the cause of mental illness, particularly schizophrenia, it would be great.'

Why did the Conservatives lose the election?

'Let's look at it the other way. We broke all records by remaining in office as long as we did. No party had ever been elected to four terms in office in modern political history. While there is no doubt that this country had gained tremendously on so many fronts as a result of 18 years of Conservative government, I think it was felt generally that it was time for a change.

'People felt that under its new charismatic leader – who had quite courageously changed the party rules – Labour was no longer under such influence from trades unions and should be given the chance of running the country. But we'll be back.'

But what will it take for the Tories to be electable?

'We must rejuvenate and reorganise our party. More importantly, we need to review our policies and to come forward with new ones which reflect the wishes and the needs of the people. That process is already starting. We have a long period in which to deliver those new policies.'

While David describes himself politically as 'an organisation man rather than any great political philosopher' he is clear that, for him, the parliamentary life is a vocation.

'It's certainly not one you should expect to make money from,' he says. 'My motivation is to get things done. If I see a good policy I want to run with it.'

David's experience on a hillside in Israel those years ago not only affirmed his commitment to human rights, it also confirmed his Christian faith. 'I'm not an evangelist,' he confesses, 'nor am I particularly fundamentalist. I'm a secular Christian. I try to avoid wearing religion on my sleeve.'

David has, however, 'always found the utmost satisfaction and fulfilment' in being a Roman Catholic.

'My father, who was a Catholic (my mother was not), ensured that I went to church every Sunday. My Roman Catholic boarding school also had a great influence on me.

'Walking where Jesus had lived confirmed all the theory of the beliefs I had learned at school and in my upbringing. It was then that my faith became real for me. Since then I believe God has used me. We are all here for a purpose – to do what God wants us to do with the talents he has given us.

'My faith gives me tremendous peace of mind. I've had many problems and crises in my life but I have always turned to him in prayer to help me out. Needless to say he has delivered. God also gives me an inner confidence that whatever I do he is there helping, guiding both in my job and in my life.'

Have there ever been times when David's religious and political convictions have collided?

'My priority in voting has always been, in the Russian abbreviation for the old Soviet Union, CCCP. Conscience, country, constituency and party. I cannot recall ever voting against my own conscience,' he says, 'although it has often taken me some time to work out precisely the consequences of what I will be voting for or against, and to reconcile any difficulties.'

David reckons the issue of how public money should be spent is the most difficult on which he is called to vote.

'There is always a very strong case to spend more money on anything and everything – the National Health Service, better schools and benefits for needy people. But we have seen past governments spend too much public money, with the result that public expenditure has decreased because people were no longer being productive.

'On free-vote conscience issues I have never had much difficulty in determining my vote, because I feel that I have a Christian conscience and my faith helps me determine my judgment.

'For example, I support moves to amend the law on abortion, to reduce the opportunities for abortion, because that squares with my Christian faith.'

And does the man who became Parliamentary Private Secretary to Secretary of State Paul Channon in the Thatcher years feel he missed out on promotion?

'I never think about it,' he says. 'If God had wanted me to be promoted then it would have happened. But he has given me other responsibilities which, hopefully, I have used to his satisfaction, so it hasn't worried me at all that I've remained a backbench MP.'

John Battle

Labour MP for Leeds West since 1987. Born in Bradford in 1951. Before becoming an MP John was National Co-ordinator for Church Action on Poverty. Opposition Spokesman on Housing, 1992 – 1994. Opposition Spokesman on Science and Technology, 1994 – 1995. Opposition Spokesman on Energy, 1995-1997. At the 1997 general election he became Minister for Energy,. Science and Technology. John is a member of the Roman Catholic Church. Married Mary in 1977. Has one son and two daughters.

The interview was conducted on 13 November 1996.

UNHOLY rows and talk of holy orders form the unlikely background to John Battle's political career. Growing up in Batley of Irish immigrant stock, the MP for Leeds West – Labour's energy spokesman – still recalls an argument one Sunday tea-time between his father and grandfather.

'My grandfather thought Harold Wilson was the worst evil on the face of the earth,' he says. 'And my father thought he was a great, enterprising young man who should become the next Labour leader, because he would win the general election.'

The effect of this inter-socialist power struggle was immediate. Sunday tea was called off and six-year-old John had to push his disabled mother home from his grandparents' house in her wheelchair.

Five years later, John left home and began training for the Roman

Catholic priesthood. He left theological college when he was 21. 'That's a life sentence in prison service terms!' he says. 'At 18, I had chosen to continue my theological and pastoral studies rather than go to university. Although it was a big decision, I have no regrets.'

As part of his priesthood training, John worked with community and tenant groups in Kirkby, Merseyside. He fitted pastoral studies, psychology, philosophy and theology around hands-on community work.

John moved from the hurly-burly of the inner-city to the peace and quiet of a silent order. While travelling around monasteries across Europe, he became increasingly impressed by the work of the early 20th-century French monk Charles-Eugéne de Foucauld, founder of the Little Brothers and Sisters of Jesus.

'He was a contemplative in a modern world – a modern saint. He encouraged people to live among the poor rather than to live as hermits.'

John went and did likewise. He returned to his native Yorkshire and enrolled as a mature student at Leeds University. Through his studies and involvement with tenant groups John found himself engrossed in politics once more. He became deeply involved in the Leeds Labour Party, got himself elected to the city council and married.

During the 1970s he was involved in setting up the first Roman Catholic diocesan justice and peace commission. He worked as a research officer for an MEP and as the first full-time organiser of Church Action on Poverty before winning the Leeds West seat in 1987.

Did he consciously decide to be a politician rather than a priest?

'No. In fact I haven't abandoned the theology and the thinking,' he says. 'I try to integrate contemplation and reflection into my busy life in the heart of the inner-city. For me, being an MP is a vocation. Traditionally, the Roman Catholic Church has encouraged its members to be involved in politics and sees politicians as called people.

'Anyone can be a politician. It's great to be able to say to youngsters, "You too could be a councillor. You too could be an MP." There's a tragic waste of potential in society, especially among the young. Many youngsters don't get the educational breaks. They don't get work so they can't contribute towards making a new world.

'Britain is an increasingly divided society. I don't want a society of exclusion zones, a throw-back to medieval times of safely fortified nobility and poor peasantry. We must tackle the massive gap between today's rich and poor. I want to challenge working practices that abuse people and treat them simply as hired hands to be picked up and put down at will.'

Does John see his mission as an MP as one of reinterpreting biblical truths for today's Britain?

'The Roman Catholic Church has traditionally been strong on social justice,' he says. 'Working people have a right to a decent wage to keep their family. Similarly people should not be priced into work. But it's not just a case of opening the Good Book and believing in a kind of fatalistic way that whatever you read there will be luminous and clear. The Bible is not an easy book. It's very challenging. You read what you don't want to read some of the time. The gospel is much more radical and fundamental than is often anticipated.

'Jesus was deeply radical. He got to the root of things. He never wrote a word down himself. He never made a political speech that's been recorded. He lived a very short life yet had such an incredible influence.

'Jesus got through to people and got to the root of their problems. The gospel – the radical word of God – still cuts through to the quick. We may not always like what it says, but its message is clear and simple.'

On a personal level, John confesses that his faith helps him to resist pessimism.

'We live in a despairing culture. My faith gives me hope. The whole message of the Bible is to say that even in the most desperate circumstances – whether it's Job or the Exile, the Passion and Crucifixion or the early Church – we must develop hope. The gospel challenges us to make sense of the Resurrection. Christianity is more than loving God and loving your neighbour. There's a more radical message – the Resurrection. If Jesus Christ is not risen, then we are not saved.

'The challenge is how to make sense of that as we go into the 21st century, when most people think that the real answers come from the National Lottery and Mystic Meg! You just can't stick it on the hoardings. You can't use the language of theology any more. For politicians, going around thumping on about God is the worst thing they can do. But you have to make sense of it in some way.'

How does he react to the secular media's interest in MPs 'thumping on about God'?

'Media interest tends to reduce morality to two key questions. Given the complexity of the questions, that is not helpful. At the same time, the media is asking us to be explicit about our reasons for being politicians. If an MP has a faith commitment he or she ought to spell it out. The trouble is, the minute you say you are a Christian someone asks, "Why should faith be brought into politics?"

'People want to know whether you are a Christian but then say, "Whatever you do, don't bring it out of church on Sunday and let it infect your life!"

'I am amazed that church leaders are hammered back into the pulpit when they speak out on secular affairs. When MPs come out and say, "Yes, my whole decision-making processes are coloured by my Christian commitment", we are hammered for daring to bring Christian thinking into politics. It's a no-win situation.

'The biggest problem is people who say they want prayer to be private and you can be a Christian provided you keep it to yourself! But the whole rationale of Christian commitment is to live differently and by your life suggest to others that they too may live differently. And that by doing so we might transform the world. It has massive political implications.

'The world is heavily secular, anti-transcendant and post-modern. The suggestion is that everything is of equal value. It makes no difference whether you change your brand of cornflakes, your car or your partner for life. They're all on a par. There's no weight in the world's morality.

'In such an accommodating culture the media has difficulty coping with people who have strongly committed currents of coherent thinking.'

If the media takes a somewhat simplistic approach to an MP's faith, MPs, John reckons, cannot afford such a luxury.

'We haven't got the answers to everything, as though God has told us what to say on every issue,' he says. 'But we must challenge the idea that everything is relative – that there are no absolutes. We must remind people that there are more important things than today's decisions. That there is a longer term perspective – a transcendent vision.'

Speaking of the longer term, what does John see as the big issue facing the next government?

'There are two big challenges. On a local level, it's how to rebuild a sense of community so people cease seeing themselves at odds with each other. The healing of social division, the restoration of a sense of social cohesion. People starting to exercise more tolerance. There's too much intolerance at every level of society at present. People are increasingly contemptuous of others. It's the winners versus the losers. And if you lose you lose your job, your house, everything.

'Internationally, the challenge is how Britain can be part of a global community. We can't just build the fortresses of Europe, south east Asia and USA and lock out the rest of the world, or hundreds of thousands of people will be condemned to poverty. People won't just die quietly and disappear.

'If global warming affects harvests throughout Africa, people will not accept the Mediterranean as a barrier. They'll get on boats and come across. So will we then have to guard the beaches? In other words, unless we reconcile the conflicts between people, between nations, between the north and the south of the globe, it will inevitably lead to violence.'

The prayer of St Francis which speaks about being an instrument of peace is more than John's favourite, it is his mission statement.

'We've got to solve things without resorting to violence,' he says. 'Holding off violence is the most crucial political imperative. That's one reason I'm in politics. My wife's from Belfast and we've seen what happens when violence becomes the route of sorting things out. It's incredibly difficult to claw things back to word-based politics. Interestingly, the Word is the key image within the whole of the biblical tradition – the Word made flesh.

'Personally, the challenge for me is to make the Word become flesh in politics! If the gospel is to liberate human beings I must ask myself, "Is it actually doing that? Are the people I represent more free in their relationships, in their love for each other, in their ability to share and to make a brand new future for the next generation? Are they celebrating the fact that they're human beings?" I'm not sure we've got to that point yet.'

So does John see a connection here with liberation theology?

'My job is to encourage people to realise their potential. The message of the incarnation is not so much believe in God but believe in the capacity of human beings. Jesus Christ becoming a human being is a signal about the value of human beings. The real tragic waste is that people don't value each other enough and don't realise their potential.

'My job is to work to shape laws and budgets that enable people to liberate their potential. They themselves can get on with changing things locally. It's not a case of saying to people, "If only you believe in God all will be well and an occasional night prayer will solve the problem". I'm asking for something more radical than that.

'I want us to challenge ourselves every day to acknowledge we are human beings with a host of brothers and sisters because we share a Common Parent. I want us to value ourselves and others more. There are no corners in which we cannot develop hope, not even in Parliament.

'People no longer believe politics can change things. We need to combat such despair. We need to restore faith in the process of politics, not just in politicians.

'All politicians, like every other group of people, will exhibit the same, if not more, failings than most. That doesn't mean you write off the vocation of politics. It means you work even harder at it.'

A view few politicians will argue with over Sunday tea.

Rt Hon Alan Beith

Liberal Democrat MP for Berwick-upon-Tweed since 1973. Born in Cheshire in 1943. Before becoming an MP Alan was a lecturer in politics and government. Deputy Leader since 1985. Appointed a Privy Councillor, 1992. Liberal Democrat Home Affairs Spokesman. He is a Vice-Chairman of the Council of Christians and Jews All Party Group. Alan is a member of the Methodist Church. Married Barbara in 1965. Widowed 1998. Has one son and one daughter.

The interview was conducted on 24 October 1996

IF those who can, do, and those who can't, teach, what are we to make of a politics lecturer who leaves textbook theory for the practicalities of Parliament?

It was while Alan Beith was lecturing in politics and government at Newcastle University that a colleague persuaded him to stand as the Liberal candidate in the 1973 Berwick-upon-Tweed by-election. 'I was already a local councillor,' says the Liberal Democrat MP, who has held his Commons seat for the past 23 years. 'Back then there weren't very many Liberal MPs and we needed somebody to carry the flag in this constituency.'

Alan's decision to be his party's standard-bearer was coloured by his Christian convictions. 'Christianity tends to encourage you to believe that if there's a job to be done and it's a job you could do, you should try to do it,' he says. 'Standing for Parliament seemed the right way of putting into practice what I'd been preaching – a way of taking responsibility.'

Alan is his party's deputy leader, but is he a man with a mission?

'Having a mission can be a bit dangerous in politics if you do not set it against the standards and requirements God places on us. You can become very arrogant about what you're doing in the name of other people. But I have a sense that being an MP is something God wants me to do with my life. In the sense that there was a job to be done, and that I'm trying to apply my Christian beliefs about what to do in society, this is God's calling.'

A sense of calling or commitment, he reckons, is essential in all MPs, whatever their beliefs. Without it, 'they can very soon lose any sense of purpose in what they're doing here. They can become embittered, mechanical and unconcerned.

'It's very hard in this job not to do some good for somebody some of the time. You'd have to be turning people away from the door to have that effect. Occasionally, MPs lose a sense of purpose or vision. Sometimes they're frustrated at not having the opportunities they think they should have.'

Although christened in the Church of England, Alan attended a Methodist Sunday school as a child. At what point did the reality of Jesus dawn on him?

'The reality was there from the age of 11 or 12,' he confesses. 'It was reinforced when I looked more fully at these things as a student at Oxford University. That was when my faith deepened.

'Mine has been a growing experience of Christ rather than a dramatic conversion. There are all sorts of stages in life when you're brought in touch with the realities of life and death. You're made to draw on these spiritual resources. You gain spiritual insight when something like that happens.

'My faith helps me deal with my own inadequacies, weaknesses and failings and not be overcome by them or despair at them. It gives me a framework and perspective from which to view life. My faith poses a challenge in political terms. I have to ask myself whether the gospel fits in with something that is politically expedient. A disadvantage of being a Christian is that it places obligations on you that you may want to cast aside. But how else would you fill the gap with the same sense that God cares about you, that there's something beyond this universe, if not with Jesus? I would find it very difficult.'

Alan, however, has no difficulty in squaring his party political beliefs with his faith.

'I've never taken the view that Christianity is compatible with only one political philosophy,' he says. 'I believe God regards people as individuals and expects them to exercise responsibility and give an account of themselves to him. I believe we have responsibilities for each other; that we should set a high priority on Christ's injunction to care for each other. With its combination of individualism and responsibility to others, the Liberal Party, for me, was the natural place to go.'

How far, though, does the deputy leader think his Party should go, if, in the event of a hung Parliament, it is invited by Labour to help form the next Government?

'I have no desire to be merged into the Labour party,' says Alan. 'That would be to lose the distinctive values we have. If you're going to participate in government, there's no use getting into a government of which you're going to be ashamed, or have reason to think you're going to be ashamed as it went on. You're better challenging it from the Opposition benches.

'Forming a government with Labour would depend not on how many Lib Dem MPs are elected but on our ability to put into practice the beliefs which are important to us. It would be of precious little use if the things we care about so deeply disappear into another party.'

And if the offer came from the other side of the House?

'Many people, including some Conservative MPs, do not want the present Government to remain in office if it needs to be supported by other parties. Nobody would thank us for keeping them in power!'

Much of Alan's time is taken up not in considering such hypotheses but in tackling complex realities. Seldom are there easy answers.

'For a Christian MP, it's not a simple case of your faith automatically telling you to vote this way or that. It would be easy if it did! Politics is about making compromises to achieve as much as possible. A dilemma Christian MPs often face is how far they should put across personal views about the sort of framework society should provide and how far society should go to prevent things.

'As a Liberal, I think freedom is a good basis on which to build society. I believe in a society in which people are allowed to do all sorts of things of which I personally might not approve. On abortion, for example, there's a genuine conflict of rights. The law does not do enough to protect the unborn child. On Sunday trading, the law must defend people's freedom to have Sunday as a special day, people's freedom to have it as a recreational day, and protect workers from being obliged to work on Sunday or risk losing their jobs.'

Should a Christian even be talking about compromise?

'Christians shouldn't compromise their personal beliefs or the gospel. But if they're seeking to govern the nation with wide-ranging points of view and seek with other representatives to achieve the best they can for a society in which different points of view exist, then there is a place for compromise.

'The law of the land can never be the same as the law of God. Society cannot be the sole agent for enforcing God's will.'

How does this Methodist lay preacher read the current interest in morality?

'A society in which you prohibit nothing delivers a message that nothing matters,' he says. 'One of the reasons people ask for restrictive laws on certain subjects is not so much that they believe the law will be an effective instrument to bring this about but that they do not want to give a bad signal to society.

'For example, when the 1967 Abortion Act was introduced, the sudden belief that 'this is not illegal any more so it must be all right' was more significant than the actual legislation!

'One of the reasons people get into difficulty about legalising cannabis is not primarily because a change in the law would have much direct effect on possession – currently it's not really enforced. It's that we would be seen to be saying to people: "It's all right. This is not a problem." That would be a bad signal to give. Any practical advantages in changing the law have to be set against very serious disadvantages of giving the wrong lead to society.

'There's no doubt, one element of the law is to provide a moral lead. But you cannot construct the whole law on the basis of giving a moral lead. The question is what contribution the law can make to morality. That's hard to reconcile with having to make the law workable.

'Frances Lawrence, wife of murdered headmaster Philip Lawrence, has identified two sides of what needs to be done. Firstly, we need to tackle the violence and breakdown in society. Secondly, she has identified individuals who need help as much as they need punishment. We need to change their circumstances. It's a cruel deception to say that by putting 20,000 more people a year in prison we will save future victims of violence. We have to offer them something better. The current political fashion is to ridicule do-gooders. But Jesus went around doing good. If we don't do good in some of these situations things will get worse.

'The mistake, however, is to ignore the fact that evil exists and that people can be drawn to it. You can't solve all the problems of crime and wrongdoing simply by getting all the social circumstances right. Some people have not had much help in learning how to overcome evil.'

In the wake of Dunblane, does he favour a total ban on handguns?

'This is a good example of the problem. Most of the Cullen Report is about how we tighten up the licensing of guns and try to identify people who shouldn't have access to them. The only argument is about how far you should go in banning handguns. There's a massive public demand that there should be a total ban. But it is wrong to pretend that this would take away the problem.

We must tackle illegal guns as well. But the public are demanding that signal. Shotguns, for example, are used in crime more often than handguns.'

While looking to Parliament to give a moral lead, has the public the right to expect individual MPs to be above reproach?

'That's an unrealistic expectation. It has no basis in the Christian doctrine of the fall of man. One of the reasons we're Christians is that we believe God welcomes sinners. We all fail. We all fall short of God's standard. The Church exists for sinners. It is not an organisation whose badge of membership is a certificate of virtue. That's even more true in politics. I want high standards of personal integrity in politics. But instead of assuming everyone in high places is incorruptible and beyond reproach, we should ensure everyone is answerable in the exercise of power and that power is not concentrated in the hands of a few people but widely distributed.'

The subject of power is, for Alan, the great challenge facing the next Government.

'Our position in Europe is a big issue. We have to ask ourselves whether we're serious about Europe. Are we going to play a full part or are we going to be so much on the sidelines that everything passes us by?

'Nationally, we need to address basic deficiencies – housing, employment, education. Without them people feel they don't have a proper share in society.'

What one thing would Alan like to change about the country if he could?

'I might once have said, "Get rid of alcohol!", because it is at the root of so many abuses. But I have to consider that many people can and do drink alcohol responsibly.

'I would like to have some measure by which people are automatically refused alcohol if it will impair their judgment or their ability to behave responsibly. I'd like some way in which that second drink tasted awful!'

Failing that, people still need to learn what is responsible behaviour – an item of further education that's high on the former university lecturer's agenda.

Stuart Bell

Labour MP for Middlesbrough since 1983. Born in Co. Durham in 1938. Before becoming an MP Stuart was a newspaper reporter, novelist and barrister. Parliamentary Private Secretary to Deputy Leader of the Opposition, 1983 - 1984. Opposition Frontbench Spokesman on Northern Ireland, 1984 - 1987 and Trade and Industry, 1992 - 1997. Second Church Estates Commissioner since 1997. Stuart is a member of the Church of England. Married Margaret in 1980. They have one son. He has one son and one daughter from his previous marriage.

The interview was conducted on 27 July 1998.

SHORTLY after becoming Prime Minister Tony Blair turned to Stuart Bell for advice. Stuart Bell – the man who'd brought the cash-for-questions affair to the attention of the House. Stuart Bell – whose revelations were the catalyst for the Nolan inquiry into standards in public life and the subsequent register of members' interests. Stuart Bell – the man behind the resignation and ultimate defeat of two Conservative ministers. What would Stuart Bell tell the new PM?

The Honourable Member for Middlesbrough told him: 'keep your promises to the electrate. And if you can't, then say so very loudly and very clearly.'

'There are other issues the Government must get right,' he says, 'but we must keep our promises. It is very important that the public do not get disillusioned with government. People were very disillusioned with the last Government, which is what gave Labour a huge majority. If people end up disillusioned with this Government then the whole nature of our democracy will tremble.'

How exactly was the former self-taught barrister involved in uncovering the 1994 cash-for-questions affair?

'I don't want to take credit for things that weren't in my purview but what happened was that *The Guardian* had printed a full exposure of Neil Hamilton and Tim Smith. At the time it was defamatory for those allegations to be repeated by anybody and *The Guardian* themselves could have been liable. I took the matter to the floor of the House, which gave it parliamentary privilege, whereby I and my fellow MPs could not be sued for mentioning it. On the back of parliamentary privilege, the media brought it to the attention of the entire country and the Prime Minister was obliged to come to the House the following day and announce a full investigation. One minister resigned immediately and the other one resigned a few days later.'

And will the consequences of 'cash-for-access' allegations be as serious?

'No, they won't. It is very much a side issue. No MP or minister is involved. It is important, however, because access to government is at issue. One of the great attributes of the Blair Government is its openness and accessibility.

'It's possible there are those who talk big but who don't have any real clout on the inside. Quite frankly, if anyone believes someone who says they can get direct access to Tony Blair or Peter Mandelson for a couple of thousand then they're a bigger fool than I am!'

With Labour coming to power partly on an anti-sleaze ticket, does Stuart think his administration is under extra pressure to be seen to be clean and upright?

'The Prime Minister has said several times that anyone found guilty of wrongdoing will be dismissed immediately. We live in a situation where a lot of stuff which appears in newspapers is, to use his word, tosh. Cash-for-access was blown out of all proportion. The Sandline business is clearly tosh of the first order – ministers were not involved in that. Nevertheless there are lessons to be learnt. There will be new codes of conduct for the civil service arising out of both of these affairs and wrongdoing will lead to instant dismissal.'

And does the public have a right to expect Stuart and his Parliamentary colleagues to be above reproach in terms of personal behaviour – publicly and privately?

'MPs should be properly accountable to the public. One of John Fitzgerald Kennedy's phrases was that people have a right to see what their Government is doing. So yes, transparency and accountability is very important.

'But one has to be careful not to preclude MPs from having private lives. Nor should we put normal and respectable MPs under particular scrutiny. In the cash-for-questions affair it was clearly wrong for MPs to receive money without having properly declared it. That was the essential point – they had received sums of money and yet not declared that fact.

'We have to be very careful not to beat our democracy to its knees by writing about MPs and other institutions such as the Royal Family in such a way that it demeans the institution. For the man in the street his MP is his last resort – the final person who can help him in any problem. If MPs as a whole are constantly demeaned all the time, our relations with those with whom we have to work – the civil service, local authorities, social security offices – will be weakened. Weakening the role of the MP by a whole series of press calumnies undermines public confidence in the Parliamentary system. That ultimately does the British public no service whatsoever.'

As Second Church Estates Commissioner, Stuart represents the interests of the Church of England in Parliament. Often he is involved in debates about Parliamentary oversight of church assets, priests' salaries and clerical appointments. His contribution in his official capacity to the debate on the age of homosexual consent was higher profile than usual. A different sand line this time. 'There must be a line in the moral sand,' reports *Hansard*. What did Stuart mean?

'Having good Christian values requires you to stand up and be counted. Parliament has to say what society is prepared to tolerate and what society is prepared to accept in terms of equality and freedom. Now where do we pitch those moral values and how do we keep them? Because there is no doubt that if we continue as we going we are going to be a very decidedly immoral society in 20 or 30 years.

'The homosexual community claim they face a great deal of discrimination at work. The Government should use the summer to draw up a bill that will protect homosexuals against such discrimination. In addition the Government should have a bill which frames homosexual rights on an equal basis with heterosexual rights. The question of the age of consent should again be left to a free vote.

'In doing so the Government should make it clear that there will be no question of allowing the age of consent to be reduced to 14; nor that there ought to be homosexual marriages; nor that there ought to be homosexual adoption of children. We should be saying we understand the sense of discrimination and are prepared to act upon it – we will go so far and no further.

'The values and nature of our society are based on family life. They are the fundamental basis which goes back to biblical times.'

Stuart's own spiritual foundation goes back to childhood.

'I was brought up with the scriptures and Jesus has always been a very living person for me. I was brought up as a Methodist chapel and still have my first Methodist Sunday school prize. When I was 14 a friend introduced me to the Church of England. When I was 17 years old I was confirmed by the Bishop of Durham, Dr Ramsey, who later became the Archbishop of Canterbury. It was an very inspiring experience which I have never forgotten to this day.

'To me, Jesus is a great friend – the ethos of the Christian religion. It is the morality and goodness of Jesus that not only keeps me going but also gives me a vision of the word. Christ's teachings are a very strong set of values, which I try to persuade everybody, so far as I can, to accept. I try, as an MP, to propound those values and to live by them. I don't see my job as one of converting people.'

Why did the man who counts serenity as one of the assets of his faith leave the security of law for the turmoil of politics?

'I was bitten by the bug,' he explains. 'I was writing a book at the time covered the French Presidential election in 1974 and went to the United States for Jimmy Carter's election. In the end I figured that I might as well get involved and I had such a commitment to it. I came back to England and stood as a Parliamentary candidate in Hexham in 1979. When I started I wasn't sure whether it was with a sense of mission or just personal desire. That worried me for some time. It was a great relief to discover that I actually did enjoy helping people!'

He describes his appointment as Second Church Estates Commissioner, following the general election, as 'another one of God's mysteries'.

'I had three jobs in Opposition. I was Shadow Minister for Trade, Shadow Minister for Corporate Affairs and Shadow Minister for Europe. (I said to myself, Tony Blair would have to sack me three times if he didn't want me in his Government.) The appointment is first and foremost a church appointment made by The Queen on the recommendation of the Prime Minister.

'The role was created by statute since a large portion of the assets of the Established Church is vested in the Church Commissioners. As such we are accountable to Parliament. I take any legislation relating to the Church of England through Parliament and see myself as the Church spokesman on matters of Church and State. Besides the more formal duties I am also available to MPs to talk through constituents' problems as they relate to church property and the like.'

And how does he feel about the suggestion that the Church and State should not be formally linked through the established Church of England?

'Disestablishing the Church would be a major constitutional upheaval,' he says. 'It would take years of legislation. The Queen in the Supreme Governor of the Church as well as the Head of State. The Lord Chancellor has an enormous role in church appointments – making some 300 appointments a year. It could only happen if Church and State thought it was in their best interests.'

Constitutional upheaval is something on which Stuart has voiced opinion before. In 1981 he wrote a pamphlet *How to Abolish the House of Lords*. Subversive or what?

'In those days the Fabian Society thought it was more attractive to say how to abolish the Lords than to say how to reform the Lords. The pamphlet actually deals with reforming the Lords and points out that you do need two tiers of government – a House of Commons and a House of Lords. Strange how things work out, because I am now involved with the bishops in the Lords and the Government is looking at the whole question of reforming the Upper House. Who knows, some of my suggestion may yet become Government policy.'

If Stuart could turn the clock back still further he would – to a time when 'people had a sense of proper values, proper respect for each other and we lived in harmony among ourselves.'

'If I could change the country overnight I would give the country a whole set of moral values,' he says. 'Television advertising is a scandal. Adverts for cars, for example, where there's a woman on the beach making love to their husband has nothing to do with the sale of a car. A woman walking down the stairs stripping off as she goes and ending up in the car with nothing on is quite wrong.

'It's not a fault of any government. It is a fault of 30 years of decline in society. If I had the magic wand I would make us all very respectful and very moral and as a consequence very much happier.'

And that, reckons the PM's confidante, is not a threat. That is a promise.

Paul Boateng

Labour MP for Brent South since 1987. Born in Hackney in 1951. Before becoming an MP Paul was a solicitor and barrister. Shadow Spokesman, Lord Chancellors Department 1992 – 1997. At the 1997 general election he became Junior Health Minister. He is the Secretary of the Council of Christians and Jews All Party Group. Paul is a Methodist lay preacher. Married Janet in 1980. Has two sons and three daughters.

The interview was conducted on 27 August 1996.

PAUL BOATENG, Labour MP for Brent South, can well understand the plight of refugees. As a teenager he was one himself.

Born in The Salvation Army's Mothers' Hospital in east London, to a Ghanaian father and a British mother, Paul moved to the former Gold Coast with his parents when he was four.

In 1966, his father – a Cabinet minister in Nkrumah's Government – was arrested and imprisoned without trial, following a military coup. Paul, his mother and his sister fled to Britain with two suitcases. They settled in a two-up, three-down council house in Hemel Hempstead. He was the only black boy on the block.

Following in his father's footsteps, Paul read law (he is still a practising barrister and member of Gray's Inn) and, in 1987, became an MP – the country's first of direct African descent. On graduating, he worked at the Paddington Law centre, dispensing advice on civil rights, housing and education. In 1977 he became legal adviser to the Scrap Sus campaign, which aimed to restrict the power of the police to stop and question people on suspicion. The black community felt the practice was being disproportionately used against black youths.

Today, as Labour's legal affairs spokesman, Paul shadows the Lord Chancellor. It is a wide-ranging brief, which includes monitoring not only practices within the profession but also public access to criminal and civil justice.

For the past year, much of his time has been taken up with the Family Law Bill – the new divorce legislation. Did he have a direct influence on the final Act?

'Yes. Many Conservative MPs were unhappy about the Bill, as were many of my colleagues. That enabled us to come to the legislative process with our own agenda: saving marriages where they could be saved, giving children new rights, changing access to pension rights and, most importantly, dealing with domestic violence.

'We were also able to do something about making the divorce process less confrontational, putting a greater emphasis on mediation so divorces are more likely to be settled amicably without recourse to the courts and to an adversarial legal system.'

What made a successful lawyer enter the somewhat adversarial world of Parliament?

'Politics is a vocation – a calling. It isn't a profession. Most people who go into politics have a vision of how they would like society to be. They want to serve, they want to help others. I wanted to contribute through a party that represents ideals of social and economic justice, that represents an opportunity for ordinary people to achieve.

'The Labour Party represented the best chance of making our society a more harmonious one – one in which there is greater justice and greater opportunity for all, regardless of race, colour, creed or birth. I want a more just society. I want a more economically successful society in which people can make a full contribution, and which doesn't put people on the scrap heap – because they are too old, because they are out of work through lack of access to educational opportunity, or because for one reason or another they find themselves homeless.'

Speaking of injustice, how big an issue is racism?

'Since the Notting Hill riots of the 50s, we haven't had race riots in this country in the sense that black people and white people have turned on each other.

'We've had riots, uprisings about inner city deprivation and the Poll Tax which have involved black people and white people, mainly young people, usually with their wrath directed at the police. That was a feature of the late '70s and '80s so far as the situations in Brixton, Toxteth, Mosside and Tottenham were concerned.

'We have seen a very considerable improvement in the relationship between the community and the police. The police are now much more responsive to the importance of community relations, so there have been steps forward there.

'At the same time disadvantage and urban decay are still very much facts of life. In fact, they are worse now than they were in the mid and early '80s. We are a more divided community now in terms of disparity of wealth than we have ever been. This is one of the great scandals of our time.

'Racial disadvantage still exists. It isn't a factor in quite the same way as it was in the '60s and '70s. Back then, the notion that you could have the likes of a Trevor McDonald on television was unthinkable. We now have black people represented at every level in our society in every walk of life. That's a good sign. There are many more positive role models – barristers, doctors, nurses, even in the police, although they still remain under-represented there.

'We can't be complacent about the rise of Neo-Nazism and racial intolerance across Europe. In my own constituency Jewish cemeteries and synagogues continue to be defiled and attacked.

'Throughout the country the number of racial attacks continues to grow. Discrimination and disadvantage are still facts of life.'

Right from his childhood the Christian faith has been a fact of Paul's life.

'Christianity has been the bedrock of my life,' he confesses. 'I came from a non-conformist background. An uncle, Brigadier Boakye, was a Salvation Army officer, and headmaster of a Salvation Army school in Ghana. It's always been part of my life, not in a preachy, repressive sort of way but as something that is a source of joy, a source of inspiration and a source of strength throughout the various trials and tribulations of my life.

'My faith also gives me a sense of proportion. Politicians address the issues of today and maybe tomorrow. Christ addresses issues that are for all eternity.'

Was there a particular moment when he decided that Christianity was for him?

'No. There wasn't. I've never actually questioned my faith in the sense of finding I no longer had it. However, there have been times when I have felt particularly moved spiritually. There have been times of spiritual growth and renewal, but my faith has always been with me.

'I have not had a Damascus Road experience. My faith has grown, become more informed.

'When you are a child you see as a child. As you grow older, hopefully you grow in wisdom and in the depth of your faith, in the depth at which you think about your faith. I have examined and considered my faith more closely and challenged myself more in the past decade than at any other time in my life.'

Upon examination, does Paul think Christian MPs are under different pressures to their colleagues?

'We have a responsibility to examine our faith, to keep it under constant review and to witness to that faith. I don't seek to ram my faith down the throats of my constituents. I am what I am and part of that is my Christian faith and belief. I happen to believe that the Christian gospel is unique and wonderful in its revelation.

'I believe that Jesus Christ is the Son of God and I bear witness to that. I seek to represent the importance of faith in our national life. One of the great sadnesses is that we have lost our vision of a nation rooted in the importance of the spiritual life.

'There is something of enormous value to be obtained by a nation in seeking to integrate the material with the spiritual. You have to try to do that in your own life and in the life of the nation.

'It's sad when we don't find time in life – personal or national – for things of the Spirit, because they are enormously important and the source of enormous joy and strength.

'Christianity is not a joyless religion, at least it ought not to be.'

If that sounds suspiciously like a sermon. It should. Paul is a Methodist lay preacher. He reckons Christianity is a can-do faith, and not, as so often portrayed by some of its adherents, a can't-do religion.

'Jesus was concerned about justice, with spiritual growth and with meeting the needs of humanity. I wish the Church would have a greater focus on those areas than in some of the things we do focus on. It would make us much more relevant to ordinary people.'

Boateng's joy in Jesus and hatred of injustice burn with an almost prophet-like passion. No smooth ride to some promised land for him. He may have a dream but he's no idle dreamer.

'Christians in politics have responsibilities,' he says. 'We must be prepared to subject our 'isms and 'ologies to close scrutiny to see if they are in tune or out of tune with higher norms and prescriptives.

'For instance, some aspects of our policy on refugees are out of tune with

Christian principles. There are many injustices in relation to the homeless which politicians and politics are just not dealing with for one reason or another. Politicians on all sides must put housing and the homeless higher up the agenda. I am challenged by failures in that area.

'There are tensions and conflicts. One has to seek to resolve those tensions and conflicts as best one can. But one doesn't do that by ducking out of one's responsibility in civic life.

'Christians cannot turn their backs on their civic responsibilities. There can be no rights without responsibility. Christians have a role to play in all parties and it is wrong to use the name of Christ in order to harvest votes.'

If there was one thing he could change about the country it would be to eradicate cynicism and the apathy it breeds.

'Cynicism is the enemy of progress. The country is in the grip of a terrible cynicism. It is destructive. It is corroding the warm heart and great spirit that I still believe lies in this great country of ours. I'm not one of those who says that it's all down to the media. We get the media we deserve. Politicians get the media they deserve. We've all contributed to it, so we all have a responsibility to do something about it.'

How does he react to what some regard as a cynical attack on his party in the form of the Conservative's 'New Labour – new danger' campaign, 'demon eyes' and all?

'I very much regret negative campaigning. I don't like it. I don't engage in it myself in my local party politics, and the Labour Party does not like it. It is an element that has crept into politics, over the past 14 years in particular, that is very, very regrettable and it's got to be fought.

'However, as a party we have a duty to expose lies. New Labour does involve new politics so we will do what we have to do to defend ourselves. We'll be strong in rebutting the lies. The 'New Labour – new danger' campaign is despicable. But I don't think people will be fooled.'

Speaking of electioneering, Paul reckons the economy will be the big issue facing the next Government.

'If we want to be a society that is going somewhere, we have to be an inclusive society. Not in terms of subsistence, or of people being dormant, but in terms of active participation. There are too many people who, for one reason or another, are on the margins. We have to create a society in which people are given an opportunity to participate. All you can do is give people opportunities. You can't make them take them.'

Trying to include people on the margins of society is something in which the former-refugee lawyer is well practised.

Colin Breed

Liberal Democrat MP for Cornwall South East since 1997. Born in London in 1947. Before becoming an MP Colin was a banker and company director. Colin is a Methodist lay preacher. Married Janet in 1968. Has one son and one daughter.

The interview was conducted on 4 November 1997.

LIFE has been turned upside down since Colin Breed won the Cornwall South East seat in the General Election. Colin took the seat from the Conservatives with a 12 per cent swing. It was, he says, a 'sweet moment'.

'For the next few days you don't think about the colossal change being an MP will make to your life,' says the Liberal Democrat spokesman on competition, energy and consumer affairs. 'You know the theory but you can't imagine it in practice. By the time I started at Westminster on the following Tuesday everything I'd treated as a normal working and family life had been turned upside down.'

Born in Wimbledon, Colin moved to Torbay as a teenager when his parents split up. When he left school he joined the Midland Bank and spent the next 26 years in retail and merchant banking. In more recent years running a distribution company in Saltash, Cornwall, enabled him to concentrate on a political career. Before he stood in his first General Election, last May, Colin spent 12 years on the district council.

Why did he stand for Parliament?

'For years I had seen first-hand how the Government had eroded the value and service of local government by rate-capping,' he says. 'I wanted to change all that, so I thought I should try getting closer to where decisions are made.'

Colin describes himself as a 'people-centred' politician and a 'keen European'.

'It is absolutely essential that I represent all my constituents,' he says. 'How you tackle difficult issues to benefit the majority is, to me, part of the fascination of politics.

'To me, a more inclusive world where we create new relationships with countries who used to be our enemies is likely to be a safer and more peaceable place. We need to create new bonds of friendship and an ability to understand each other's situation across the world.'

A single European currency is vital for Britain's future prosperity, he reckons. 'We read of splits in the parties over the single currency, who's for it and who's against it, but we should also be told how going in or staying out will affect the people of this country.

'It's nonsense to reduce the argument to a fight between parliamentary personalities or an emotional attachment to the £1 coin, which not so long ago used to be a note! To say we should fight for the pound is absolute nonsense. It's only a medium of exchange. It's of no more value than any other currency.'

So what are the advantages of the single currency?

'It's essential for a single market to operate with a single currency,' he says. 'Although our main trading blocks are America, the Pacific and Europe, our home market is not the UK, it is Europe. To operate different currencies in the same market is illogical.

'There will be differences in standards of living between member states as there are in America, where California is richer than many countries and Missouri is much poorer, yet they both use the dollar. But our economic future depends on European trade. Not being in the single currency would put us at an enormous disadvantage.'

Doesn't Colin's 'keen European' face present a conflict of interests when Spanish trawlers fish in Cornish waters?

'I must always be on the side of the people I represent even if I sometimes don't agree with them. However, Cornish fishermen have been a pawn in a game played by successive governments in respect of the Common Agricultural Policy.

'In the past Britain has given away fishing benefits to gain other agricultural concessions. The conservation of fish is not just a British or a Spanish issue, it is a world problem. It is in everybody's interest for fish stocks to be preserved. That can only be resolved by people recognising their responsibilities to future generations and coming up with workable solutions, bearing in mind the impact on local economies today. It won't be solved by fishing wars.'

As a teenager Colin went to the youth club at his parish church in Torquay. It was the time of The Beatles and The Rolling Stones. He describes his Christian upbringing as 'pragmatic, robust and unapologetic'.

'Every church youth club had a rock band,' he says. 'It was great fun. When I was 15, people at the church started pressurising me to be confirmed. I didn't have any inkling to be confirmed. I didn't know what it meant really. I was told if I wanted to remain in the youth club I'd have to be confirmed so I said "thank you very much", walked off and didn't go again.

'When I started work I met a girl who was the organist at a Methodist church. She made it quite clear that if I wanted to see her I had to go to church. I went to the Methodist church and was made extremely welcome. Before long I was committed.

'When I was 19 or 20 I moved to Cheltenham with my work, leaving my friends and organist girlfriend Janet behind. It was while sitting alone in my tiny flat 100 miles from home that I realised I was going to church for deeper reasons than just wanting to see Janet. It was then that I made my decision. I acknowledged that God had always been with me. I found a new church and trained to become a local preacher.'

Now, married to Janet for nearly 30 years, how has Colin's faith developed?

'The longer I live the more I determine that what happens to me is through the hand of God. There have been some very hard times, for instance our first child was stillborn. But I am convinced that everything that has happened has worked together in some way to make us the people we are.

'As a lad I used to leave school on Friday afternoons and go to the courthouse to pick up the maintenance from my father. More often than not I went home empty-handed. We had to survive on money from my paper round and my mother's cleaning job. Now as an MP I get many letters from single parents trying to bring up children on their own. Because of my past I can identify with what they're saying.'

Colin readily agrees, however, that it is often only with hindsight that we recognise the hand of God.

'At the time it does cause strain and you probably say things you don't really mean. That's when prayer and others praying for you enable you to get to the point when you can look back and say, "OK, if I can get through that, I can get through anything."

'I worry less now about things that might happen to me tomorrow.

What is important is doing what I believe to be right, even though in the short term that might mean a degree of hardship.'

Still a Methodist lay preacher, Colin restricts his preaching engagements to a few Sundays a year, 'usually when somebody's been let down'.

'If I could preach only one sermon it would be when Jesus spoke of himself as the Son of God who had come to serve, not to be served. To me that sums up what I believe my service is – that whatever position you're in you are there to serve and not to be served.

'My faith gives me a sense of purpose. It is a standard by which I measure what I am thinking and doing. There are many major decisions that come an MP's way, where you are battered by different views from opposing pressure groups and individuals. My faith helps me sort out what my position is.'

And does his position ever find him in conflict with his party?

'Yes, I shall vote against reducing the age of homosexuality to 16. I wouldn't have reduced it to 18. I know there's the question of discrimination but I believe that homosexual acts are wrong.

'I accept that it is part of some people's make-up but we all have within us all sorts of urges we have to control. Some people have an enormously strong heterosexual sex drive that needs to be controlled. Others have to keep a strong urge to steal under control.

'A person can be a Christian and gay. The issue is what they do about it. People with all sorts of tendencies may well, when they become a Christian, decide to impose restrictions and controls upon their behaviour.'

Does he agree with his party on abortion?

'The big debate is whether life begins at conception or at birth,' he says. 'Losing our first baby has fashioned my view as to when human life exists. At that time I had to register a birth, even though our baby was dead. I found the whole experience very difficult. I was required by law to register a corpse as a birth. The way I saw it our child was not able to survive outside the womb. So for me human life begins at birth, not at conception. After all, one is not required to register a conception!

'On the wider issue I am utterly opposed to abortion being used as a method of birth control. However, I recognise there are good reasons why some embryos need to be aborted.'

For Colin, the public does have the right to expect its MPs to be above reproach.

'If people put themselves forward as elected representatives and have the opportunity to use that power then we should rightly expect them to have the moral scruples not to use that power for personal gain. We should be able to expect them not to put their personal interests above those of whom they represent.

'Similarly, sexual impropriety is no more acceptable here than it is anywhere else. However, perhaps the way Westminster operates – the excitement of power, late nights and separation from family – provides an atmosphere unlike other places. Given that there are some 4,000 people working in the House of Commons, I doubt that the percentage of sexual misconduct is greater than that in any other office. It's just more highlighted. That, of course, doesn't mean it's right. It's just a fact of life.'

Before the election there was talk of the LibDems doing a deal with Labour in the event of a hung parliament. How does he see his party's relationship with Labour now?

'We would like to build cross-party support on a number of issues and we support those we believe to be in the best interests of the country. The most obvious one at the moment is Europe and I welcome the opportunity to work with Labour and Europhile Conservative MPs to further Britain's cause.

'There are a number of other long-term issues which need more cross-party co-operation. On the question of pensions, for instance, any decisions this Government takes will affect people in six parliaments time. We can't have people investing large amounts of their income into pension plans if in 10 years time the government of the day changes the law and reduces the value of those investments.

'It is vital for cross-party views to influence long-term policy decision-making.'

But with a majority in excess of 170 isn't the brutal fact of the matter that the Government doesn't need to consult with LibDems?

'True, but even they recognise that although they had a landslide victory last May their share of the vote nationally was only about 1.5 per cent more than the Conservatives.

'The first-past-the-post system produces not only landslides but also minority governments. It is generally accepted that governments lose elections rather than others win them. In five years time Labour need only a two to three per cent swing against them and they'll be denied the second term that has always eluded them.

'I believe Tony Blair is a pragmatist. It is in Labour's interests to change the system.'

The even bigger issue facing the Government, according to Colin, will be how they can introduce a wide-ranging programme of legislation without losing the goodwill of the people.

'They could, of course, rely on their majority to get things through the House,' he says. 'Changing society at a pace which maintains the trust of the people is a very difficult balancing act. But if they rush too far ahead of the British public, they'll find themselves out of favour.'

Tony Colman

Labour MP for Putney since 1997. Born in Norfolk in 1943. Before becoming an MP Tony was a director of the Burton Group and GLE. Member of Treasury Select Committe since 1997 Tony is a member of the Methodist Church. Married Juliet in 1989. They have two sons. He has four sons and two daughters by previous marriages.

The interview was conducted on 10 September 1997.

LABOUR's Tony Colman is one of three millionaires who contested the much-publicised Putney seat at the general election. Of the others, former Conservative minister David Mellor lost his seat and Referendum Party founder Sir James Goldsmith has since lost his battle against cancer.

It was, says Mr Colman, a dirty fight. 'Shooters Alliance supporters spent the entire campaign attacking David Mellor on the basis on his opposition to handguns. I made it clear I was right alongside the opposition to handguns but they felt they wanted to target him.

'The sneering, simplistic approach of the Referendum Party did British politics no good. There was far too much unnecessary mud-slinging.

'David Mellor attacked me again and again about my personal life. The scenes at the count, with hundreds of photographers climbing around the tables and the chanting of supporters when the result was announced, was appalling.

'My criticism of David Mellor was not his affair itself. His wife Judith has forgiven him, after all. What to me was wrong was that he trooped his family in front of the cameras and said there was nothing wrong.'

Marital infidelity, Tony reckons, is not necessarily a reason to resign.

'It is money that corrupts, no personal relationships,' says the member of the Treasury Select Committee. 'MPs should not be involved in any financial peccadilloes. The public has a right to expect MPs to be above reproach in their dealings.

'But I do not believe a failed relationship or a marriage breakdown means a person cannot be a good MP. If handled the right way there should be no need for an MP to resign from a parliamentary post or from the House.'

Getting into the House was a boyhood ambition for the dairyman's son from Sheringham.

'My father fell ill when I was young and from the age of 11 I worked hard to support my family. There was enormous poverty in the area just after the war. The village was owned by one man and we had no running water, no electricity, no gas and no sewerage. All we had was an enormous amount of milk! It was a tough life.

'We lived in a tied cottage. My father was a strong member of the Labour Party and of the National Union of Agricultural and Farm Workers. He was the only person on polling day who would tell for the Labour Party. We were the only place in the village that put up a Labour poster. When he fell ill and the herd was sold he lived in fear that we could be thrown out of our house at any time.'

It was seeing this fear at first-hand that shaped Tony's political ambition. It would be the 1975 Tied Cottage Act that brought him into politics. 'I was determined that if I got involved in politics I'd make sure nobody would suffer the way my parents did,' he says.

With an Anglican father and a Salvationist mother, Tony was sent to the Methodist church.

'It was a happy compromise,' he says. 'My mother, Beattie, still worships at The Salvation Army in Sheringham and I have been a Methodist ever since. I have benefited enormously from growing up with three Christian viewpoints. I'm not sure I could wear Salvation Army uniform though. It must be very difficult, particularly for younger people.'

At 17 Tony left home for Cambridge University. When he graduated he headed for Africa to work with industrial giant Unilever. He spent the Biafran War years in Nigeria as a merchandise manager buying goods from all over the world. He is particularly pleased that the factories he set up are still producing goods for the Africa market.

Tony returned to England in 1969, teamed up with Ralph Halpern and built up what became the Burton Group. In 1976 he became a director, responsible for such High Street names as Principles, Dorothy Perkins and Top Shop.

Around this time he also became involved in politics. Incensed by the inequality in which families could be put out of tied cottages he helped the Tied Cottage Act get onto the statue books.

He subsequently served on a CBI committee, joined Jim Callaghan's Price Commission, became the chairman of the Low Pay Unit, failed to get elected to parliament in 1979, was elected onto Merton Council in 1990 and became its leader in 1991.

Business, meanwhile, thrived. Sadly, his marriage did not.

'I had two marriages that failed because I was working too hard,' he confesses. 'For four years I was a single parent as I brought up my children from my second marriage.' He has since re-married.

What does it feel like for Tony to have achieved his ambition?

'Initially I was euphoric,' he says. 'Since then it's been: what have I done! For only the second time in my life I feel helpless. I'm accountable for everything and responsible for nothing. People look to me for help, yet I don't have the power of decision-making. All my business life I had the last word. I made the decisions. Now I don't. It's very humbling.'

The other time Tony felt like this was as a teenager.

'As a child I'd won some cups for Bible knowledge. But when I was 13 I realised that however good or brilliant I thought I was I needed help. It was during an annual Children's Special Service Mission that I welcomed Christ into my life. I immediately sensed I had somebody who would be with me throughout the rest of my life.

'I felt a very real voice from within. He changed me. I became a much softer person. My attitude to my parents changed. My attitude towards myself changed.

'I'd seen myself as an unlovable person because I was aggressive and stroppy. The joy of discovering that Christ loved me was fantastic.'

It was out of Christian conviction that Tony headed for Africa after university.

'I knew I should be involved in Third World development, not become a minister,' he says. 'Even now I spend about half my time dealing with Third World issues.

'My faith gives me a benchmark in terms of the policies which I would like to have. And it also gives me worries that my children might not see Christ the way I do, that they might not share my strength of faith. I have been through some very bad and frightening times but I've always felt Christ has been with me.'

Tony joined the Christian Socialist Movement in the days when it attracted few members.

'It has almost become fashionable now for Labour Party members to be in the CSM,' he says. 'I admired the fact that John Smith and Tony Blair were Christians living out their faith in service as MPs. I thought I should try to do the same. I'm not here to make money. I'm not here to make a career – I've got nothing to prove. But I came into Parliament with a sense of practical mission. I want to deal with the power brokers and get a good deal for the poor. I'm here to work not just to talk.'

Tony agrees that there is almost a revivalist feel to the way in which his Government has 'hit the ground running', and that others share his sense of mission.

'There is a sense within the Government that we will deliver that which we have promised, that we are part of a crusade. Delivering on promises has a spiritual quality.

'The cancelling of Third World debt is something on which I shall be pressing the Government hard. Similarly I believe in a right to a roof over your head. We need a massive increase in social housing in this country. We have to make sure that young people are not disadvantaged in our society by living on the streets or in abject conditions.'

Through his long association with the Low Pay Unit Tony is a supporter of the minimum wage.

'I shall be working hard for the introduction of the minimum wage,' he says. 'The way we'll do it is by getting people back into work. As a result the social security bill will drop and revenue from income tax will rise, making money available for the minimum wage.'

What does Tony say to those who accuse New Labour of abandoning its working class roots?

'The working class doesn't exist any longer,' he says. 'What we have now is a two-class system – a classless society and an underclass. In industry hierarchical management has basically gone. Businesses are built around teamwork. Trade unions are there to protect people from bad employers. A strike is a sign that all sides have failed. Unions play an important part, as does the CBI. The two should work together to build a better future.'

But isn't it a contradiction that someone who has made a lot of money should stand as a Labour candidate?

'I tried to be an MP in 1992 but perhaps my strongly capitalist background was unacceptable to some of the selection committee. Today things are different. I am very much New Labour.'

'This country has to rethink its way forward. Unless we celebrate the making of wealth, we will not make wealth. We must carefully regulate how we make wealth and we must ensure everyone shares in it.

'There are many business people who have a sense of community and want to deliver a better society for this country and for the world. They must be encouraged – not face tax increases or be put out of business.

'The public are not fools. They know economic problems are not solved just by putting up taxes. They know jobs don't appear out of thin air. We have to encourage companies to review and renew their working practices so wealth is more evenly divided.'

Tony is no fool either. He knows that a wealthier society does not equal a better society. There is a moral agenda to be faced.

'There is no hidden government agenda, either on moral issues or on the raising of taxes. We fought the election as New Labour. We will govern as New Labour.

'We must help the poor nations in terms of writing off their debts,' he says.

'My view on abortion is that the present law is correct.

'On homosexuality, it's very sad when people feel they have to hide their sexual orientation. You have to be content with yourself. It's wrong to pick on a particular part of the community. Homosexual people should have the same rights as heterosexuals. People in a same-sex relationship should be able to worship the Lord.

'Euthanasia is difficult. I believe in living wills. I have had friends who've suffered terminal illness. Like C. S. Lewis, I believe there is a point of pain beyond which God would not want us to go, especially as we have the ways to ease the passage into the next world.'

So far as the immediate future is concerned Tony reckons pensions will be the biggest issue facing his Government.

'The problem is,' he explains, 'nobody wants to pay for them. This problem has to be dealt with. It will not go away. You've got to have a proper basic pension, available to everybody. For instance, many people do not understand about Income Support. There are some 1.7 million pensioners who don't realise they could get another £14 a week on their pension.

'It is essential that poorer pensioners have a right to live in dignity and not have to worry about putting their fire on if they are cold. We should not go back to a poor house mentality.'

If he could change one thing about the country overnight it would be for everyone to discover 'a true belief in God'.

'That would change society dramatically,' says the man for whom principles is more than a brand name.

Jeffrey Donaldson

Ulster Unionist Party MP for Lagan Valley since 1997. Born in Kilkeel in 1962. Before becoming an MP Jeffrey was a partner in a financial service and estate agency. Member of Ulster Unionist constitutional talks negotiating team since 1991. Party Trade and Industry Spokesman. Jeffrey is a member of the Presbyterian Church and worships at the Baptist Church. Married Eleanor in 1987. Has two daughters.

The interview was conducted on 10 June 1998.

HE is the man who held up history. That, at least, is how *The Times* described Ulster Unionist peace negotiator Jeffrey Donaldson on the morning after the long-awaited Good Friday Agreement. Leaving Stormont 'in disgust' and 'resisting fiercely' was how another broadsheet saw the Lagan Valley MP's 11th-hour misgivings about The Agreement. Is that the way it was?

'I wasn't the only one,' says the mildly-spoken father of two, who at the time had been an MP a little less than a year. 'Almost half the Ulster Unionist negotiating team shared my view. There were two basic problems: the release of terrorist prisoners and the decommissioning of terrorist weapons. And I'm talking both sides.

'To give early release to terrorist murderers places a different value on the lives of their victims than, for example, the value of the life of a woman who has been murdered by her husband following a domestic row.

'I also have difficulty with the idea that people who have been connected with terrorist organisations could become ministers in a Northern Ireland assembly without a clear, unequivocal end to violence and the decommissioning of weapons.'

An experienced politician once declared: 'When I think I've got the answer to the Irish question, they change the question!' Does Jeffrey – the Ulster Unionist Trade and Industry Spokesman – believe the Good Friday Agreement will bring lasting peace?

'On one level there are still terrorist organisations who haven't called a ceasefire. So they're likely to continue with violence.

'From a Christian perspective I think real peace will come only when man is reconciled to God. Real peace will come only in this world when the Lord Jesus returns. Conflict between people will continue to be with us because violence is a product of sin. There will never be real peace in Northern Ireland until God re-establishes his Kingdom on earth.'

Although Jeffrey belonged to a churchgoing family (attending Sunday school and Boys' Brigade as a lad) it wasn't until 1989 that he and his wife Eleanor 'committed our lives to the Lord Jesus'. It was, he says, the end of a long journey.

'I knew something was missing in my life,' he says. 'But for a time I didn't know what it was. I thought I was in control of my life, but I wasn't really.

'I remember being at a funeral for a colleague who had been murdered by terrorists. We were singing "Abide With Me". As I looked at the coffin, all of a sudden it hit me: what if that was me? What if I had been killed, whose victory would it be?

'God spoke to me that day and brought me to the point where I recognised and acknowledged my need of salvation – salvation through a personal faith in the Lord Jesus.

'I had to come to the point where I was prepared to hand over my life to Christ. Eventually I did so and since then my life has been wonderful and rewarding. Over the years it's been great to see my relationship with God become more and more enriching.

'Some people think it's going to church on a Sunday that makes you a Christian. It isn't. Being a Christian is about having a personal faith in the Lord Jesus Christ. It's about having a personal relationship with him and being prepared to surrender your life to him.'

Of the many things his faith gives him Jeffrey reckons the greatest is 'a relationship with a Heavenly Father whom I can turn to in the deepest valley and on the highest mountain'.

It is, he maintains, through that relationship that his political life finds focus.

For many years Jeffrey wanted to be an MP. When he was 21 he was agent to Enoch Powell. At 23 he was the youngest ever member of the Northern Ireland Assembly. When he became a Christian he was prepared to give up his political ambitions. Instead, he says, it was while he was working as a financial adviser that God made it clear to him that Parliament was where God wanted him to be.

'I see being an MP as very much part of God's calling for my life,' he says.

'I feel that I have been elected not only to serve the people I represent but also to serve the Lord as an MP. For too long Christians have avoided politics. But God calls us to be lights in a world of darkness. And light needs to shine in politics as much as anywhere because Parliament is where laws are made.

'I am not the kind of person who tries to push his faith onto someone else. I believe very simply that you live out your faith and that it is through practical example that people can be changed.'

But even given a Christian presence in the shaping of legislation, won't people behave in certain ways: right or not, legal or not? In other words, we cannot legislate for morality.

'Maybe, but the Government has a responsibility to set certain standards and those standards should be influenced by the faith our nation holds, which is a Christian faith.

'Yes, some people will break those laws just as we all break God's laws. Humans by nature are sinful. But that does not mean we as a nation shouldn't set high standards for moral behaviour. Christians can't impose their will on parliament any more than they can on society as a whole. But God works through us to touch society.

'MPs themselves should set an example and provide moral leadership to our nation, on a personal level and as legislators in setting the standards and the rules for our society.'

The example of some so-called Christians over the past 30 years of violence in Northern Ireland has led many people to reject Christianity on the basis of hypocrisy. If that's how Christians behave, they say, no thank you very much! But, says Jeffrey, The Troubles is not a religious war.

'It is a conflict of political identities,' he says. 'Religion gets mixed into that because most unionists are Protestants and most nationalists are Roman Catholics.

'Very often the terms Protestant and Roman Catholic are used to describe the opposing factions in Northern Ireland. By so doing they create the impression that this is a religious war. But that's a misnomer. People don't kill each other simply on the basis of their religious beliefs. No

Christian could justify taking the life of another person because they disagreed over some theological point! It is evil that's behind the violence, not the gospel.

'God's grace is at work in Northern Ireland – in the lives of individuals, in society at large. There's no doubt that the 30 years of violence have left very deep scars on the people of Northern Ireland. Many people as a consequence of the emotional trauma of the violence in Northern Ireland have turned to Christ. Many others have rejected Christianity. But one must not lose sight of the reality that it is the grace of God that leads to salvation, not just some intellectual decision made by man or woman.

'I have no doubt God's grace has been at work during all of the troubles of the last 30 years. I have met some lovely Christian people who have lost loved ones at the hands of terrorism. To see and to hear their forgiveness is a marvellous thing.'

Jeffrey, who himself has lost two family members through terrorism, readily acknowledges that the healing process is far from easy and far from over.

'There are many open wounds in Northern Ireland, many deep scars,' he says. 'For the victims of violence, those who have suffered quietly for years, the healing process is going to take a long, long time.

'Politicians can reach a political agreement and people can vote for that political agreement but peace comes only when people's attitudes change. Peace comes only when the men of violence decide that violence is wrong.

'We're not there yet. There are still people who believe violence is justified. There is still evil in our society.'

As one who has to be careful about his personal security (he has received at least one letter bomb) how does Jeffrey cope with what has gone and what might come?

'I know my life is in God's hands,' he says. 'That gives me the strength to do the things I do. Terrorists might try to take my life, they might try to attack me but I can call upon God's protection and that means an awful lot to me.'

His first year in Parliament has been eventful, to say the least. As well as being involved in peace talks Jeffrey leads his party in the debates on the legislative implications of The Agreement. He is, however, keen to do his best for those who elected him.

'Spending time with people who come to talk about health or education issues might be less glamourous than appearing on television but it is the most important work a backbench MP can do.

'Of course the media don't focus on the advice centres and weekly surgeries but I place a high priority on my constituency work. And whatever the intenennsity of political activity in Northern Ireland in the future I will try to look after my people.'

If there was one thing Jeffrey could change in the country overnight, it would not be to deliver peace. Well, not directly.

'Obviously I think the greatest life-changing experience is for a person to give his or her life over to the Lord Jesus Christ. But I'd also like prayer to become a priority. I'd love Christians individually and collectively to be revitalised in praying. Prayer, more than anything else, changes things. Prayer changes people.'

When in Westminster Jeffrey values the opportunity to meet and pray with other Christian MPs. As well as belonging to the Parliamentary Christian Fellowship he is a member of a small group which meets regularly to pray, discuss and study the Bible.

'There are six of us,' he says. 'Two Conservatives, two Labour, one Liberal Democrat and one Ulster Unionist. The friendship and fellowship are marvellous. Hopefully the fact that MPs from four different parties can be friends in spite of their political differences is in itself an example of what is possible through Christ.'

For such understanding to happen on a larger scale it seems history, Jeffrey Donaldson and the rest of us will have to wait just a little bit longer

David Drew

Labour and Co-operative MP for Stroud since 1997. Born in South Gloucestershire in 1952. Before becoming an MP David was a senior lecturer at the University of West England. Chairman of Backbench Committee for Agriculture, Fisheries and Food since 1997. David is a member of the Church of England. Married Anne in 1990. Has two sons and two daughters.

The interview was conducted on 16 June 1998.

THE British public loved the humorous compliance of fictional MP Jim Hacker in the television comedy *Yes, Minister*. But, according to Labour and Co-operative MP for Stroud David Drew, we have no time for real-life MPs who are yes-men.

'It's better to let people know what you think rather than jump through hoops trying to keep in their good books,' says the man for whom 26,170 voters said yes last year. 'Even if they disagree with what you're proposing to do, at least they know where you stand and respect you more.

'I can be a rebel when I feel there is a purpose,' says the anti-poverty campaigner who didn't back his government on the proposal to introduce university tuition fees. 'There are times when you've got to go with your conscience, despite the pressures on you to comply.

'The whips are there to get the Government's business through the

House but unless you're prepared to stand up and be counted on occasions then you're not a very effective politician, let alone someone who has strong convictions.'

However strong his or her convictions, an MP, reckons David, can't always be voting against his or her party. To do so would be seen as a sign of unreliability.

'If you get known as one of the usual suspects you lose your influence. You have to balance your reasons not to take the official line against the fact that you need to keep your influence. Once you become marginalised and unable to get people to listen you are a far less effective weapon in terms of your political pursuits.'

There are ways of making one's opinions known other than in the voting lobby says the man who describes himself as 'a great believer in a consensual approach'.

'It's a misconception to believe that voting is the only way in which you can express your conscience. You will try to get to Government ministers, you will try to work with colleagues to form an alternative way of doing things. You will compromise as much as possible to bring about the greater good. Sometimes you have to bite your tongue. But at other times you have to stand up and be counted because clearly if you believe in something strongly enough then it is wrong not to pursue it.'

Not only do people not want yes-men it seems they don't what er-men either.

'The worst thing an MP can do is sit on the fence on every issue,' says the chairman of the Backbench Agriculture Committee. 'You can't abstain on a regular basis. You have to make your mind up.'

There was no definitive occasion that helped David decide to try for Westminster. He joined the Labour Party when he was 17, became a district councillor at 29 and entered the teaching profession after graduating from Nottingham University.

In 1992 he failed to win the Stroud seat by some 12,000 votes. Five years later he was a lecturer at the University of West England.

He describes the moment he realised he'd won his parliamentary seat as 'a shock; a pleasant realisation that years of activity and weeks of frenetic pressure had come right; daunting and a touch fearful'.

As a Christian David sees his being in Westminster as part of God's plan for his life.

'In politics you have to have self-belief, you have to be committed. But God also gave me peace of mind and the encouragement to keep going,' he says.

David has been a Christian since he was young – a keen worshipper, singing in the church choir, actively involved.

'When I left home and went to college I tended not to go to church very much. I wasn't committed at all. It wasn't that I had become a non-believer, it was more a question of life taking me in a different direction, which tends to happen with adolescents leaving home. It was only later that I rediscovered my faith.

'There was no sudden realisation. It was a gradual deciding that it was nice to go to church. I met a number of ministers who were very persuasive. It was a natural rejoining with my spirituality.

'Jesus to me is the Son of God but he's also someone who came to this earth to teach us and to raise the good things that are achievable in life. He didn't come so much to tell us off as to tell us that we can have a quality of life if we stretch ourselves spiritually as well as materially.'

Constituency duties allowing, David worships in his parish church every Sunday. Although Sunday is a busy day – taking services at a local hospital, spending time with his wife, Anne, and their four children, occasionally being the guest speaker at another church – David appreciates the chance to be able to 'concentrate on God's will'.

His faith, he says, 'gives me peace of mind, helps me make better judgments, enables me to withstand the many pressures and has led to developing some very good friendships across the political spectrum'.

There are, he acknowledges, great dangers in reading into Scripture one's particular political viewpoint. 'The strength of the Bible is in terms of its stories, which give you wider principles to tackle issues.

'Trying to be too specific can be absurd and dangerous. Jesus is not New Labour! Jesus lived in a different era. Through his parables he spoke on behalf of the poor and the dispossessed and so on. But that isn't necessarily a party political issue, that's simply an issue of how everyone treats each other and that's far more important.'

As an advocate of the consensual approach how does David answer those who think Christians should stay out of politics because it can involve compromising one's principles in the interest of self-preservation?

'I don't subscribe to that view,' he says. 'Christianity must involve itself in all aspects of life. Christians should be people who behave better than their counterparts, but this is sometimes not the case!

'If they are not willing to engage in the political process then how can they educate others about what is right and wrong?

'Yes, politics is a tapestry of pressures, problems and opportunities, as is life itself, but one's Christian faith should enable one to face the dilemmas rather than deny the right to engage. There again, if nobody got involved in politics we wouldn't have a democracy, and that would be unthinkable.'

How does David's faith help him personally engage in debates over moral issues?

'I tend to take a mainstream view in terms of the Christian approach to issues such as abortion, euthanasia and capital punishment,' he says. 'But I find it difficult to pinpoint it as the definitive Christian approach.

'I am not in favour of abortion but it is an unfortunate reality in our society. I am not in favour of capital punishment because I believe in the sanctity of life. Euthanasia I oppose, again because I believe in the sanctity of life. On lowering the age of homosexual consent I am a bit idiosyncratic. I believe that the age of heterosexual consent is too low because of the pressures that are put on young people in terms of their sexuality. I believe in equality but I would make 17 the age. I know I'll be seen as completely off the wall but young heterosexuals are as much under threat as young homosexuals.'

Looking at personal behaviour a little closer to the home of democracy, does David think the public can reasonably expect their MPs to be above reproach in their public and private dealings?

'It's difficult to say what we mean by beyond reproach but I think there is a standard of behaviour that should be upheld. In this place you tend to be a bit of a hedonist – enjoying the palace bars and the social life – or you tend to be a workaholic.

'I tend to veer towards the latter. Given the workload of an MP, I don't know how some members get time to do all these other things. While in one sense it's a matter for their own conscience I do think they owe an obligation to their electorate to meet certain norms of behaviour.

'Eventually the electorate will decide that member's fate. If constituents think they have been badly let down they will not elect that member next time round. The way to counteract the general disdain for politicians which well-publicised misdemeanours generates is for MPs to be seen to be doing their jobs on behalf of others well.'

Although he personally made a stand against the introduction of university tuition fees, does David think New Labour as a whole has lost touch with the traditional working class?

'I don't think we have these monolithic groupings like working class, middle class and upper class any more,' says the Christian Socialist Movement member. 'There is much more movement between the classes. I also think it's a myth to pretend that working-class people would necessarily feel as strongly as some middle-class people on issues like lone parent benefit.

'The fact is people on council estates in my constituency don't feel very altruistic towards people who have different problems to themselves. In the same way society as a whole is very fractured. It's easy to become very selfish and self-interested.

'It's not down to what the Government is or isn't doing. It's more a question of antipathy, of marginalisation and of exclusion.

'To think that any government can deal with those things just with a few policy tweaks is a myth. A lot of people are feeling very isolated – they wonder what the point of the political process is. Somehow we must try to engage with them and bring them back in. And that's a much deeper issue than adopting a particular policy or introducing a particular initiative.'

Although he has purposely chosen not to specialise in education ('you lack objectivity if you don't distance yourself from your past') the ex-teacher does see education as one of the issues the Government needs to get right.

'Too many kids have had a raw deal,' he says. 'I sympathise with teachers over the increased bureaucracy they have to deal with but the simple fact is that a lot of kids have had a raw deal from their schooling and that's where Government efforts have to go. There's a lot of talk about how the general standard of education in this country is very good. But some children have been short-changed

'Our education system fulfils the expectations of people who know where they are going – people who have had the opportunities. We need to widen those opportunities because in the next century anyone who is unskilled or poorly educated will be unemployed inde nitely. As a Government we must tune our policies to prevent that happening.

'The wider issue is how we are to bring the dispossessed and excluded back into society. We must attack poverty, both at home and on an international scale. The developed world is notorious for speaking loudly but doing little in reality.

'I'm very pleased that we've made some inroads in terms of international development but it is slow progress because you have to take the rest of the world with you. Eradicating poverty would turn this country into a more understanding and reasonable place to live.

'If I could change one thing about the country overnight, however, it would be to reverse the decline in active involvement in Christianity. If more people rediscovered their Christian faith their lives would be more meaningful and by dealing with poverty and helping those who live in despair the world would be a better place for all.'

And how many people wouldn't want to say yes to that?

Rt Hon Frank Field

Labour MP for Birkenhead since 1979. Born in London in 1942. Before becoming an MP Frank was a director of the Child Poverty Action Group. Appointed a Privy Councillor, 1997. At the 1997 general election he became Minister of Welfare Reform. Resigned following cabinet reshuffle, 1998. He is Chairman for the Council of Church and Associated Colleges All Party Group. Frank is a member of the Church of England.

The interview was conducted on 19 December 1995.

'I'M a radical,' says Frank Field, Labour MP for Birkenhead since 1979, when asked to describe his politics. 'I believe in the sacredness of the individual. Throughout my career I've campaigned for issues such as council-house sales, the abolition of the union block vote, the ending of fraud in the social security system and for welfare reform.'

Frank fought his first election – for Buckinghamshire South – in 1966 at the age of 22. He is now chairman of the Commons Social Security Committee, which is responsible for monitoring the biggest departmental budget – £90 billion of taxpayers' money. Frank is also involved in looking at the work of the Child Support Agency and social security fraud, as well as suggesting policy developments.

'I've always been interested in politics,' he says. 'I enjoy being able to do things which I think are worthwhile. I have the chance of meeting people and freedom over my day, which most people don't have. Above all, being in Parliament gives me a platform. After all, why should anybody take one's views about reforms seriously, if one can't get elected?'

Just as he has long been interested in politics, so he's been involved with the life of the Church.

'There's no time when I wasn't a Christian,' he says. 'I was brought up as a Christian but I've never had the certainty that some people have of a conversion experience. Mine is a constant struggle with doubt. My faith is based on the probability that the Christian way of explaining the world is a better, more coherent, more rational way than any other explanation. Therefore I accept it.

'I am attracted to R. S. Thomas's poetry because it's about struggling with uncertainty, old dogmas being thrown away and being given no handrails to survive on. The stumbling block is, does God exist? Once you can get past that then all other arguments – such as, was it a virgin birth? Was there a resurrection? – are minor points compared with the existence of God, because all things are possible once you can surmount that barricade.'

On a personal level, what does Christianity give this self-confessed 'traditional Anglican'?

'The Christian faith gives me a framework. Apart from the passing pleasures of friendship, how can one make any sense out of this life if there isn't a greater coherence than our little brains can give it? And that's what comes from Christianity – I get a sense of coherence. I can understand a bit more about our purpose for being here, and how we should live our lives.

'We've got a fight on our hands to ensure that the rumour of God survives in this country. Ecumenical politics – trying to get a uniform Church – leaves me cold. It's the politics of decline. It's looking inwards – rearranging the chairs on the *Titanic* before it goes down – rather than facing the cruel hard reality that each year more people are prepared just to be nominal church members. Churches seem to go to any length rather than accept this growth in nominalism.

'Ecumenism is one of the escape routes from the harsh reality. I wouldn't spend any energy trying to put groups together. If it's God's wish, it'll just happen. Part of the wonder of God is the diversity of expressions of Christian worship. All are equal. All are equally valid. None of them should be despised, none of them should be elevated, none of them should be curtailed just because it doesn't fit into some wonderful plan of unification that someone has thought up.'

Here is a politician speaking on religious affairs. In the past, when the

Church has spoken on political matters MPs have been among the first to tell it to keep its nose out. Can religion and politics ever mix?

'The two worlds are indivisible,' says Frank. 'The more serious Christian MPs never said that the Church shouldn't become involved in politics. What they did say was that it should know its case better. If the Church comes into the political arena it can expect a boxing match. It can't expect to come in and be treated differently, just because it's the Church.'

Has Frank ever had a personal struggle in deciding which way he should vote?

'One can exercise conscience on occasion. That is seen as being eccentric. But politics is about team-play. This place couldn't run if it were comprised of people who were always exercising consciences – doing their own thing. People have to make up their minds what they want to be, part of a team or out on their own.

'I may not be typical in this but I've been in opposition for so long I've always had great freedom in voting the way that I wish. For example, I voted for affirming union rights at GCHQ not because I'm an avid trade unionist, but because I don't believe people should be pushed around. But I was sacked from the front bench for doing so, because the party thought it wasn't advisable to vote on these matters, even though there was a vote taking place.

'There are a couple of occasions I feel ashamed of. For example, I strongly supported the first three union reform acts – I thought it was intolerable the ways the trade unions were behaving. I didn't vote for them because I was under siege and my own party was trying to sack me. I knew that if I gave my critics something else to attack me over, my supporters in Birkenhead would have felt that they couldn't cope and would get rid of me, thus giving my Trotskyite opponents the chance to win the seat.

'Moral issues are often decided in a grey area. I feel I was compromised on that occasion. It was a matter of judgment. My conscience was in the middle of it all and I decided not to exercise it but to behave in another way. That was one occasion when I've done what I've not wanted to do.

'What was so shameful was that those trade union reforms should have been Labour ideas. It shows how divorced we were from our voters. As it's worked out, I'm still here, the party has survived, the Trots didn't win Birkenhead and they've been almost exterminated from the Labour Party.

In the cut and thrust of national politics, is there a noticeable difference between Christian MPs and their non-Christian colleagues?

'I'm never conscious there are particular groups of Christian MPs and non-Christian MPs. We are a non-church nation, so there would be lots of people who might regard themselves as Christian but who wouldn't immediately stand up if you asked them. Part of our culture is a sense of reserve. I don't think the British like people endlessly parading themselves around as though they are better than other people.

'Although we are a non-church nation, we still have the intellectual capital that came from Christianity which affects what people regard as right and wrong – certainly in this place, perhaps more clearly than in other institutions.'

Speaking of right and wrong, what does he think about those MPs who are involved in political sleaze?

'It's regrettable. It's inevitable. This place isn't an island, it's representative of the whole country. There's sleaze going on out there, so it would be amazing if the House of Commons were somehow gated in the Garden of Eden.

'That doesn't excuse the behaviour here. Rather than going down the Nolan route, I think it would have been better if the Speaker had expelled people and ruled from the Chair what is not compatible with being an honourable member of this place. In one of the instances, I would have expelled for ever the people concerned.

'When one particular allegation of sleaze was raised, I was, for the only time in my career, ashamed to be a Member of Parliament. I thought it was appalling. While there is a tendency for the public to tar all MPs with the same brush, most voters think in moderately good terms about the ones they know, but collectively they think about us in rather bad terms. We have a very powerful press and MPs are frightened of being done over by the press. That worries me more than the sleaze does.'

Over the years, Frank has done some writing of his own, publishing books, journals and papers. His ambition is for his ideas on the reform of the welfare state to come to fruition.

'If there were one thing I could change about the country it would be the welfare system,' he says. 'If the next government is to be a great reforming government it will have to deal with welfare. Its budget is out of control. It may not be the most crucial issue but you won't get others right until you get this right. If we get every other policy right but fail to tackle welfare, the next Labour government will be derailed.

'We should have a welfare system that rewards you if you work hard, rewards you if you save and rewards you if you're honest. At present, it does the opposite. It's increasingly creating a nation of people who know how to work the system. In that sense it is dangerous and doesn't deserve to survive in its present form. We should be promoting the virtues of honesty, hard work and thrift, which is crucial for any society which is going to survive in the next millennium.

'The morality of the country has changed in my lifetime. People are less honest. Parliament can address it not by preaching but by practical activity. That's why welfare reforms are so important, because by reform you give a powerful message on how people should behave, and people have shown themselves willing to respond to that. It's no good preaching about honesty, hard work and savings. You need a system which encourages that and penalises the opposite.'

How does Frank see the Church contributing to his scheme of things? 'If it wants to comment it ought to do so from a theological stance. Its entry would be that any system created by human beings has to be based on a proper appraisal of human nature – both our fallen quality and our potential for redemption. That's the Church's special contribution.

'The Church has been entrusted with the most important message that mankind has ever been given. It looks as though that message is going to die out in this country. All our energies should be about preventing that happening. The number one priority for any church leader should be: "How do we teach about the faith?".

'We know faith is a gift. But it does appear that the Holy Spirit finds it easier to bestow that gift if we know something about what faith is. Hence, we ought to be thinking about how we teach it, and the most crucial area here is schools.

'We ought to take seriously the safeguarding of church schools and the opportunities the National Curriculum gives for teaching RE. At present, we do neither. And we stand condemned.'

Rt Hon Derek Foster

Labour MP for Bishop Auckland since 1979. Born in Sunderland in 1937. Before becoming an MP Derek was in marketing, a youth and community worker and Assistant Director of Education for Sunderland Borough Council. Parliamentary Private Secretary to Leader of the Opposition, 1983 – 1985. Opposition Chief Whip, 1985 – 1995. Appointed a Privy Councillor, 1993. Shadow Chancellor of the Duchy of Lancaster, 1995 – 1997. Chairman of the Employment Select Committee since 1997. Joint Chairman of the Education and Employment Select Committee since 1997. Chairman of the Parliamentary National Prayer Breakfast, 1998. He is a member of The Salvation Army. Married Anne in 1972. Has three sons and one daughter
The interview was conducted on 22 February 1996.

AS a teenager, Derek Foster played on Sunderland's street corners. Unlike many of his contemporaries, he did not confine himself to football but also played in a Salvation Army band.

Derek reckons taking part in kerbside services turned out to be a stepping-stone towards politics. 'I was really painfully shy as a young boy,' he confesses. 'I couldn't put two words together in public. I saw people doing this and it was a skill I greatly admired. But I couldn't do it. So, I prayed hard that I would be able to speak in public.

'My life was transformed at 13 when I got converted. Not only did my new-found faith give me a sense of purpose, but also I found that within 12 months I was actually speaking in outdoor services. (Sometimes I thought God had done too good a job on me because it was soon difficult for people to shut me up!)

'It did wonders for my self-confidence. As a result I began to get interested in academic work, rather than just football and cricket. I have The Salvation Army to thank for my eventually getting to Oxford. Without that transformation in my life I wouldn't have been serious enough.'

The movement as a whole, and the example of his Salvationist grandmother in particular, had a strong influence on Derek. His early involvement with The Salvation Army not only led to him setting his sights on university but also opened his eyes to a needy society.

'Playing in the band in the east end of Sunderland introduced me to a kind of poverty which was new to me,' he says.

'In common with many men of his generation, my father had long spells of unemployment. He was a shipyard worker and my mother worked in a shop. They moved to Surrey in search of work and returned to the north-east just before I was born. I grew up in an atmosphere of unemployment and saw the scars of poverty.

'We were a poor family. The most my father earned in his life was four pounds ten shillings a week. He was permanently sick for the 12 years prior to his death at the early age of 51. Although there was no money in our family, through playing in the Army band I saw a different kind of poverty, one I never knew existed.'

Far from forgetting his humble upbringing when he went to Oxford, Derek found that reading philosophy, politics and economics strengthened his resolve to bring about change.

'One of the things that sticks with me is that some fellow-students spent as much on a *night's* dinner and entertainment as my father earned in a *week!* The inequality and injustice of some people having to work extremely hard to eke out a living, while others had a much easier time of it, began to press themselves upon me.

'Reading accounts of life in the mines and mills of the 18th and 19th centuries – the conditions women and children worked under – also made a big impact on me. It struck me this was not the best way of organising society.'

In 1972, Derek, then a youth and community worker in the new town of Washington, was elected to Sunderland County Borough Council.

'I was working with families living in difficult areas,' he says. 'I'd reached the limit of my ability to get things done. So I looked for how I could have more influence in changing living conditions. Getting elected to the council seemed to be the most logical step.'

Moving from council chamber to Westminster back bench was not so deliberately planned.

'Although the idea of getting things done at a senior level had always intrigued me, I didn't see myself as a politician,' he says. It was while chairman of the North of England Development Council, a body set up to secure new investment in the region, that Derek increasingly found himself meeting mandarins in Whitehall and lobbying MPs at Westminster.

'I was getting sucked in more and more,' he recalls. 'Then, by accident, I discovered there was a vacancy for the Labour party candidacy in Bishop Auckland. I had no contacts in the town and no introduction to the local party, in addition to which another contender already had 17 nominations.'

From this unlikely start, Derek won the candidacy and went on to win the seat in 1979. His parliamentary progress to date includes terms as Opposition front bench spokesman on social security, parliamentary private secretary to Neil Kinnock and Opposition Chief Whip.

Currently shadow to the Chancellor of the Duchy of Lancaster, Derek monitors the Government's relationship with civil and public services. He is also responsible for preparing his parliamentary colleagues for the mechanics of government – nuts and bolts issues such as how government departments work; the function of functionaries.

What function would he personally like in a future Labour Government?

'Having come this far in opposition, just to be sitting round the top table, having influence on shaping Government policy and, hopefully, managing to change the country in the direction that we would like to see it go would be fascinating and well worth doing,' he says.

Before becoming a man with a Ministry, does Derek see himself as a man with a mission?

'Yes, undoubtedly. As a Salvationist, I'm very proud that The Salvation Army has always tried to minister to people's physical and spiritual needs. Indeed, the whole thing is seen as a piece. For me, it's impossible to separate religion and politics, because I wouldn't be a politician but for having been a Christian first and my social awareness having been awakened. Wanting to do something about the problems of poverty I'd seen on Sunderland street corners eventually drove me into the political arena.'

On a personal level Derek cannot separate religion and politics. But what about nationally?

'To expect the Church to be silent on social, and even political, issues is a wrong construction of what Christians and the Church is about,' he says. 'However, although the Church can enter into political argument it is well advised not to affiliate itself to one particular political party. Christians are to be found in every political party and that's absolutely right. Some Christians are reluctant to enter politics because its cut-and-thrust nature is not their style.

'By nature, I'm a conciliator. Conciliation and reconciliation is part of the political process. Politics exists to resolve conflicts which exist within society. I think some Christians shrink from that because they feel there's something unsavoury about getting stuck into conflicts.

'I'm of the opposite opinion. I think Christians have an obligation to get stuck in to conflicts and to assist people to resolve them – along the lines of "Blessed are the peacemakers". That's always been a strong motivating belief for me.'

Is there one Big Issue that Derek would like to see a future Labour Government tackle?

'Poverty is a huge issue and it will be important for us to get to grips with it,' he says. 'But perhaps even more important is the need for everyone to feel a part of the country they live in.

'We all need to feel we're important. People want to have a say and feel part of shaping the future Britain. They are very patriotic. They want to feel they are making an important contribution to it, as well as seeing progress for their own families and for their own communities. It's crucial for us to re-establish trust between people and Government.'

Speaking of which, what does Derek think about the Nolan report into personal standards in public life and the Scott report into Government involvement in the sale of arms to Iraq?

'I'm delighted that both inquiries were set up. As someone who was involved in local government, I was appalled when I came to Westminster and found standards were so lax by comparison. In local government there are standing orders which preclude all kinds of activities which within Westminster are regarded as acceptable.

'People should come into politics to serve the country and their constituents. They should not be motivated by the idea of making a lot of money. The public is rightly incensed if they perceive their representatives using the tag "MP" to feather their own nests!'

That doesn't mean Derek thinks MPs should have no outside interests. On the contrary, he thinks that knowledge of the wider world gives an MP greater credibility, within and outside the House.

'A lot of organisations,' he continues, 'seek our assistance in trying to get certain changes in the law. All of this is offered voluntarily without any thought of monetary gain. This is perfectly legitimate – part of the legislative process. I'm entirely relaxed about the existence of the whole range of lobbying organisations.

'However, you have to know whether MPs are making money from advocating the cause of others. You need to know whether an MP is speaking in his own or his constituents' interests – or in the interests of the company which is paying him.

'I think Nolan will help to rebuild public confidence in MPs. But it will take some time before the public perception of sleaze is eradicated.'

When Derek was Labour Chief Whip, his job was to marshal his colleagues to vote. Did he ever ask people to vote against their consciences?

'Political parties are most reluctant to force a person to vote against his or her conscience. On issues such as capital punishment and abortion there has always been a free vote.

'That's absolutely right. But there may be other occasions when individual colleagues feel that a certain issue has become a matter of conscience for them. A sensible Chief Whip tries to take that into account.

'You try not to force people to do things about which they are deeply unhappy. On the occasions when people are very reluctant to support their own side all you can do is to use all the personnel management skills you possess to try to persuade them. You don't always succeed, but mostly you do.'

While acknowledging that a Christian can speak out on any issue, Derek pinpoints poverty, housing, and family values as the concerns closest to his heart.

'Giving an individual the sense that he's important within society and that he can make a contribution to it is a Christian issue. I don't want a society that treats individuals as dispensable – as things that can be swatted to one side without any thought. We need companies to realise that their workers are their most important assets; companies that care about training and the contribution their workers can make. Companies which do not take joy in getting rid of people.

'The idea that it's a macho thing to boast about the number of people you've got rid of is totally alien to me. Organisations should be developed in such a way as to husband their most precious resource – people. It must always be a last resort to get rid of people. Even then, all efforts should be taken to ensure that they're found alternative opportunities.'

Here's a Labour MP talking about the importance of the individual. Is he dispensing with the traditional socialist emphasis on community?

'Not at all. I was a community worker at one time, so I'm entirely committed to community. But I believe the individual only flourishes within groups – not on his or her own. We're all members of groups. The part you play within the community is part of the recognition and the self-esteem that you get. There are some things that the individual can do for him or herself, but there are many things which you can only do by associating with other people.

'A group being able to protect the individual and encourage the full development of the individual is at the heart of truly understanding what politics is about. Communities exist in order to encourage individuals and families to develop fully. The individual cannot exist on his own.'

As a Christian, Derek is very much aware that he, too, cannot exist on his own. What does his faith give him?

'Many things. One of the things I prize greatly is the ability to deal with set-backs, because in the political life these occur regularly. It's not a life for the comfortable. So I value being able to draw upon strength other than my own to get through the daily problems and the great crises which arise from time to time. I continue in faith and optimism that I'm working towards a better future for the people I represent.'

Michael Foster

Labour MP for Hastings and Rye since 1997. Born in Hastings in 1946. Before becoming an MP Michael was a solicitor. Member of Standards and Privileges Committee since 1997. Michael is a member of the Methodist Church. Married Rosemary in 1969. Has two sons.

Interview conducted on 7 July 1998.

THERE are two MPs named Michael J Foster in the House of Commons. Both were elected for the first time in 1997. Both are Labour MPs. One is an anti-fox-hunting campaigner, the other the receiver of misdirected mail. This is he. Michael J Foster, Honourable Member for Hastings and Rye.

Taking the occasional mistaken identity in good heart, Michael is as fervent in his convictions as any anti-blood sport activist.

'Tony Blair isn't my boss. God is,' says the 'ecumenical Methodist'. 'As a Christian, I want to make things better for not only my family and my neighbours but also for people I will never know – people in India or wherever. Politics is the way you have some influence in changing society. If you just want to campaign then stand outside the Houses of Parliament and wave a banner. But if you want to change things then you try to get inside and compromise.'

Christians in the House

Compromise? Should Christians be involved in the business of political wheeler-dealing and compromise?

'I'm not ashamed of compromise,' says the self-confessed 'principled but pragmatic' Socialist. 'We achieve most by understanding what our opponents are saying and reaching mutual agreement. That way we go forward rather than take two steps forwards and one back.

'It would be wrong to compromise on Christian principles to achieve an objective but compromising on policy issues is not unchristian. If politics isn't a place for Christians I don't know where is. One of the encouraging things to discover when you first arrive here is just how many MPs profess Christianity.'

Before he became an MP, Michael practised as a solicitor, specialising in employment law. Today he is a member of the Standards and Privileges Committee, the Commons's watchdog which monitors members' privileges – such as being ably to speak freely in debates without fear of facing defamation claims – and ensures members maintain high standards in public life. How reasonable is it for the public to expect their MPs to have a higher standard of personal morality than the rest of us?

'Anyone in leadership has obligations because they are a role model for others. It is right that MPs should aspire to high standards. It is reasonable to expect MPs to be honest in their financial affairs. They shouldn't get paid twice for doing the same job. That's where the Standards and Privileges Committee comes in and looks at the issues which are of public concern.

'The other big question is whether an MP's private life is of genuine public concern. I think it is. How, for instance, can the public trust somebody who is dishonest to their spouse? Politics is not the only area where that applies but being in the limelight people tend to look to MPs more.

'That's not to suggest that some MPs won't fall short of those standards. Parliament doesn't require a standard in private morality as a condition of entry. It's up to individuals to decide what is below the level of acceptance. Concealment is the thing. Jesus reserved his strongest words for the hypocrites.'

Michael first learned about the words of Jesus at The Salvation Army in his home town of Hastings.

'I was brought up in The Salvation Army. (My mother, Dolly, is the longest-serving member in Hastings Temple.) I didn't have a Damascus Road conversion but I do remember that at about the age of eight I decided for myself that I wanted – in the words the Army used in those days – to give my heart to Jesus. That's not to say, of course, that from them on I was exempt from sin and temptation – although I think at the age of eight you think you might be! From time to time over the years I've felt the need to ask God to renew that gift when I have started to take it back. I've often asked him to help me do what's right.'

One of his early Sunday school lessons, Michael reckons, still keeps him in good stead.

'My faith gives me confidence in my decision-making. We were taught a very simple test for whenever had to make difficult decisions – ask yourself the question, what would Jesus do? It sounds very simplistic now and I know that Jesus didn't necessarily have the issues of single parents to cope with. He certainly didn't mention homosexuality and there was no cloning. But while you need to update his commands, he is probably the best agony aunt you can look to for answers to today's problems. Christianity – through the Bible, through discussion with other Christians and through prayer – does give a modern approach to almost every single social issue if you look for it.'

Michael explains the fact the two Christians, MPs or not, can reach different conclusions on each of those social issues as part of our God-given free-will and the fact that 'Jesus simply gave us the framework'. His picture of Jesus as an agony aunt might appear irreverent to some but he's not being flippant.

'For me Jesus must always be a friend,' he says, 'but he is also the Governor. It's important that we remember him as Someone who is a just God. One day we will all be judged. I like the image from the hymn 'There's a kindness in God's mercy'. Sometimes as humans we're too harsh with ourselves and with our fellow men. We are too bent on justice rather than kindness. That might be interpreted by some people as being soft but I interpret that as being a Christian.'

Like many believers, Michael finds encouragement and inspiration from reading the Bible. He finds the parables of Jesus, especially the parable of the talents, particularly appropriate.

'The parable of the talents is a good example of where Christ tells us that he expects us to use the talents we have and that we'll be rewarded for doing so. That's something which the Government wants to work on. Like the master in the parable, we want to give people the opportunities and the responsibility of making the most of who they are. That, to me is at the heart of Christianity is about.'

People have, he reckons, more opportunities under New Labour than under previous incarnations.

'Far from betraying the working class, we have fulfilled the possibility for the working class, if by that we mean people who live essentially by their labours. Labour principles remain constant. It is about opportunity; looking after the poor; and creating wealth for the benefit of the many and not just the few. None of that is possible unless we accept that we have to produce the goods. There has to be a cake to be divided. New Labour recognises human frailty – that people work better if they are looking not only to their community but also to themselves and their family. We want to harness people's personal efforts to benefit the wider community. None of us by ourselves can own a National Health Service. Few can afford a bus company. But by encouraging individual endeavour and increasing personal – and thereby Government – wealth society as a whole will benefit.'

The Christian Socialist Movement member sees his being in Parliament as the coming together of personal ambition and God's will for his life. Although he has not been there long his Christian conscience has already been tested.

'The first occasion was over the Government's support for the bombing of Iraq if UN weapon's inspectors were not allowed access to installations by Saddam Hussein. That was a tough decision. In the end I vote with the Government because I was ultimately persuaded that if nothing was done then the world would be at risk. In the event the bombers weren't sent. But UN Secretary General Kofi Annan subsequently said that it was the threat of force coupled with diplomacy that brought about a peaceful resolution. Of course, you don't know that at the time you're voting. And I found it extremely difficult to walk through a lobby and say I support the possible use of force.

'The other occasion was over the Government's decision to remove an additional income payment to single parents. Again there were conflicting moralities. Is it right to give preference to single-parent families and, if not, how do we make sure that the children in such families do not suffer? The issue was effectively resolved in the end by the fact that we came up with wider measures which gave incentives to single parents. As Tony Blair puts it: better a hand up than a hand-out. And that fits in with my Christian principles – charity isn't necessarily the answer. Opportunity may be.'

On the wider front can Parliament ever legislate for public morality?

'No, it can't. But legislation gives out the message that certain things are OK. For example, I voted for the reduction of the age of homosexual consent. The only argument against it that I had to think hard about was what message will lowering the age give? I know that just because something is lawful, it doesn't make it right. If it were we'd have a law banning adultery because adultery breaks up more families and creates more misery that ever a reduction in the age of homosexual consent would do.

'Legislation can only do so much and you need to be careful that you don't send out the wrong signals. Maybe in the longer term, as in the case of women's votes and the abolition of slavery, public opinion is changed by changing the rules.'

Opponents of the lowering of the age of consent feared that Parliament would eventually give way to further gay lobby demands such as a further lowering of the age to 14 and same-sex relationships being recognised in property, probate and marital legislation. Is that the way things will go?

'I know of no MP who would support a lowering of the age of consent to 14,' he says. 'This was an issue of equality and, in determining that, MPs needed to decide whether there were overwhelming reasons for denying it. I did not think there were. That doesn't mean to say that I support homosexual – or heterosexual – sex at 16. There were many MPs who would rather have seen the age of consent raised to 18. Or as I rather glibly suggested 43! But that isn't practical. We have to accept that folk are sexually active at 16; that homosexual sex happens at 16 and, therefore, that youngsters of 16 and 17 need to be protected from predators without the fear of being criminalised if they report it.

'It wouldn't be Christian marriage but there should be some formal recognition of homosexual relationships. A priest once put it to me like this: if we were to remove the cement of society's acceptance of heterosexual relationships, how would heterosexuals behave? The chances are, he reckoned, they would behave like animals. The tie of faithfulness and public acclaim would disappear and they would behave badly.

'Therefore, if as Christians we believe that faithfulness and honesty and long-lasting relationships are important then to deny the cement of acceptability to those who are in such same-sex relationships is likely to encourage promiscuity.'

Homelessness is the one thing about the country Michael would change overnight if he could.

'One of the greatest blights on our society is that 400 or 500 people will be on the streets of London tonight. I am delighted the Government is addressing this problem. I know The Salvation Army and other churches are doing their bit but if there were to be an instant miracle (I don't believe in magic wands) it would make us all feel good to know that nobody is homeless.'

While waiting for the miracle, what one issue must Michael's Government get right.

'It sounds boring but we must get the economy right,' he says. 'If we don't we'll be back to the days of boom and bust, and we won't be able to achieve all our social ambitions. We want an education system we can be proud of. We want a vibrant National Health Service. We want to look after our pensioners. We want to help alleviate Third World poverty. But it all depends on getting the economy right.'

And with that Michael Foster leaves to out-fox those who mistake him for someone else.

Rt Hon John Gummer

*Conservative MP for Suffolk Coastal since 1983. MP for Lewisham West, 1970 –
1974. MP for Eye, 1979 – 1983. Born in Stockport in 1939. Before becoming an MP
John was a publisher and a company director. Minister of State, Department of
Employment, 1983 - 1984. Conservative Party Chairman, 1984 - 1985.
Paymaster-General, 1984 - 1985. Appointed a Privy Councillor, 1985. Minister of
State for Agriculture, Fisheries and Food 1985 – 1988. Minister of State,
Department of Environment 1988 – 1989. Minister of Agriculture, Fisheries and
Food, 1989 – 1993. Secretary of State for the Environment 1993 - 1997. John is a
Catholic. Married Penelope in 1977. Has two sons and two daughters.*

The interview was conducted on 30 October 1996.

SINCE becoming a Conservative MP in 1970, John Gummer has held many
positions of responsibility in the House of Commons. Government Whip,
Parliamentary Secretary, Lord Commissioner of HM Treasury, Paymaster
General, Minister of State, and Party Chairman preceded his promotion to
his present responsibility – Secretary of State for the Environment – in 1993.

Coincidentally, that was also the year John left the Church of England
for the Roman Catholic Church. Sitting 16 floors above contradiction in his
Marsham Street office, the Anglican clergyman's son explains why he felt
he had to move from one house of the Lord to another.'I believe Christ

84

founded one Church,' he says. 'When I believed the Church of England ceased to see itself as part of that church by making its own rules, it seemed to me it was in the same position as a whole range of other sects (I use the word technically). When it stopped claiming to be part of the Church that Christ founded many people felt it was impossible to remain Anglicans. It was the fact that the Church of England thought it could decide for itself rather than anything to do with the nature of specific rules that made me leave.'

At the time, the church was publically debating woman priests, the Virgin Birth and the Resurrection. Did those debates colour his decision to leave?

'I did not leave over the issue of the ordination of women. I am agnostic as to whether women should be priests or not. It's not an issue that terribly moves me. What does move me absolutely passionately is the question of whether the Church is the Church or not. The Church of England has decided that it is easier for it not to seek to uphold the nature of the whole Church, but to become a group on its own.

'The Church of England hasn't made a definite pronouncement about issues like the Virgin Birth. But what it has said is that it *could* do. In other words, rather than maintaining its traditional view that it is part of the Catholic Church – divided visibly by history but not in faith – it decided it was going to make up its own mind. Unilateralism is bedevilling the Church. It always comes when a generation thinks it knows better, and always ends up in division.'

Looking back to the beginnings of his faith, growing up in a vicarage, how did he becoming a Christian?

'I think you grow and retreat,' he says. 'There have been long periods of retreat and coldness. There have been periods of very fast revelation in the sense of understanding more clearly and growing awareness. Outside factors have an effect on that. Sudden impressions and people that you've known have an effect too.

'In the end, you catch the faith from Christians, through glimpses of Christ in the Gospels or through the teaching of the Church. Man's relationship with God is a personal relationship. The concept of a divine being who becomes man is an important part of an understanding of how religion is communicated. Christianity is communicated in that personal way. Not that I believe in the sort of personal religion where you make your mind up about which bits you take and which bits you don't!'

Did the Right Honourable Member for Suffolk Coastal ever feel he should have entered the ministry of the Church rather than the Ministry of Agriculture?

'I grew up in the sort of atmosphere where becoming a priest was an ever-present possibility,' he says. 'But I never thought I had the necessary vocation.

'I've always wanted to be an MP. Having been brought up in a vicarage,

I'm very fond of the idea of looking after a patch and caring for people's interests and concerns. The fact that every week I can look back and say I was able to help someone in my constituency is a very rewarding thing. It makes up for all the knocks.

'Secondly, there are particular issues about which I feel very strongly. One is to help build in Europe the kind of relationships which will ensure we will live together as nations in the future instead of going to war. When I came into politics Britain was not playing her part in Europe. Now she is and her world role is much greater. That gives us a real chance to make some changes in the world.'

Does he see being an MP as his vocation?

'Cardinal Newman was right when he said that God has a special work for each of us,' he says. 'I don't see being an MP as different from other jobs. In fact, I get rather annoyed with people who think it is. You can, for example, have a vocation to be a carpenter. It's then a question of being a good carpenter, or honest carpenter, of doing your best and playing your part. In that respect, MPs aren't any different from anyone else. One should do the job as well as one can.

'I find it disagreeable when people feel there's something unsuitable about being an MP. The overwhelming majority of MPs of all political parties are not in politics for any other reason than to try to serve the people they represent. Like many people in other jobs, we passionately believe in certain things. That's a perfectly genuine and proper role to play in society.'

What does his faith give him?

'That's difficult, because I'm terribly conscious that one should be looking at it the other way round. We live in a me-centered society in which everybody asks about their rights. Faith isn't me-centered. The question suggests that you have a faith because it does something for you. I hope that's not true. The hymnwriter was right in saying: 'My God, I love thee; not because I hope for Heaven thereby, nor yet because who love thee not are lost eternally.'

'While it's true we do have all sorts of temporary reasons for shoring up our faith, in the end, faced with the stark reality, I believe because I *have* to believe. The figure of Christ looming over the ages is a figure which is devastatingly demanding. Many of the truths of the gospel are uncomfortable. In the end you have to say, "I believe".

'Of course, you believe with different intensities and with reservations from time to time. I don't like the word pilgrimage because it suggests always going in the one direction.

'The trouble with the Christian life is that you're going backwards and forwards all the time, a bit of an advance here and a bit of a fall-back there.

The faith is about catching it and having to say: "In the end I have to make a decision. I have to accept either the claims of Christ or the claims of somebody else". Therefore it's not about what faith gives you, it's what faith demands of you.'

How does the MP who for 13 years was a member of the Church of England General Synod see the increasing media interest in politicians' faith?

'It's a pretty quick turn around,' he says, chuckling. 'I've spent most of my life being told how much better it would be if one never talked about it. I think this is a passing interest. It arises from a general realisation that many post-war theories have clearly not worked.

'The idea that "I have a right to break up my marriage", "I have a right to be happier" and so on has resulted in enormous social pressures and been a huge disaster.

'Newspapers have an idea there's a lot of unhappiness in the country. So they're thrashing around to see what the answer is. There are debates about school discipline and family life. You can't even use the word family. You have to interpret it now. People don't take the family for what most sane, sensible human beings have taken it to mean down the ages. We have gone through a period in which the once much-prized notion of motherhood and the nurturing of children has been cast aside.

'Time was when both husband and wife were proud that the wife's prime duty was to bring up the children. They would have felt rather ashamed if, for one reason or another, they hadn't done that. Now the thing is entirely the reverse. We have created a world in which women are almost embarrased to say this is important to them.

'Consequently, there's a feeling in society that we've got all the things we wanted. People are better off than ever before. Even the poorest define poverty in a way which would have been utterly impossible in the days of William Booth. But people are discovering that the material quality of life doesn't deliver what they thought it would. They are thrashing around. And if you're going to thrash around, politicians are a pretty good target.

'One has to start from the assumption that religion is much more important than politics. The thing that worries me about this link is that very often politicians, having decided what their political views are, claim Christian support for it. That is intolerable. Christianity is about the acceptance of truth and the application of truth in one's daily life. People making different judgments based on their faith is part of our God-given creativity.'

So, to use his earlier analogy, are Christian MPs recognisable more by the way they go about their business than the policies they pursue?

'Yes, although there are certain issues which (and I don't want to unchristianise anyone) seem to me to be absolutely impossible for

Christians to accept. A Christian can't be a fascist or a communist, because the central tenet of both is unchristian. But you can be a member of any other political party.

'I think it's impossible for Christians to support abortion. The Church clearly teaches that abortion is unacceptable. A Christian who votes for abortion and doesn't seek to stop it and protect the child, seems to me to be taking an intolerable position.

'You have to oppose any issue which is manifestly contrary to Christian teaching. However, at the heart of serious Christian concerns there is space for Christian judgment.'

As MPs warm up for the general election, the Environment Secretary sees warming of a grander scale as one of the big issues facing the next Government.

'Global warming is a reality,' he says. 'We're going to have to change the way we live if we are to ensure the planet is here for our children. The idea of reducing taxation on home heating is wholly contrary to any concept of stewardship of the world's resources and any concern for protecting us from the effects of global warming.'

Is he suggesting VAT was put on domestic fuel out of concern for the environment?

'I pressed for it,' he asserts. 'The cost of heating has fallen very sharply and because people have increasingly turned up the heat rather than put a jumper on, we've got to ensure sensible use of the world's resources, while also finding a way of helping the poor.

'That's why we introduced a more than compensatory amount on pensions and spent huge sums on home insulation. We've spent much of the money raised through VAT on fuel on energy-saving activities.'

Is there anything he would like to change about the country?

'I'd like to change the language,' he says after a long pause, 'so we no longer talk about rights, and talk only about obligations, because my rights are actually my obligations. Emphasising my rights is a grasping, grabbing, self-centred view. That is corrosive. If you emphasise my obligations and your obligations then we're being generous.

'God's generosity is one of the great marks of Christianity. We need to recover a sense of thankfulness for that generosity. We are created beings. We have no rights, but we do have obligations. Because we are created by a loving God our obligations are about loving relationships with other people.'

Now there's an environmental policy few would disagree with.

Simon Hughes

Liberal Democrat MP for Southwark North and Bermondsey since 1997. MP for Bermondsey, 1983. MP for Southwark and Bermondsey, 1983 – 1997. Born in Cheshire in 1951. Before becoming an MP Simon was a barrister. Simon is Chairman of the Parliamentary Christian Fellowship. Simon is a member of the Church of England.

The interview was conducted on 11 April 1996.

THE QUEEN pays income tax, thanks to Simon Hughes. In July 1991 the MP for Bermondsey and Southwark tabled a motion requiring the monarch to pay tax on personal income. It was not so much an act of disloyalty, more the action of a man who is fiercely intolerant of injustice.

'We live in an unjust world where resources aren't fairly shared,' says the Liberal Democrat spokesman on Urban Affairs. 'I didn't come into parliamentary politics to defend the status quo but to make the country a fairer and more just society. I want to make the *world* fairer and more just – to help people better understand the ideas of stewardship and individual responsibility. The Queen paying tax was one small but symbolic campaign towards that fairer society.'

While Hughes wants his message to reach the upper echelons, his

89

motivation comes from life at street level. When he lived in Bermondsey in the days before the emergence of yuppie developments he saw injustice first-hand.

'As a church youth club leader, I knew how difficult it was for local people to get their voices heard, how the system conspired to thwart people's aspirations. People were living in overcrowded houses with leaky roofs. They were blighted. But they couldn't get moved – the system said no. People could never find anyone who would deal with them.

'I saw how frustrated and demoralised people were. Families on estates were under great pressure – with lack of play space for energetic youngsters and so on. This led me to think that we've got to be able to do better. It was really a belief that people in the inner city were being completely oppressed, suppressed and repressed and that this was not fair or just.'

Having enjoyed the space and freedom of the countryside as a child, Simon wanted to do something to improve inner-city life. He stood for election to the Greater London Council in 1981. Although the electorate did not return him to County Hall, it did return him to the House on the other side of the Thames in a by-election two years later.

What evidence does the former barrister have that he has improved the lot of his constituents during his time in Westminster?

'The job of politicians is to enable individuals to live their lives to their full potential and to provide a structure for society that supports people when they are in need. The most consistent way I feel I have been of use is to help people who tell me I'm their last resort.

'There are many individuals and families who we have been able to help practically across the whole range of social needs – social security, housing, employment, education or health. I hope I've played a part in getting local stations built on the Jubilee Line extension, which will boost the local economy. We are currently battling to ensure there's no reduction of local health provision at Guy's and St Thomas's hospitals'.

Simon's mission for social justice also stems from his faith. Brought up in a Christian family and confirmed in the Church in Wales, Simon reaffirmed his faith shortly after leaving Cambridge University.

'While at a conference I met Christian converts from all over the world. Seeing the faith of those who had come newly into Christianity, and the difference it had made to them, inspired me. I realised Christianity wasn't just a matter-of-fact everyday thing one should just take for granted.

'I decided, there and then, that my faith would come first in my life, and I have tried to hold on to that ever since.'

Simon describes himself as a 'non-denominational evangelical Christian'.

'For me that means two things,' he explains. 'The Church is one Church. Denominations have been the bane of the Church's life. My Saviour didn't say anything about denominations. Technically I'm a disestablished Anglican, but I refuse to be labelled an Anglican or a Nonconformist.

'I'm evangelical because I believe that one of my jobs is to spread the gospel and to bring people to Christ – to evangelise as and where appropriate.'

Does he think the Church and politics can happily coexist?

'No, not happily. They should always make life more difficult for each other. The gospel is about permanent truths and the best ordering of society, whereas politics is run by fallible human beings who have a range of motives, including party interest, self-interest and self-preservation.

'Trying to be selfless, far-sighted and non-sectarian is very difficult for politicians. Christianity is always a challenge to them, but politics should be just as much an area for Christians to get involved in as anywhere else. There are no no-go areas in God's world. It is a nonsense if people don't seek to apply their faith to politics.

'I can't hide behind theology. I must try to apply theology to the real world. As a Christian MP, my job is to seek to bring the Kingdom of God to this earth as soon as possible, without being arrogant about it.'

If Christianity is a 'challenge to politicians', what challenges does Simon face as a Christian politician?

'Being honest about your own views, about the policies of your party and about your opponents. It's very easy to distort what your opponent might say just slightly, or leave things out or put things in to one's own advantage. There are challenges about being silent when you should speak up. There are difficult Christian and ethical issues, such as divorce, abortion and homosexuality, where the challenge is to work out what is the best legislation.

'For example, I believe abortion is wrong. But something that is wrong may nevertheless be something that somebody decides to do for their own reasons. MPs have to legislate for a society where people often do wrong things. Therefore, I voted for abortion to be legal up to 24 weeks, because if I had voted against abortion altogether it wouldn't have stopped abortions. I had to come to an ethical decision, which I did after much prayer, struggling and talking through. This is what I mean by applied theology.

'Sometimes I get slated. People write in, saying, "How dare you vote for abortion – you're a Christian!" I reply by saying that while the Bible has the "thou shalt not kill" principle, which is something I seek to apply to myself and others, I recognise people can be driven to do things which they know are wrong but they do it in spite of themselves.

'So it's often a case of choosing between the lesser of two evils. The fundamental thing to realise when you're in Parliament is that you can't legislate for obedience to God's commands – even when you're clear in your own mind what obedience would mean for you and for others. People don't become obedient to God's commands because you legislate!

'South Africa, for example, has abolished apartheid in law. But that hasn't eradicated prejudice in people's hearts. You have to legislate in a way which enables people to make their decisions better, in a more informed way, yet recognise we are all personally accountable to our Creator. MPs and legislators can't take that responsibility away from people. We have to legislate for a humanity that makes mistakes all the time and give people the structure whereby they can pick up the pieces. That's the dilemma. I'm legislating both for people who are not Christians and for Christians who make mistakes!'

Is there room, then, in British politics for a Christian party?

'Yes, but it would be a bad idea. The history of Europe shows Christian parties have become more right wing, and many Christians of the left feel they couldn't belong. The gospel is about being radical and not conservative, about being progressive and not reactionary, and therefore to drive Christians into parties that are seen to be reactionary is unfortunate. So I would regret it if there were a Christian party and that's why I haven't joined the Movement for Christian Democracy.'

What about Tony Blair's widely reported Easter piece in *The Sunday Telegraph* where he said that a person can't be a Christian and vote Conservative?

'Tony Blair didn't actually say that. What he *did* say was that his faith led him to the view that he was to be on the left, and for him it meant he couldn't be Conservative. But he accepted that other people were perfectly honest and honourable Christians who were led to be Conservatives or Liberals, or have other positions. He made it very clear that it wasn't for him to say: "My politics are the only answer." I think that's right and I defended him on that basis. As politicians we must recognise that Christian faith will lead people into different directions so far as party politics is concerned.

'Faith doesn't lead you to a specific manifesto. Faith doesn't give you a crystallised set of policy proposals for the next election. The Christian faith is about principles and the practice of those principles. It doesn't say, for example, that the best way of raising tax from home buyers is to set mortgage interest tax relief at 25 per cent.'

Being the LibDem parliamentary spokesperson on health, community relations, urban affairs and young people's issues gives Simon a wide view of national life. What one thing would he like to change?

'I'd like to see everyone housed properly. That is an entirely deliverable political objective. In a five-year term of Parliament there could be decent housing in Britain. Nobody need be in squalid accommodation.

'The one job in Government I'd like is to be housing minister, to ensure that in a rich nation we didn't have so many people sleeping on the streets, or living in overcrowded or inadequate housing. All that's lacking is the political will.

'I'd like to be able to reduce the difference between the haves and have-nots throughout the world, correcting the injustices that breed individualism. I'd like every country to make it a government objective to reduce the gap between the rich and the poor, globally. At present the rich, strong and healthy are walking away with all the benefits of a world which was given to us all to share.'

Would becoming Minister of Housing be the fulfilment of a personal ambition?

'I don't have a job ambition. My only ambition is to be a better MP for the people I represent. I don't plan to be here for ever. If we were to have the chance of being in, or sharing in, Government and if somebody offered me a job I think I could do and wanted to do, then I'd accept it.'

Speaking of which, how does he see the possibility of his party forming part of a minority government after the next election, along the lines of the Lib-Lab pact of the late '70s?

'Unless we were sufficiently big to make the ratio between us and Labour fair, it would be better for us to be supporting the things we agreed with, and opposing the things we didn't, from the Opposition benches. If there were just a few of us, even 30 or 35 MPs, we would have very little influence on policy, yet we would have to take responsibility for every decision. That would be the worst of all possible worlds.

'Given that politicians are in Westminster to be in power, if we had 50 MPs and the Labour Party were to offer to collaborate, we should consider it carefully. That way we could be an effective influence. Unless there was electoral reform, the better way of doing that would be to agree beforehand with Labour what we could and couldn't support them on.'

Before dwelling too much on the heady notion of having jam tomorrow, is this MP one of those eating beef today?

'Yes,' he says, smiling. 'I like it. I've tried to be responsible in the House with my colleagues and not be alarmist. Those who press the panic button are over-reacting. Beef is as safe as anything else that comes out of the butcher's or from the supermarket. I don't think we should be overly frightened. In life you can never protect yourself against every eventuality. And there are many things that are less safe than eating beef, so the answer is yes!'

Joan Humble

Labour MP for Blackpool North and Fleetwood since 1997. Born in Skipton in 1951. Before becoming an MP Joan worked for the DSS and the Inland Revenue. Member of Lancashire County Council, 1985 - 1997. Joan is a member of the Orthodox Church and worships at the Methodist Church. Married Paul in 1972. Has two daughters.

The interview was conducted on 18 November 1997.

LITTLE did the National Front supporter realise that putting a leaflet through Joan Humble's letter box would put her on the road to Westminster. But that's precisely how the career of the Labour MP for Blackpool South and Fleetwood began.

'My husband, Paul, picked it up and chased after the man who had delivered it,' she says. 'Fortunately he didn't catch him. He said, "I'm not going to let these so-and-sos push any more leaflets through my letter box." So we got a spare Labour poster from a house opposite and put it in the window. After the election the secretary of the local party called asking if we would join. So we did.'

Joan grew up in Keighley, crossing the Pennines to go to Lancaster University where she specialised in ancient and medieval history. While at university she met and married Paul, and on graduating went to work for the DHSS. When they moved to their present home in Preston Joan got a job with the Inland Revenue.

'I've now done the two most unpopular jobs in the world,' she smiles. 'Working for the tax office and being a politician!'

Although she admits she would have dissuaded National Front workers by displaying Conservative or Liberal posters had they been available, joining the Labour Party was a more considered decision.

'To me the Labour Party has always represented the interests of a wider community and not just the interests of a few,' she says. 'I'm a great believer in society. I believe we should all contribute to the best of our abilities to help other people. We were all created equal and we all ought to work together.'

But hasn't New Labour deserted the interests of the traditional working class?

'Society has changed,' she says. 'The Labour Party recognises that the old class divisions no longer apply. Even when I went to grammar school in the '60s, class didn't apply as once it did.

'There was the doctor's daughter, the lawyer's daughter, the bank manager's daughter, but the rest of the girls came from backgrounds like mine. My father worked on the buses and my mother worked in the mills.

'Besides what does middle class mean today? What concerns me is the development of an under class. People who have never worked, people who live in poverty. The Labour Party wants to give those who depend on welfare benefits reasonable prospects of work. We want to get the long-term unemployed back into work.

'Many of this country's teenagers have given up hope of a decent job. And given up hope altogether. That's awful! We need to give them something to hope for.'

Joan became a Lancashire county councillor in 1985 and chaired the social services committee for the seven years prior to her election last May. It was, she says, a succession of events rather than one defining moment that spurred her into standing for Parliament.

'Our two daughters had grown up,' she says. 'The time was right. For 12 years I had seen the rules and regulations of central government affect what I could do in local government. I wanted to be making the rules so other local councillors didn't have to make the harsh decisions I had to make.

'It was also a period of enormous excitement within the Labour Party itself. I wanted to be part of the New Labour changes - improving society, preparing it for the next millennium.'

Despite the realities of separation from family, late-night debates and mounting unease about some Government proposals, the excitement at being an MP has not worn off.

'We really did, in the words of that phrase, "hit the ground running". In the first few weeks we banned handguns, legislated for money to be transferred from the assisted places scheme to provide for more infant school teachers, and had referendums for the Welsh Assembly and Scottish Parliament.

'While the initial excitement and momentum has kept me going, I'm very much aware of the difficulties many of my constituents face. Many people have very high hopes of this Government. They want us to wave a magic wand and transform the country instantly. They will have to be patient. Some of the changes will take some time.'

But isn't the Government's insistence that it will deliver on all its election pledges and do away with sleaze, while exciting – refreshing even – a trifle naive?

'The Labour Party has always been open and honest about where our money comes from. Perhaps in the instance of Bernie Ecclestone's £1 million donation to party funds we were naive to suppose that having openly declared that the motor racing boss had given us money, we assumed the public would accept that any decision on tobacco advertising in motor racing would be taken purely on the basis of whether it is right or wrong.

'But I hope we can re-examine the whole basis of party funding as a result of this episode. That way the electorate can have their faith in politicians restored.

'I don't like the way in which the status of politics and politicians has declined over recent years. Politicians are disparaged because people have seen too many who have not lived up to the high standard that I personally think we should attain. MPs should offer leadership and live up to higher standards. We are, after all, referred to as "Honourable Members".'

Honourable and Right Honourable Members, according to Joan, are entitled to a private life. It is only when a private failing affects an MP's capacity to do their job that the public should expect to hear of it.

'What I am much more concerned about is public probity,' she says. 'I believe in open and honest government. There should be no financial irregularities. When stories of an MP's private life hit the papers I worry that innocent people get hurt.

'I am against hypocrisy. Those who preach about family values shouldn't practise adultery. But it's also important to remember that Christians don't always live up to the high personal standards they set themselves. Certainly none of us should be judgmental about those who fall in love with someone other than their husband or wife.'

Joan, whose husband is also a Christian, describes her religious upbringing as 'unusual'.

'My parents came to this country after the Second World War as refugees from Yugoslavia,' she says. 'I was raised in the Orthodox faith, which is wonderfully elaborate and is one of the earliest Christian churches. My parents were keen for me to have a religious education so they sent me to the local Church of England Sunday school. As a child I found this mix of high and low church fascinating but bewildering.

'As I grew older I developed an academic interest in the development of the Christian religion. I enjoyed reading about the development of the early Church and how the Church fragmented. So my faith has not always been focused on one particular denomination. My parents instilled in me a belief in God. How that belief is then demonstrated is secondary.'

Unlike many young people Joan did not rebel against her spiritual upbringing when she left home.

'My parents taught me very well the importance of family, moral values and moral certainties based on Christianity,' she says. 'It was so matter of fact – this is a common sense way to run your life and it is one that will succeed. It is absurd to rebel against that which is common sense!

'They also encouraged me to find my own faith and were sympathetic on the occasions I didn't want to go to church. Faith and belief were not just something that happened in church on Sundays, they were part of everyday life.'

As well as giving her 'strength of character', Joan reckons her faith also gives her 'a centre to my life' which, among other things, supports and guides her in the bringing up of her children and in her political decision-making.

In an increasingly busy schedule she is grateful for times when she renews and strengthen her faith through worship. Despite being an irregular churchgoer, Joan is very sure of what Jesus means to her.

'First and foremost, Jesus to me is the Son of God,' she says. 'He is the incarnation of our faith on earth. Jesus was also an historical figure who dealt with what was happening in the politics of his own world.'

She says there have not yet been occasions when her faith has conflicted with her party's voting requirements.

'So far I have voted on issues that were included in our manifesto but there may well be difficult choices coming before us,' she says. 'There's the question of how Third World debt should be dealt with. And issues of personal morality. We will be looking at the age of consent for homosexuals and we might be revisiting areas of abortion law.'

How will she vote on those issues?

'I will vote for the age of homosexual consent to be lowered to 16,' she says. 'The present law is discriminatory. The few of my constituents who have written voicing dissent tend to be those who are against homosexuality altogether.

'Abortion is a very difficult issue. I am reasonably happy with the current provisions. But any women who has felt life grow within her has to view abortion with repugnance. Fortunately I have never been in a position to have to contemplate it. If abortion is to be undertaken it should be the last resort in particularly difficult circumstances. It should not be regarded as a birth-control method.

'While medical advances will probably mean that we have to look at abortion time limits, I would prefer to address it from the perspective of doing more to reduce the number of unwanted pregnancies. We should be providing more education on sexual health.'

Joan readily admits she finds medical advancements in euthanasia and genetic engineering frightening. She would, she says, consult those with first-hand knowledge before casting her vote.

'On the surface some aspects of genetic engineering like preventing degenerative disease seem sensible,' she says. 'What we have to decide is what is acceptable and what is not. That's scary!

'We are now getting stories about genetically modified vegetable crops. How are they going to affect us? Many experts believe BSE came about because we fed meat to cattle, effectively turning vegetarians into carnivores. We have to be very careful. We shouldn't allow scientists to run away with their discoveries and then present us with implications we don't fully understand.'

As a member of a European standing committee Joan spends much of her time in Westminster dealing with European legislation on agriculture and fisheries. With that and her work as secretary to the Backbench Departmental Committee on Culture, Media and Sport she is able to represent two of the main industries of her constituency – Fleetwood fishing and Blackpool tourism.

It is the boosting of local economies through the welfare to work programme that Joan sees as the biggest challenge facing her Government.

'Welfare to work and the New Deal are central to what we want to achieve,' she says. 'New Deal is our promise, from this coming April to get a quarter-of-a-million 18 to 25-year-olds back to work. From June we shall be addressing the needs of the over-25-year-olds.

'It is a key issue in my constituency,' says the mother of daughters aged 17 and 20. 'We have many young people who have never had any hope of employment. We will be offering those who failed at school the chance to go back and get themselves qualified. Our local colleges are very enthusiastic about the scheme.

'We have to get more people into work. We need to improve the economy and provide more jobs. Only then will we have the resources to improve the NHS, education, transport and social services.'

A busy time ahead, then. And all because the lady was given a leaflet.

Ieuan Wyn Jones

Plaid Cymru MP for Ynys Môn since 1987. Born in North Wales in 1949.
Before becoming an MP Ieuan Wyn was a solicitor. Plaid Cymru Whip, 1991
– 1995. Spokesman on Welsh Affairs. Ieuan Wyn is a member of the Baptist
Church. Married Eirian in 1974. Has two sons and one daughter.
The interview was conducted on 28 January 1997.

SEVENTY years ago, when Britain's Empire covered atlases in pink, the
primary aim of the newly-formed Plaid Cymru was to achieve dominion
status for Wales within the Commonwealth. As today's domestic political
map changes to red the party's sights are on Wales becoming a self-
governing European nation.

'There's a great deal of misunderstanding about what Welsh people are
arguing for,' says Ieuan Wyn Jones, MP for Ynys Môn.

'There's a general feeling that transferring power away from
Westminster to Wales will break up a unitary state but we need to have
our own identity. Uniformity is something which destroys people's
capacity to develop in their own way.

'Wales is a nation and as such it needs its own institutions. The Welsh
Office was set up in 1964 and has some £7bn to spend on domestic issues

like roads, health and education. But although there has been devolved administration, the people of Wales do not have the political power to decide how that money should be spent. We want a transfer of power to a Welsh-elected body which would have the responsibility for all legislation and, eventually, for the raising of taxes.'

Only after receiving a clear mandate from the people of Wales through a referendum would there be an autonomous Welsh Parliament. Welsh extremists burning holiday homes receive no sympathy. Only condemnation.

'The use of violence and other unconstitutional methods is something we cannot support,' he says.

Ieuan Wyn, with his wife, Eirian, and their three children, made Angelsey his home in the mid 1980s and has represented the island since 1987, retaining the seat with an increased majority in this year's general election.

It is, he reckons, essential to live among his constituents. 'I can't imagine how MPs can do the job unless they live in their constituency, or at least spend a significant proportion of the time there. That's the only way they can represent their people properly,' he says, pointing out that his mother was born in his constituency, as were some of his father's family.

A solicitor by training, Ieuan Wyn traces his interest in politics to his childhood. His father was a minister. Welsh chapel not Whitehall cabinet.

'My father was a quarryman before he became a Baptist minister,' he says. 'His passion for politics – both he and my mother were Plaid Cymru members – led to a great deal of discussion within the family. He was also interested in the relationship between the social aspects of his work and the need to try to change people's lives for the better.'

Ieuan Wyn 'never really seriously contemplated' going into the ministry.

'I was never pushed by my family into thinking along those lines,' he says. 'For me it was never an inevitable consequence of being a minister's son. Politics was a much more natural course for me to take, although – belonging to a party that has only a few seats in Westminster – being an MP is not something you can plan for from an early age.'

While hesitating to describe his parliamentary career as a calling – 'although you want to improve the lives of people whom you represent' – he does see it as a mission.

'It's a constant battle to remind yourself why you were sent here in the first place and what you want to achieve,' he admits.

'But I feel strongly that although we live in a time of increased communication people are becoming increasingly alienated from the political process. Unless MPs keep in touch with their electorate the system will fall into disrepute.'

How did growing up in a manse affect his Christian faith?

'Having a minister as a father you either become a firm believer or a rebel. I was never tempted along the rebel road,' he confesses. 'I can't remember a time when I didn't believe in Jesus.

'I was baptised when I was 15 or 16. There have been times when I've had doubts, and not just in childhood or young adulthood. But they've never been serious enough to cause me major problems.

'There has never been a time when I haven't been regularly worshipping, although because of the life I lead it has sometimes been difficult.

'There have been times when I've felt closer to God than at others. When I was 18 or 19 I read the Bible again and again. Although I was thrilled by what I read I felt very inadequate at trying to model my life on Jesus.

'I'm still trying to live up to Christian ideals and it doesn't get any easier. My faith is the basis of my life. It's important for me to try to translate the fact that Jesus is my redeemer into my everyday life.'

There are, Ieuan Wyn admits, occasions when he has struggled with his faith and his vote. Few moral issues are clear cut.

'Abortion has been the most painful issue for me to deal with in my 10 years in Westminster. I came here thinking the law should be tightened. I felt the 1967 Abortion Act was too liberal. Then I began to consider the arguments.

'On the great moral issues there is a tendency to be black and white. Part of my lawyer's training is that nothing is black and white. There are always shades of grey and you have to listen to both sides of the argument. The more I listened the more I became convinced that my original view was wrong.

'I talked to people whose views I respected – my mother, my wife, my friends who shared my Christian beliefs – and had to work very hard in coming to a view that I was eventually comfortable with.

'I don't believe abortion should be available on demand but I do realise there are circumstances which make it necessary on medical grounds, such as when the life of the mother is in danger. Part of the difficulty is that the abortion issue has been clouded by the fact that people regard the current legislation as allowing abortion on demand. I don't.'

On other moral debates Ieuan Wyn has voted against Sunday trading, resists relaxation on euthanasia, wants to tighten the law on pornography and voted for the age of consent for homosexuals to be lowered to 18.

'That was another difficult issue to decide,' he says. 'One of the virtues which is very important for me is the virtue of tolerance. I don't want the law to be a stick with which to beat people with whom we disagree.

'You cannot legislate for moral behaviour. Dogmatically forcing people into codes of behaviour through legislation is wrong. Nor should the Church use the law to force its morality onto people. The Church would be better listening to people and trying to persuade them to change their behaviour.

'The law should establish a basic set of principles which society generally believes – no stealing, no murder and so on – but moral guidance should be left to the Church not to the law.

'Jesus' teaching focuses on people having freedom of choice, with each choice having its consequences. People sometimes say to me that to decriminalise something is to say you're in favour of it. But that's not the case. You don't have to agree with people about the way they behave but you do need to give them a choice.

'Drugs, for example, are ruining people's lives. It's not confined to inner city areas. I've been trying to help young people in my own community who are coming off drugs. The effect of drugs on young people and their families is massive.'

While calling for greater tolerance, does Ieuan Wyn include the public's view of MPs, or should people expect a higher standard of moral behaviour from their MP?

'People should not regard their MPs as being different from ordinary people. We *are* ordinary people, we just do a different job. The public is entitled to expect the same moral behaviour from their MP as they expect of themselves. Judge us by your own standards.

'The difficulty is that, living in a goldfish bowl, MPs are scrutinised more closely than other people. If an MP falls from grace it's headline news but if John Citizen does it, it doesn't make the papers. Of course people want to look up to their legislators but all of us are susceptible to the same temptations, whatever we do.'

Given that power is considered to be an aphrodisiac, are the temptations greater in Westminster than West Wales?

'I've not found them to be greater here than anywhere else,' he says. 'Basically man is a fallible being and some will succumb to temptations whatever circumstances they are in. The hardest thing to bear about being an MP is being separated from your family.

'If an MP sets him or herself up as a happy family man or woman and then it's discovered that's not the case, the constituents are entitled to draw their own conclusions and take the opportunity to get rid of their MP. But there's an awful lot of pressure put on MPs which is unfair.

'People cannot expect their MPs to be perfect. If they do then they're making a great mistake because we can only reflect what is out there in society at large. We are only human and we all make mistakes from time to time. Some of us make mistakes in the glare of publicity, others do not.'

Is the Church right to involve itself with the lives of politicians or politics in general?

'The Church has a great responsibility to speak out on big issues,' he says.

'But not in a party political way. Part of the reason why the Church is facing a dwindling role in society today is because it has kept quiet. It needs to rediscover its own mission in making itself relevant to people's lives.'

It is the relevance of politics, however, that Ieuan Wyn sees as the big issue facing the new Government.

'People, especially the young, are increasingly feeling alienated from politics,' he says. 'MPs are not tackling the big issues of the young. We need to make politics relevant to young people and give them opportunities for participating more in politics – to change the system to accommodate them. Young people tell me they don't see the point of voting. Often politicians aren't talking the same language as them.

'The big issue for young people is the protection of the environment. They don't hear politicians talking enough about making it a safer world to live in by protecting the environment. We need to change that.'

If making the world a greener place helps recapture the interest of disaffected young people, the man whose party once wanted to be another bit of atlas pink will not be complaining.

Martyn Jones

*Labour MP for Clwyd South since 1997. MP for Clwyd South West, 1987 –
1997. Born in Cheshire in 1947. Before becoming an MP Martyn was a
microbiologist in the brewing industry. Opposition Whip, 1988 – 1992.
Opposition Spokesman on Agriculture, 1994 – 1995. Chairman of the Select
Committee on Welsh Affairs since 1997. Martyn is a member of the Church
of England. Divorced. Has one son and one daughter.*

The interview was conducted on 19 November 1997.

ZERO tolerance tops the agenda for the Government's view on crime. For mild-
mannered Martyn Jones, MP for Clwyd South, it is tolerance that tops the bill.

'Morality is being tolerant,' says the Labour member for the north Wales
seat. 'To me the ultimate sin is harming other people. I suppose I can lose
my temper with the best of them and regret it in the cool light of day, but
that is humanity. The one thing I can't tolerate is intolerance! I don't like it
in myself and I hate it in others. You can't be moral and intolerant.

'That doesn't mean anything goes. We can't allow people to be
persecuted, for example. To me, being a Christian means being tolerant.'

As befits a Welsh MP whose birthday is on St David's Day, Martyn is

Chairman of the Welsh Affairs Select Committee. He also chairs the Population and Development Group. A microbiologist by profession, he specialises in the environment and agriculture.

Before he entered Westminster in 1987 Martyn worked as a quality control adviser in a Wrexham brewery.

'As a moderate drinker, I don't think there is anything wrong in responsible drinking,' he says. 'But in one way I was glad to get out of alcohol production.'

When he first arrived in Westminster Martyn was surprised to discover that his scientific training could be useful in politics. But why did he make the move?

'I've always been one of those people who wants to take things apart to see how they work. I got into politics because I could see that society wasn't working properly and I wanted to change things. I have no illusion about how much one can do to change society but I think things get better by inches rather than feet.

'I started a staff union in the brewery because we were having trouble from senior management. I then joined the Labour Party in 1977, even though I could see we were going to lose the next election. I realised that I had to do something about it.

'I became secretary of the branch and then secretary of the constituency. Although I hadn't considered standing for election when I joined I stood in the 1981 county council election and won. It was the first time the ward had had a Labour councillor.'

Six years later Martyn won the then Clwyd South West seat from the Conservatives and has been in Parliament ever since. Wanting to make a better society is still his overall mission.

'There's no one political theory or philosophy which has the answer to everything,' he says. 'I suppose true Christianity comes closest. Even that needs people to be involved in the political system for it to work.

'I'm a member of the Labour Party because it is the party closest to my beliefs. It's not perfect. But I don't believe anybody who says they believe everything their party stands for. That cannot possibly be true.'

Is there any sense in which Martyn sees being an MP as a divine calling?

'That sounds a bit too grand,' he says. 'I'm very wary of people who are absolutely certain about their mission in life. But looking back at the ways things happened, it seemed very easy to get here – although I'm sure in reality it wasn't. But I pray regularly and ask for God's guidance to do his will.

'I like to think I'm doing God's will, but I'm not sure. I like to think that he is helping me make things better but I honestly don't know.

'I know I'm not as good a person as I should be. But I think that if I am doing the job slightly better than somebody else might have done then maybe that's the reason I'm here.'

Some of the most testing times, he reckons, come not from political opponents but from political friends.

'One of the things that is common to all MPs is that we want to be liked. I know I do,' he says. 'It's great when the majority like you. But the true test of character is when a substantial chunk of your electorate or your party leaders don't agree with your stance on an issue.'

So how does an MP cope with the fickleness of politics – being flavour of the month one minute and out of favour the next?

'It is very difficult,' he confesses. 'John Smith appointed me to the Opposition front bench. I was the spokesman on agriculture, food and rural affairs. I loved it. Tony Blair took me off. That is a blow to your self-esteem. Was I not doing the job properly or was it merely that I didn't vote for Tony Blair for the leadership? Who knows? You can never be certain of how well you are performing in the House of Commons.

'I enjoy being at the despatch box and making speeches but I don't like the personal insults. I am not an aggressive person in that way. There are too many people in this place who measure a person's worth by their aggression in the chamber. To me politics is about being inclusive, not aggressive.'

Martyn, who voted for the more traditional Labourism of John Prescott in the 1994 leadership election, describes himself as a 'convert' to the Blairite camp.

'I see the best of moderate left politics being put forward by some of the attributes of what we call New Labour. I don't like the name but I utterly support the ideas of constitutional reform and more open government. Plans for the Welsh Assembly and Scottish Parliament are wonderful because they will devolve power to the people who are best able to make the judgments.'

What does he say to those who suggest that New Labour is all image and smiles and doesn't really represent the true socialist working class like it used to?

'I don't think the Labour Party has ever truly represented the working classes in the country,' he says. 'It has always been driven by middle-class intellectuals. At its best Labour has been a party which has helped the working classes through reforming society as a whole. Today we have an underclass that needs support. To me true socialism is true Christianity.'

Martyn was brought up in a 'not very church-going but basically C of E background'. He was a regular at the church youth club. Today he describes himself as non-conformist. 'Although I attend church fairly infrequently these days. I don't think the established Church is the kind of Christianity I believe in.'

However, there have been occasions when Martyn has discovered God's closeness, when faith has come alive for him.

'Some years ago I had moved away with my job,' he says. 'My marriage was on the rocks. It was a very hard time. I realised I needed something inside. I went to church and prayed for help. As I did so my relationship with God, which until then had been very superficial, became very personal.

'Sadly, I am now divorced but it was through the trauma that I found God to be real. Today my relationship with my ex-wife is cordial and, most importantly, I have been able to keep a very good relationship with my children. It was the thought of losing contact with them that drove me to God. I couldn't have borne losing them.

'Now my faith is an anchor to my life. I find when I pray for others or for guidance for myself it works. It's uncanny! It's amazing!'

There are, Martyn reckons, no issues on which the Christian voice should not be heard. Even though there is usually more than one Christian voice on any issue.

'One of the most difficult areas for me is abortion,' he says. 'I get letters from people who I'm sure consider themselves Christians (and are maybe better Christians than me) saying that as a Christian MP I should make abortion illegal. This is one of those situations where I have to make a difficult choice and stand by it.

'I believe in a woman's right to choose. A woman deciding between an abortion and her unborn child's right to life will make her decision partly according to her conscience. I don't think it's up to me to legislate for that woman's conscience.

'The present system might be being exploited but it is too glib to say we should restrict abortions because there are many people who are desperate to adopt children. That is not an answer. There are no easy answers. But giving a woman the right to choose is, to my mind, just as Christian a response as wanting to do away with abortion.

'The same is true for all moral issues. The person who tells me they have an easy Christian answer is usually somebody with a very closed mind or a blinkered attitude. It would be wonderful it we had Christ here to tell us what to do. But given that he is not I have to try and assume that he is leading me to some kind of knowledge on these matters.

'I was, for instance, always against euthanasia until my father became extremely ill. Although he wasn't ill for long, he was suffering. He was 89, semi-conscious for practically a month and didn't recognise anybody in the family. It made me wonder if we should be able to release people from these circumstances. I still don't know the answer but I've moved from being against to being not so sure.'

Early in his Westminster career Martyn was able to bring his microbiology background to bear during the celebrated Edwina Currie salmonella-in-egg-production scare. Today's question is genetic engineering. How far should we go?

'There are huge potential benefits,' he says. 'What concerns me is that research is being driven by financial profits and not by benefit to society. They can co-exist but there are dangers when money becomes the primary goal, as we have seen with BSE.'

As a champion of the virtue of tolerance, which he readily admits can be taken to unhealthy extremes, does he think the public should tolerate misdemeanours by individual MPs?

'In terms of financial probity, absolutely not,' he says. 'MPs should not misuse their position for personal gain. The public perception of MPs and sleaze has devalued politics. We should be above all that and be seen to be above all that.

'But I don't think the public has a right to expect us to be moral paragons of virtue. That would be hypocritical. Actually I don't think the pressure comes so much from the public as from the tabloid press. The general public actually expect us to be human.

'The fuss about the £1 million donation to party funds from the motor racing industry was the media clutching at straws. No MP was behaving improperly. As a militant non-smoker I am against tobacco and tobacco advertising, but the Government realises there are jobs at stake. An immediate ban on tobacco advertising would put people out of work. That can't be right. Better to let the motor racing industry find new avenues of sponsorship over the next three or four years.'

It is the handling of money – taxpayer's money – that Martyn sees as the big issue facing his Government in their first term.

'We need to be able to manage the economy while at the same time deliver a lot of the social benefits we promised. Striking the balance between keeping our promises and maintaining a strong economy is going to be critical for us.

'The trouble is, people are impatient. I get people in my surgery saying, "You've been in power for nine months. Now, where's my dosh?" I have to tell them there isn't any dosh because we're keeping to the Tory's budget at least for two years.'

So, while New Labour reforms come to fruition, the electorate will have to show tolerance

Tessa Jowell

Labour MP for Dulwich and West Norwood since 1997. MP for Dulwich, 1992 – 1997. Born in London in 1947. Before becoming an MP Tessa was a social worker. Opposition Spokeswoman on Women, 1995 – 1997. Opposition Spokeswoman on Health, 1995 – 1997. At the general election she became Public Health Minister. Tessa is a member of the Church of England. Married David Mills in 1979. Has one son and one daughter

The interview was conducted on 20 February 1998.

WAITING to see Tessa Jowell MP in her Brixton surgery is like waiting in a barber's shop. There's a constant stream of people wanting a 10-minute interview with her.

If the wallcharts are anything to go by Tessa's constituents worry about eviction, harassment and housing benefits.

From time to time Tessa pokes her head out of her pokey office with a 'Who's next?' The corner-shop advice centre might well once have been a hair salon but for her people this is the last chance saloon.

'I'm their last resort,' says the MP for Dulwich and West Norwood. 'It shouldn't be so, but that's the destructive and inhumane way bureaucracy works.

'I have people for whom the bottom has fallen out of their lives. There's no reason why they shouldn't be able to get the information they need on, say, their position on the housing list without having to get their MP involved. But as wrong as it is, that's the way it is.'

The white-glossed panelling of the advice centre is, Tessa admits, a world away from the opulent Palace of Westminster.

'It's also a world away from life as a Government minister,' says the Minister for Public Health. 'But this is the real world. There must always be a connection between the pain, suffering and endeavour of people struggling against the most awful odds and the life in Westminster. I couldn't be an MP if I didn't try to help people. Spending every Friday in my constituency enables me to stay rooted in the real world. It helps me understand the hopes, fears and troubles of those I represent and see how we need to shape policies and priorities on a broader scale.'

Before she was elected as the MP for Dulwich in 1992 Tessa was a social worker. What made her want to become an MP?

'Many of the people I saw as a social worker are now my constituents,' she says. 'I got tremendous satisfaction during that time but I could do only so much. Many people need big solutions. They need a government that understands the corrosive effect of poverty and unemployment. A government that recognises the importance of parenting for children and of feeling safe from crime.

'One person's ability to deliver all those solutions will always be limited. But governments can do it. I decided – I suppose I was driven – to try to make a difference to people's lives through getting involved in the bigger political process. I wanted to put something back into society.'

As a Government minister Tessa has the opportunity to do just that. Part of her responsibility is to tackle the root causes of ill health.

'Dealing with the causes of bad health are much more intractable and extensive than prescribing remedies,' she says. 'Those who are poor, for example, are much less likely to enjoy good health than those who are well off and in secure employment.'

There is though, one presumes, only so much the public will stomach. A Government ban on chips would greatly improve the nation's health but it's not exactly a vote-winner.

'People would be pretty miserable, wouldn't they?' she agrees, with a smile. 'And the Government would be unpopular. But seriously, with public health it's very important to move forward with public consent. We can give people information about what might be good and bad for their health but whether anyone takes notice of it is a private matter.

'So long as private behaviour doesn't create public risk the Government doesn't interfere. We are not prepared to act like the nanny state – telling people how they should live their lives. Rather we will encourage measures to bring about improvements in health.

'Take smoking, for instance. We're seeing an increase in the number of young people – especially girls – who smoke. It's very important that we stop this trend. Nicotine is highly additive. Tobacco companies know that most people start smoking before they are 20. Not surprisingly their marketing efforts are targeted at recruiting young smokers.

'By banning tobacco advertising and the promotion of tobacco we are doing what we can to protect young people from that pernicious effort. We're also looking at creating a schools smoking-awareness campaign, evaluating quit programmes from America, strengthening health education and promotion and getting good information to teachers and parents.

'Even that might not be enough. We need to influence the models, the magazines and the movie-makers. They need to think twice about the effects of glamorising tobacco for what are quite vulnerable and susceptible young minds.'

Last year the minister was the subject of intense personal criticism after the Government decided to exempt Formula One racing from its tobacco advertising ban. The media made much of her husband's links with motor racing despite an official statement recognising that the minister did not have a conflict of interest. How did she cope with being the subject of criticism?

'In politics you just have to live with it,' she says. 'It was extremely unpleasant and I wouldn't begin to pretend that I enjoyed it.

'Stories appeared saying we weren't going to ban tobacco advertising, which was ridiculous. But I felt serene in my soul because I knew I had done nothing wrong. Indeed I believed that what we were doing as a government was right. I just kept my sights fixed on the critical meeting of European health ministers where, as promised, we delivered the framework for a ban on tobacco advertising. I felt terribly proud of that.

'These crises pass and we are probably a stronger family as a result. And yes, I'd go through it again if I had to, if it was for something that I believed was right.'

As well as support from family and friends Tessa found strength in her faith.

'My faith was a great comfort. I did get comfort from prayer and contemplation. I held on to the fact that the situation would pass. In moments like that you hope you're being watched over, don't you? I certainly felt like that at the time. I also reminded myself that as a family we were united, we were healthy, we were happy and we had people who loved us.

'Faith, for me, shouldn't simply be passive. It should be active. It should inform and drive the way I live.'

When she was a child Tessa's family were 'infrequent churchgoers'. Her paternal grandparents were 'very active Methodists' and Tessa went to Sunday school. Faith, she says, is something she has grown up with.

'I have always felt that there was a sort of force beyond myself and that I had a spiritual as well as material aspect to my life,' she says.

Three years ago Tessa was confirmed. The details, she insists, are not for public consumption through the media.

'Yes, as an adult I have thought more deeply about the Christian faith,' she says, 'but I regard that and how I practise my faith as private.'

In her public life, however, Tessa readily recognises the influence of her faith. 'As an MP I aspire to do what millions of people do privately and often without recognition – get involved in community activities in pursuit of the common good. That's where my political belief and my Christian faith overlap.

'Not that we Christians have a monopoly on wanting to be a force for good. As my incredibly diverse constituency makes clear, there are forces for good in people of all faiths and none.'

What does Tessa say to those people who maintain politics is no place for a Christian because it can be a nasty business and is full of compromise?

'That is complete and utter nonsense! Absolute nonsense! Politics is what the people in politics make it. In my experience politics is populated by decent people who want to do good and want to make the world better. There is an undue level of cynicism about. I hope we as a Government will be able to rehabilitate politics.'

When it comes to casting her own vote in support of her party Tessa has never had a crisis of conscience. Might it happen?

'It's all hypothetical. I would never vote for the death penalty but nor would my party. Equally I would never support racist legislation but nor would my party. So no, I don't think it will. Again, traditional issues of conscience are matters for a free vote. You make your judgment in the light of your conscience and after careful thought.'

If she had the magic-wand ability to change one thing about the country in an instant it would be to remove unfairness.

'It's a big ambition,' she admits. 'But I have never forgotten when my daughter, my first child, was born. Four other babies in the ward were born that day. The next day I remember looking at five little cots lined up in the middle of the ward. Five babies – all the same age, all fit and healthy, all looking almost identical. The fact struck me that the circumstances of their birth would be the most powerful determining factor of their subsequent opportunities and quality of life.

'One baby was going to be received into care, one was going home to a bed-and-breakfast hotel, two were going to securely provided-for homes and one was going home to a family where the father had just lost his job. That moment gave me an absolute focus for my motivation in politics – to tackle unfairness.'

One area of unfairness so far as the public is concerned is hospital waiting lists in particular and the state of the NHS in general. The minister speaks about the need for preventative care. She knows the poor are at a disadvantage when it comes to health. Why, then, can't the Government spend Lottery money – money the public has given – on building more hospitals, on cutting waiting lists?

'First of all the NHS is funded from taxation,' she says. 'We all pay into it and so we should. Secondly the Lottery funds the extras over and above.'

But many people feel there is no 'over and above'.

'Let's wait and see. We inherited waiting lists at their highest level and have made absolutely clear that the present position is completely unacceptable.

'We have not been in power for long. It will take time to turn things around. I am involved in talks about fulfilling our promise to reduce waiting lists.

'Managing waiting lists is not just about money. It is about tough and determined management and the resources that we have. I don't want an NHS which is funded by Lottery money as if it was an optional extra in our nation's life. I want a health service which is funded by government in recognition that it is our most treasured and important national institution.'

Nevertheless there are people who are suffering through want of money. If individuals had the money they'd have their operations done privately. The Government has received millions through National Lottery taxation. Instead of building millennium domes, why can't we have millennium hospitals?

'Since we've been in government we have announced 16 new hospitals. There are more to come. But modern health care is not just about hospitals. It is about community provision, improving GP surgeries and getting more treatment out of hospitals and into the community.

'Judging us by the number of hospitals built will be only one way in which people can judge the quality of health care. By the time of the next election we will have delivered on our pledge to treat 100,000 more people off the waiting lists compared to the last election.

'Waiting lists will be shorter than they were on 1 May 1997. We will also make sure that, regardless of where they live, a modern and dependable health service will be there when people need it – a health service that will treat patients on the basis of need and not on their ability to pay.'

And with that Tessa's surgery closes – until next Friday.

Ruth Kelly

Labour MP for Bolton West since 1997. Born in Northern Ireland in 1968. Before becoming an MP Ruth was a journalist at The Guardian and economist at the Bank of England. Ruth is a member of the Roman Catholic Church. Married Derek Gadd in 1996. Has one son and one daughter.

The interview was conducted on 21 January 1998.

THIS time last year Ruth Kelly was a young lady of Threadneedle Street – an economist at the Bank of England. Having studied at Oxford and the LSE she rose to become deputy head of the bank's inflation unit. Today, as Labour MP for Bolton West, Ruth is a member of the Treasury Select Committee, a cross-party group of backbenchers which monitors the work of Treasury ministers, cross-examines the Chancellor and scrutinises the, er, Bank of England.

Prior to her time in the City Ruth was an economics journalist on *The Guardian*. Today she is on the receiving end of media coverage. The irony is not lost on her.

Given that MPs tend to treat the media with anything from caution and suspicion to outright fear, how does it feel to be the hunted rather than the hunter?

'Very strange,' she says. 'I think if I were to go back to journalism I would have a different attitude. On the other hand the media does fulfil a valuable role. Obviously it has its excesses but we do need scrutiny of government, and the media is a very effective way of carrying out that scrutiny. The media can also do great things for people and for governments. It is not always counter-productive. It is just a question of knowing how to handle it.

'For example there has been an awful lot of misinformation about the Government's motives over cutting lone parent benefits. The whole area of welfare reform has been brought to the public's attention piecemeal. The overall vision for the future of the welfare state has not been communicated.

'Although I have total faith in the top people on the question of welfare reform, the way it has come out is partly the Government's fault.'

So we're being told bits as the Government thinks of them without being told what the answer is?

'Exactly. The problem is that that approach is part of government. We are in the middle of a huge debate about welfare reform. And as some parts of it come out they are inevitably taken out of context. Without the big picture it's really no surprise that the media picks up and runs with these stories. The problem is people then get very afraid and fearful of the future. And that's a tragedy.'

Would it be better then if governments waited until they arrived at their final solutions before presenting them to the electorate through the media?

'That's part of the problem,' says Ruth. 'It will never all be sorted out. Four or five years in office is not a long time. People expect you to start addressing issues right away and want to hear of your progress sooner rather than later. A free press is the price democracy in general and politicians in particular have to pay, even when we don't get the whole truth up front every time.'

Although Ruth started getting interested in politics when she was a teenager it was not until she left university that she gave serious consideration to becoming a politician.

'At the Bank of England I was very much carrying out government policy,' she says. 'I wanted to be involved in *making* policy or at least representing constituents' interests and trying to shape policy. I wanted to do more than carry out government orders. I wanted to make them.'

Like many MPs Ruth arrived at Westminster with a sense of mission.

'I wanted to change the world,' she says. 'I'm sure a lot of MPs think exactly the same. I wasn't content to sit by and let things happen around me. I wanted to be part of changing society.

'Mass unemployment, for example, is a disgrace. Even as a small cog in a big machine I want to do something about it.'

Ruth readily agrees that being in a position to 'do something about it' involves dedication and sacrifice from members of a Member's family. Since winning her seat Ruth has become a first-time mum. Her husband, Derek, has given up his Labour Party job and is training to become a teacher. ('He wanted a profession that would be compatible with my career in politics because we think it's very important for a child to have at least one parent at home in the evenings.') And they split their time between Ruth's Bolton constituency and London.

There are, she admits, many times she would rather be at home with her family than at Westminster. How does she cope with the conflict of interest?

'It hits me most during the long evenings when MPs have to be on site to vote,' she says. 'Very little productive work gets done and you never know when the division bell will ring. It's particularly frustrating when we're under a running three-line whip, which means that every day from 3.30 until 10 or 11 o'clock at night we have to stay on site until the last vote. That takes its toll.'

So being an MP is not quite as glamorous as one might think?

'No it's not! It never totally loses its glamour because being an MP is exciting and a great privilege with many opportunities. I feel quite a sense of achievement just at being here. But there are a lot of dull moments as well!'

What also helps Ruth through the duller moments is the conviction that she is where God wants her to be.

'As a Christian I believe we all have a calling. I can't easily put it into words but being an MP is right for me and in that sense I feel it is my calling. You wouldn't be here unless you really believed this was the place for you.

'I was brought up as a Roman Catholic and I am still a practising Catholic. I was a rebel as a teenager, of course. I think everybody was. It would have been strange not to have been. But I never lost my faith.

'If anything, my faith is stronger as a result of the rebellious stage. Jesus, to me, is God-made-man and is our first encounter with God. I try to follow his example.

'The great question of life is: Why are we here? I am now much clearer in my own mind about why I am here and what people are supposed to do, which is to live to the best of their ability and do God's will.'

Among other things Ruth's faith, she says, gives her a sense of purpose, courage and compassion. 'I know I should be working at it more than I do but I pray every day. I am a regular churchgoer and I try to see things around me with a lot of faith. It's probably too early to tell whether it is as easy or more difficult being a Christian MP than a Christian financier. I am sure there will be very difficult questions ahead.'

Indeed there will. While MPs vote on moral issues according to personal conscience rather than party whip, Ruth recognises that some issues are far from clear cut. She is, however, absolutely clear where she stands on abortion.

'I don't believe in abortion,' she says. 'That doesn't mean that as a politician I am going to start campaigning to stop all abortions. I do understand that abortion has become accepted in our society and that many of these issues need much more subtle approaches than just outright banning.

'If Parliament outlawed abortion tomorrow it would have a riot on its hands. That would help nobody. I would prefer to see resources put into supporting people who have children. I don't think the support systems are in place. It's often very difficult for people who are abandoned by their partners, who have been kicked out of home, who are so financially impoverished that they think they can't afford to bring the child up. That's how public policy can help.

'I don't want a return to back-street abortions. But the problem goes deeper than that. We have to change society's attitude to the unborn child. Hopefully over time that will happen. I look forward to the day when people don't have cause to consider terminating a pregnancy, even when a child might suffer severe handicap.

'I can understand people who are driven to abortion. And we are right to have compassion and sympathy with them but I don't think abortion is the right answer. It is not a necessary evil. It is wrong.'

If abortion is a difficult issue, homosexuality, according to Ruth, is 'probably one of the most difficult questions of the age'. How does she view the proposal to lower the homosexual age of consent, which is due to come before this session of Parliament?

'In general people are sexually active far too young – whatever their sexuality,' she says. 'It is almost impossible to legislate for personal morality but I don't like the idea of promiscuity.'

How does she react to the idea that Christians shouldn't be involved in politics because it is based on the principle of compromise?

'Life is about making compromises,' she says. 'One of the reasons it took me so long to join the Labour Party was because I had to work out how much I would have to compromise. Eventually I decided that to achieve anything in this world you have to commit yourself to particular projects and operate within certain restrictions. One consequence is that you might be involved in a project you don't wholly believe in. But if you want to change anything you have to accept those limitations. Even though I don't agree with everything it says, the Labour Party, to me, is the best on offer.'

And would having more Christian MPs make for more ethical government?

'It is very easy to call yourself a Christian,' says Ruth. 'What you need is not necessarily more Christians but people with strong values who are prepared to stick to them.'

How long, then, is Ruth prepared to stick around Westminster? She acknowledges the commitment of her husband. She treads a compromise between parenting a toddler and perusing a Treasury report. Will she be there 30 years from now?

'I have no plans to leave,' she says, with a smile. 'At least not at the moment. At some point others might decide that I should go. On the other hand I won't stay if I don't think it's right.

'How will I know? One way would be to work out whether I have achieved certain goals. The downside of that approach is that just by being here and doing my best I believe I am making a difference.

'Another way of looking at it would be whether I feel particularly attracted to a different way of life. But it would have to be a job where I could make a difference and be even happier than I am now. Central to that happiness would be my family. I don't want them making unreasonable sacrifices.'

Looking only four years into the future what does Ruth reckon to be the big issue facing her Government?

'There are two big issues,' she says. 'Europe is important because it affects the number of jobs, the prices we pay in the shops and people's overall standard of living. What's not clear is whether Europe will make a big positive difference, a small positive difference or a big or small negative difference to people. That's what the arguments are about. Britain's future prosperity rests in getting it right with Europe.

'At home the welfare state is not working. We spend huge amounts on benefits but get very little in return because too many people are in poverty, on very low benefits or out of work. They want to be able to contribute more positively to society. It's vital we reform welfare so people can bank on having fulfilling, decently paid jobs.'

Rt Hon Peter Lilley

Conservative MP for Hitchin and Harpenden since 1997. MP for St Albans, 1983 – 1997. Born in Kent in 1943. Before becoming an MP Peter was an economic consultant on overseas aid projects in developing countries and then a partner in W. Greenall & Co, advising on investment in the oil industry. Parliamentary Private Secretary to Chancellor of the Exchequer, 1984 – 1997. Economic Secretary to the Treasury, 1987 – 1989. Financial Secretary to the Treasury, 1989 – 1990. Appointed a Privy Councillor, 1990. Secretary of State for Trade and Industry, 1990 – 1992. Secretary of State for Social Security, 1992 – 1997. Deputy Leader of the Conservative Party since 1997 Peter is a member of the Church of England. Married Gail in 1979.

The interview was conducted on 27 June 1996.

PETER LILLEY, Secretary of State for Social Security, will never buy a National Lottery ticket. Perhaps being responsible for spending £90 billion a year – 40 per cent of central government spending or £15 per working person per working day – is excitement enough.

Whichever way he figures it, the man in charge of the caring sector of the Government knows his policies aren't always an instant success. 'The biggest challenges are to ensure that this huge sum of money really *does* go to people in genuine need. And helps people out of dependency and back into work,' he says. 'It ought to be possible to meet the obligations we all have for the better off to help the less well off.'

For the Right Honourable Member for St Albans, that means reform. How does he sees the future of the welfare state?

'I'd like it to grow in a way in which, increasingly, provision for the risks and vicissitudes of life are met by people's own resources,' he says. 'We are succeeding in building up private pensions. Two thirds of people who retire now have their own pensions on top of the state pension. More people are insuring themselves against the risk of losing of their jobs. This has the twin advantages that people want to help themselves if they can and accept the need to help those who can't. In so doing they have to save money and that strengthens the economy. This provides the wealth for us to meet the needs of an ageing population.'

But isn't that a privatising of the welfare state by any other name?

'I describe it as the transition from a welfare state to a welfare society,' he explains. 'There is always going to be state provision, but there will also be a greater amount of private provision. For example, we have recently uprated the basic pension in line with prices and encouraged people to build additional pensions on top of that. If the state had taken over that function and raised the basic pension so it was going to provide help for everybody, we would have had far less money to channel to those who, for one reason or another, have been unable to help themselves.

'Because the bulk of people have provided extra pensions themselves, the state has been able to boost the help we give for elderly people to the tune of well over £1 billion extra a year. This makes possible focused help on those on greatest need.'

If focusing help on those most in need is his cardinal rule, what changes will he make to Child Benefit, awarded to every mother in the country regardless of need?

'Child Benefit is something I've had to give a lot of thought to,' he says. 'I can't imagine a system where you didn't recognise the costs of having children – whether in the form of Child Benefit or child tax allowances.

'Child Benefit money is not there for the state to spend on something else – to help the elderly or the disabled. It is a recognition of the costs of bringing up children. It isn't my priority for reform because, with a roughly constant number of children in the country, it's almost the only element of my budget which isn't growing.'

Getting more people off state benefit will, in Peter's opinion, be the biggest issue facing the next Government.

'At present the earning power of people with limited or no skills is not much greater than the amount of money they could get on benefit. We need to create jobs so people can get a decent living, support themselves and bring up their children without having to spend their lives on benefit. The problems are easy enough to define. The solutions are not!'

Peter, who, apart from Prime Minister John Major, is the longest-serving department head in the Government, has long experience of tackling tricky problems – he studied physics at Cambridge University.

'Even before I went to university, I knew I wanted to be a politician, if I could. Although I thought I might be able to contribute something, I was far from certain that someone with no connections, such as myself, would ever be able to do so.'

Peter, describing his youthful ambition as 'a dream rather than a prospect', made his parliamentary entrance 'with a sense of vocation rather than mission'.

'We shouldn't be too high minded, though,' he reckons. 'Politics is a mixture of vocation, self-gratification and simple enjoyment. But if you didn't have the vocation, you wouldn't put up with the hours, the effort, the insults and the indignities.'

Before becoming an MP, Peter was an economic consultant working on aid programmes in under-developed countries in Africa and Asia. As his interest in politics grew, he realised he couldn't pursue British politics from the jungles of Tanzania. He returned to the City, specialising in North Sea oil investments.

He now heads the Government's response to benefit claims from asylum seekers, many of whom come from parts of the world where he once worked. His aim, as always, is to target benefit to those who are genuine.

'Anyone who comes to this country as a refugee, or claiming to be a refugee, will continue to get benefit while they're here. Unless and until they're found not to be a refugee.

'Those who were abusing the system – illegal immigrants and people who had entered the country as businessmen and travellers and later claimed asylum – are no longer entitled to benefits.'

Benefits also used to be available to asylum seekers if, having been turned down, they then appealed against their decision. Now they'll have to win their appeal *before* they get benefits.

'We shall be treating foreign asylum seekers on a par with British citizens,' says Peter. 'If they succeed in their appeal, their benefits will be backdated to when they first made their claim. So people who helped them will know that they'll get reimbursed – if they've been backing a genuine case.'

Given his experience of working abroad, is there ever a conflict between his head and heart when dealing with this issue?

'Yes. Because, although the vast majority of people claiming to be asylum seekers are not genuine refugees in the accepted sense of the International

Geneva Convention, they come from countries which have enormous problems. I can well understand them preferring to live here.

'There's a mass movement of people across the world which is exploited by very unscrupulous people. They are creating human misery by encouraging economic migration from poor to rich countries. This process is fuelled by access to the benefits system, which was only ever intended to help a small number of people who are genuinely escaping persecution and torture.

'No government or party would allow unlimited immigration to this country. What we have to do is try to ensure that those countries can prosper and develop. My experience in working in them is that, given a free society, free economy, open trade and investment with the rest of the world, they could.

'But that doesn't mean I'm lacking in sympathy for the economic migrant. Though I describe them as bogus refugees because they are not what they purport to be, they are, nevertheless, human beings who want to live in a more prosperous country. One can't blame them for that. Neither can one say that it gives them an automatic right to benefits.'

Peter was brought up in a Christian family and at the age of 12 started to specialise in science.

'Whereas others of my generation were brought up to think there was a clash between science and religion, I realised there wasn't. Science reinforced my faith rather than undermined it.

'Christian faith is like a pair of spectacles. It enables you to see more clearly what is happening in the nature of good and evil that otherwise you would see only fuzzily.

'I can't remember a conversion experience,' he confesses. 'It was more of a process.'

Describing personal faith as 'the most important thing in the life of any Christian', he's quick to point out he hasn't been gifted an exclusive divinely-inspired manifesto.

'No political party has a monopoly of Christianity. I have lots of Christian friends in other parties and don't deny them their authenticity, even though I disagree with their policies. Faith influences the objectives you pursue. I probably have the same objectives as Christian colleagues in other parties. We differ as to the best way of achieving them.'

Peter also acknowledges faith's influence on his personal morality.

'It's tempting to put your career ahead of the things you believe in. Politics is often thought of as being a dirty game. Opportunities arise to slip down to the level of the cheap jibe or offensive remark, which I'm sure I've often succumbed to, but I know I shouldn't. As a Christian, I'm under a greater obligation to try to be honest and reasonable about opponents, and avoid attributing to them evil motives, which is a natural temptation in the hurly-burly of politics.'

When it comes to voting in the House, Peter admits to having had times when he's had to question his motives.

'There have been times when I've had to judge whether I'm right to pursue a certain course or whether I'm doing that just to preserve my political position. So far, I've resolved them all without going against my conscience.'

Talking of conscience, does he think the electorate has a right to expect a higher standard of moral behaviour from its national leaders?

'We *all* ought to be virtuous,' he says. 'Adultery is a bad thing. But to a Christian, funnily enough, it is much easier to recognise that we are *all* sinners. We *all* do wrong things. I go to church on Sundays, kneel down and say the General Confession. The presumption is, therefore, that I've done wrong things which need to be confessed.

'It's not terribly surprising to find that a number of MPs are not perfect paragons of family virtue. We all ought to be. Some of us have failings in other spheres, which don't happen to be of such an interest to the press and that's a relief to us!

'But none of us is perfect. There will always be shortcomings, whatever standards are set. What we ought not to do is condone wrongdoing or suggest that just being in high office is virtuous in itself. To expect angelic standards from people in public life is also nonsense.'

And how high would the Secretary of State like to go?

'I've never made any secret of my desire to be Chancellor of the Exchequer, one day. But I don't think Kenneth Clarke need get over-nervous just yet!'

Might he, perhaps, like to take up residence in the house next door to the chancellor's?

'I wouldn't complain,' he laughs. 'If it was offered, I wouldn't refuse. Any politician who tells you his ambition falls short of that is not being honest.'

The next Conservative Prime Minister? That really would be hitting the jackpot!

Peter Luff

Conservative MP for Mid Worcestershire since 1997. MP for Worcester, 1992 –
1997. Born in Windsor in 1955. Before becoming an MP Peter was a public
relations director. Parliamentary Private Secretary to Minister for Energy,
1993 – 1996. Parliamentary Private Secretary to Minister for Prisons, 1993 -
1996. Parliamentary Private Secretary to The Lord Chancellor, 1996 – 1997.
Chairman of Agriculture Select Committe since 1997. Peter is a member of
the Church of England. Married Julia in 1979. Has one daughter and one son.
*   The interview was conducted on 12 February 1996*

FATHER-OF-TWO Peter Luff, Conservative MP for Worcester, is at the
heart of a sex scandal involving teenage girls. This, however, is not another
tale of a weakness in Westminster.

Last month Peter highlighted the explicit sexual content of some
teenage magazines read by children as young as eight, when he tabled a
bill requiring publishers to put minimum readership ages on the front
covers of their publications.

'Sex is great,' says Peter, over a cup of Earl Grey. 'It's one of God's greatest
gifts. As a Christian, I would say its best place is within marriage. But these
magazines degrade sex. That's what I find offensive. They turn sex into just
a chemical exercise of gratification. The matter-of-fact message for girls is

you go out to the pub, have a couple of drinks and go to bed with your boyfriend – just another aspect of everyday life. This approach is destroying the mystery of one of the greatest gifts of God.'

It was while on a family holiday last summer that Peter became aware of the reading diet of many teenage girls.

'My 10-year-old daughter wanted something to read. We picked up a copy of *Shout* magazine. It looked perfectly innocent and harmless with pictures of pop stars and animals. My wife just happened to glance at the problem page. It was dealing with marital infidelity and pornographic photographs. She said to our daughter, "I'm terribly sorry, Rosie, you're not reading this!"

'In retrospect, that particular magazine wasn't terribly offensive but we were shocked. It was the first time we'd been exposed to the contents of some of these magazines. When we got home, my wife talked to one or two friends and discovered there were other titles which were causing parental concern. I bought one or two and was absolutely horrified.'

One aim of Peter's bill is to make other parents aware of what their children are being subjected to by some magazine articles. He has no aversion to responsible sex education or to healthy sexual attitudes. But for Peter, given that the age of consent is 16, what might be useful to know at 21 is unnecessary at 13. Thirteen-year-olds shouldn't have to read about 'position of the fortnight', fruit-flavoured condoms, the techniques of oral sex or how their pop heroes lost their virginity – the typical content of these magazines.

'I want a way of giving parents more information about what their kids are reading,' he says. 'I suggested publishers should say on the front cover what age they are writing for. I've objections towards most of these magazines but my biggest objections are directed against *More!*

'According to the publishers, *More!* is aimed at 19-year-olds. I don't believe them. They are being less than honest. I think it's aimed at 14 and 15-year-olds. The design style is not as sophisticated as women's magazines. It looks almost identical to *Sugar*, which is aimed at 13-year-olds. I think they're trying to encourage younger girls to read it. If the publishers are aiming at 19-year-olds and up they should say so on the front cover.'

But aren't these magazines providing useful advice?

'The publishers defend these articles by saying they're providing essential advice to young girls: "Parents and schools have let kids down with sex education, we've got to give them something..." There is some truth in that. Some of the things they say are quite useful, but that's more typically found in the sponsored supplements. The magazines themselves are not offering helpful advice. It sounds very plausible when you haven't read them.

'I accept that the halcyon days of *Jackie* have gone for good and there are issues they ought to explore which they wouldn't previously have explored, but they've simply gone much too far. If we're to protect family life in this country we can't have this kind of incitement to early sexual activity.

'The argument of dissemination of important information is bogus. They are selling sex! The publishers' honest defence should be "we're making a lot of money out of this and we don't want to lose any sales, thank you very much", which is what drives the newer titles in the market.

'I suspect the older titles are unhappy at what's happened and are following reluctantly in the footsteps of *Sugar, More!* and *Bliss. Just Seventeen* has had a difficult time because, in response, it's becoming more explicit.'

What reaction, though, has Peter had?

'The campaign has touched a nerve in the country. I've been overwhelmed by support from a wide range of interests – Christians, non-Christians, parents and non-parents, journalists, retailers ... I'm particularly pleased because we tend to think society has become less decent.

'I've had 400 letters of support and only a handful – from advisory centres and the magazines themselves – expressing opposition. I believe people are crying out for basic Christian principles, family values, moral values to be reasserted. I thought there'd be a big liberal backlash but there wasn't.'

But won't the very action of putting age indications on magazines make them more desirable to younger readers – a forbidden fruit – and thus boost sales?

'In the short term, maybe. But that's arguable, because young girls are reading them already. The long-term effect will be to make parents more informed about what their children are reading.'

Strangely – given that his campaign could cause a slump in sales – Peter has the support of retailers.

'Newsagents strongly support what I am doing because they don't like the moral dilemma they're placed in by these magazines,' he says. 'Newsagents can refuse to stock top-shelf adult magazines. But with these it's more difficult. They also want to have something to protect them from attacks by irate parents.'

To Peter, *More!* and the like are no better than girlie magazines in the way they portray women.

'Girls, through these magazines, are being brought up to believe that there's only one route to personal fulfilment – sex and looking good for their man. That's appalling! There's a distinct poverty of aspiration in these magazines. They're saying that all a girl should live for is to please her boyfriend. That's degrading to womanhood. It's sexist.'

In some ways, he reckons, they are worse.

'With top-shelf magazines you know what to expect. They're not pretending to be something they're not,' he says. A pre-teen girl buying a magazine for a picture of her pop idol only to read in detail about how many lovers he's had is, in Peter's view, being treated less than honestly.

His concern for family values extends to other media.

'I'm concerned about all influences on children, not just teenage magazines,' he says. 'I'm very worried about children having TVs in their bedroom which are not controlled by their parents. I'm worried about programmes like *Blind Date*. I'm glad to see the Independent Television Commission censured *Blind Date* over the way it was becoming explicit.

'I'm worried about the lyrics of pop records. Last year, one of my constituents said his 12-year-old daughter came home with a record which was about having oral sex with your mother. The man was furious when he heard it. I campaigned to have the record withdrawn from sale, which eventually it was.'

While Peter's bill received cross-party support and generated nationwide public interest, it is unlikely to become law. It has, however, in some measure served its purpose by raising public awareness and parental displeasure.

That done, Peter moves on to the next item on his agenda. Minutes before taking up his new appointment as Parliamentary Private Secretary to the Lord Chancellor, he replied to my quesion asking for his views on the divorce legislation he will be helping to guide through Parliament.

'Fault-based divorce hasn't helped, I'm quite clear about that,' he says. 'It's led to increasing acrimony in relationships and has been very bad for the children involved. Where a relationship is dead, ascribing fault has only made the situation worse.

'The principle of mediation, which the bill proposes, is good, although I'd like to go further and include conciliation. Ending a relationship without acrimony is better for the children. But the best thing of all for children is if the couple doesn't split up in the first place! Even some well-balanced children find divorce impossible to come to terms with.

'I'd like to see the Government give more money to the marriage guidance service, Relate, which helps people stay together. Also the Church, and indeed the Jewish and Muslim faiths as well because they share the Christian view of the sanctity of marriage, should be giving forth a very clear sound on this. I'm afraid I think sometimes there's a lack of clarity, particularly from the Anglican church, on these issues.'

Peter is uncomfortable with the idea of being branded a moral crusader or 'some kind of nut'. While he is convinced that Christians should be involved in politics, he's not happy with the notion that his faith could itself be a vote-winner.

'Winning votes is not what I'm a Christian for,' he says. 'Telling the world you're a Christian and not using it to political advantage is a difficult balance to strike.

Christians in the House

'I'm an Anglican by habit, but a Christian by conviction,' confesses Peter. 'My father died when I was eight years old and at the time I had a very strong sense of God's love and protection. I knew that my father had passed on to something better. I derived such comfort from my faith that I've never seriously questioned it since.

'My faith came alive when I was at Cambridge University. Although mine is a deeply-held faith, I find it difficult to talk publicly about it. I would, for example, find it very difficult to stand up and deliver a personal testimony.

'Politicians, like anyone else, must bring their faith with them to their daily life and use it to inform the decisions they take,' says the man who once considered becoming an Anglican minister. 'We must reflect whether the motives behind policy decisions are pure. We should never claim scriptural authority for anything we're seeking to do. The best we can hope for is to be able to say to our Maker: "I did my best, I hope I got it right." '

If actions really do speak louder than words, we will be hearing a lot more of Peter Luff.

Ken Maginnis

Ulster Unionist MP for Fermanagh and South Tyrone since 1983. Born in Northern Ireland in 1938. Before becoming an MP Ken was a teacher. Spokesman on Defence, Security and Employment, 1994 – 1995. Spokesman on Defence and Home Affairs since 1995. Ken is a member of the Church of Ireland. Married Joy in 1961. Has two sons and two daughters.

The interview was conducted on 12 November 1997.

'ATTENTION! Attention! There is a fire in your area, leave the building immediately and go to your assembly point.'

Not even a 'this is not a drill' fire alarm stops Ken Maginnis from finishing his point about decommissioning terrorist weapons. Other occupants of his Millbank office block have long since vacated to the comforting sight of fire engines gleaming under Westminster's sodium lights. Ken, it seems, is used to not moving until the building does.

'If I had the power to change just one thing about the country, I'd remove the weapons,' says the Ulster Unionist security spokesman, whose Fermanagh and South Tyrone constituency includes Enniskillen and Dungannon and borders the Irish Republic on three sides.

'Once you get rid of terrorist weapons there's no need for armed soldiers on the streets. You won't get people volunteering to be terrorists if you can't put a nice Armalite or an AK47 in their hand. There is nothing that would be as good for Ireland as a whole as to have wholesale disarmament. I would give anything for the guns. I'd give my life for the guns!'

Nine times it has nearly come to that. Having been on the receiving end of parcel bombs it takes more than a fire alarm to get Ken Maginnis excited.

Father-of-four Ken spent 16 years as a primary school headmaster in his native County Tyrone before he entered the fiery furnace of Ulster politics.

It was 'a series of coincidences rather than one particular incident' that put him on course for Westminster.

In the early '70s Ken became an Ulster Defence Regiment company commander. On one occasion he went to speak to a group of Unionists about getting some anti-Catholic graffiti removed. 'At the meeting the Divisional Chairman of the Unionist Association jokingly said it was nice to see me at a Unionist meeting and that I should go along to my own ward meetings.'

A few months later Ken did and after a few more visits was selected to fight the May 1981 council elections. Three months later he stood in the by-election following the death of the local MP, IRA hunger striker Bobby Sands. Although Ken lost, he was invited to stand for the Northern Ireland Assembly and gave up a 23-year teaching career when he was elected in October 1982. The following June he won the volatile Westminster seat.

Was becoming an MP a calling?

'I suppose that is really a matter of faith,' he says. 'I don't want to suggest that I am here to be the salvation of Ireland or anything like that. But I am maybe here to bring a bit of sanity to the process from time to time. I have a knack of saying what I mean. People aren't confused by what I am saying. That's necessary in politics.'

Ken had a 'very traditional' upbringing in the Church of Ireland.

'I was brought up to know not to tell lies and not to steal. You knew the Ten Commandments and faith wasn't complicated.

'There is a fundamentalist element within Christianity which talks of being born again, which suggests a Damascus Road conversion for us all. I am not sure that ever happened to me. I grew up, I went to church, I went to Sunday school, I taught in Sunday school, I taught the Bible class, I did my bit in the Scout movement, I was confirmed when I was 16 and that was an important time for me. It was the occasion you took responsibility for your own life.

'When I married and moved back to Dungannon I was made a member of the select vestry and put in charge of the church's stewardship campaign. Not exactly religious fervour, but I'm a very practical person.'

Ken readily admits that sectarian violence among a nation of churchgoers is a bad advert for Christianity. And the Church, he reckons, is losing opportunities and influence.

'The rector or the priest used to be at the heart of his local community,' he says. 'Today too many clergymen adopt an intellectually pompous attitude to the ordinary fellow – the person who doesn't quite understand why he believes what he believes but believes it nonetheless.

'Take the Orange Order, for example. I'm not an Orangeman but in the past Orangeism was a great force for stability. It had a very strong religious affiliation. It kept a lot of young people who were totally frustrated at governments seemingly giving in to terrorism from taking the law into their own hands.

'Most Orangemen were in church every Sunday and were faithful to their church. Nowadays the younger generation of clergy find it unfashionable to become lodge chaplains. We're not getting the honest-to-God grass-roots Christian clergymen. Consequently, as the older element of Orangeman passes on, the Order is in danger of becoming sectarian for the simple reason that the only religious influence now is fundamentalism.

'I don't mean evangelical zeal. I totally approve of that. But the kind that believes that now is the time for us to judge who and what is right and wrong and God must wait his turn.'

Living close to violent death, what does Ken's faith give him?

'I think it has enabled me to take life as it comes,' he says. 'I don't know whether I am a fool but I have never felt the need to be afraid of the IRA. I have never allowed myself to be protected by the police. By the time I became an MP I had soldiered for 12 years and I wasn't going to let myself be tied down with bodyguards – to be told I couldn't visit certain parts of my constituency because some IRA men might be there.

'There's no doubt my faith helps me to face up to that type of thing. It's easy to say that in respect of my own survival. Whether it would be strong enough to face up to one of my family being seriously ill or facing the sort of tragedy that so many parents have had to face, I don't know. I hope it would. I don't want to find out.

'I greatly admired Gordon Wilson's attitude and forbearance at the death of his daughter at the Enniskillen Remembrance Day bombing. But just saying "I forgive" is not enough. Forgiveness is something that has to be accepted as well as given. I think God says, "I forgive you if you accept." To me accepting forgiveness involves repentance and a change of heart.'

Repentance, he reckons, is also the key to lasting peace in the province.

'We have had some 2,200 murders by the IRA,' he says. 'They and other terrorist organisations must move from an Armalite-and-ballot-box policy to one totally reliant on the ballot box.

'The IRA must have a change of heart and a change of motivation. They know they cannot win a war. They have never been freedom fighters. They are simply callous people who use terrorism for political advantage. For there to be real peace Republican leaders have to begin conditioning rank-and-file members to renounce violence.'

Despite his insistence on the need for metamorphosis, Ken dismisses the idea of spiritual revival being the answer to The Troubles as too simplistic.

'I also learnt other stories from the Bible,' he says. 'When, for instance, the Temple was abused, Jesus took a whip and drove out the perpetrators in stark and stern terms. He didn't have much good to say about those people. Likewise we would be wrong to say that all people are redeemable. Some aren't – those, for example, who refuse to obey the command to love your neighbour. Now, as then, society has to maintain rules to discipline those who refuse to conform.

'The Government must also be disciplined in its response to terrorism. Terrorism can be overcome. We don't want a shoot-to-kill policy because that becomes state terrorism. I would always be opposed to that. But there should be encouragement for the legitimate forces of law and order to use the necessary level of force to regulate society in keeping with the wishes of the greater number across both traditions.'

Almost uniquely within Ulster Unionist MPs, Ken is against capital punishment. Given his hard-nosed approach to terrorism, isn't that unusual?

'My thinking has been guided by the New Testament account of the woman who was to be stoned for committing adultery. What particularly impresses me is when Jesus says, "Let him who is without sin cast the first stone."

'Of course, times have changed, but Jesus established the principle. As a Christian my responsibility is to apply that biblical principle to today. But make no mistake, I am not a softy when it comes to prisons. Punishment is reasonable; recompense is reasonable – sadly they don't play a big enough part within today's prison regime. Similarly, there doesn't appear to be any shame now about having been in prison. Terrorist prisoners even become folk heroes!

'Quite frankly, some people deserve to be branded because of the horrendous crimes they have committed – cold-blooded murder, child abuse and so on.'

How does Ken line up on other moral issues, some of which are likely to come before this Parliament? Should, for example the age of homosexual consent be lowered to 16?

'I am old-fashioned. I believe the biblical teaching is still as relevant today as it was in Old Testament times. I reject the whole notion that homosexuality is acceptable. Nobody will convince me that all the homosexuals who flaunt themselves at the rest of us have some sort of gene that has gone astray. I just don't believe it.

'I hate to say this but I would find it very difficult to have my children in my home if it turned out that they were practising homosexuals. I find it repulsive and hence I can't legislate. Nobody can legislate for what goes on behind closed doors. But people are not emotionally and spiritually mature enough at 16 to be given total freedom for their own lives.'

But isn't it only natural justice to give 16-year-old homosexuals the same rights as 16-year-old heterosexuals?

'I wouldn't have wanted my children to be indulging in heterosexual activity at the age of 16!' he says. 'Because homosexuality is an unnatural practice we should go for a higher age limit. I would set the age limit at 21. That way society will have shown that it doesn't approve of homosexual activity. But maybe society does now, God help us!'

Ken would not like to see abortion outlawed but he is against convenience abortions.

'I have always thought that abortion is very sad,' he says. 'I have seen too many people lose children they wanted. I know how terribly sad it is. I shudder at the thought that people would voluntarily and with no just cause fail to accept responsibility for a life they have created.

'The current notion that a woman's body is her own and she can do what she likes with it is a very selfish attitude and one I disapprove of. It would be better if the medical profession made judgments based purely on clinical necessity and not on convenience.'

When it comes to euthanasia, however, Ken has a different view on medical ethics.

'I can identify with people suffering from a disease who want relief from their pain even though the increased dosage will ultimately lead to their death. I believe people should be able to use whatever science and medicine provide in order to be able to die with dignity.

'But the idea of doctors setting up computer programs for people to kill themselves, or committees which will decide when it's time for us to die is dangerous.'

Ken deals with the question as to whether the public should reasonably expect their MPs to be above reproach in one word – leadership.

'If leadership means that MPs have to make more sacrifices than Joe Bloggs then so be it. We have an obligation to meet the general expectation of our constituents.

'They don't expect me to be on the take. And they don't expect me to desert my wife.

'There will be occasions when MPs are unhappy and become incompatible as far as their spouse is concerned but that is a personal thing. After all, an MP can be as unhappy as the next person. Where it is wrong is when an MP's self-belief dominates their sense of right and wrong, when arrogance creeps in.'

And what is the biggest issue facing the Government?

'It's so easy to be perfect in Opposition,' he says, after 15 years on the Opposition benches. 'But the Government is becoming accident prone – over money from the tobacco industry and in its handling of Northern Ireland, for example.

'I keep hearing that New Labour has hit the ground running. It'll have to get its balance very soon,' he says, sounding the alarm.

Seamus Mallon

MP for Newry and Armagh since 1986. Born in Northern Ireland in 1936. Before becoming an MP Seamus was a schoolmaster. Member, Northern Ireland Assembly, 1973 - 1974, 1982, 1998. Member, Northern Ireland Convention, 1975 - 1976. Deputy Leader, SDLP since 1978. Member, Irish Senate, 1981 - 1982. Member, New Ireland Forum, 1983 - 1984. Member, Select Committee on Agriculture, 1987 - 1997. Deputy First Minister, Northern Ireland Assembly since 1998. Seamus is a member of the Roman Catholic Church. Married Gertrude in 1966. Has one daughter.

The interview was conducted on 30 July 1998.

'NEVER believe history books,' says Seamus Mallon from behind his Stormont desk and his smiling Irish eyes. The subject is the behind-the-scenes story of how he was appointed Northern Ireland's Deputy First Minister back in July. With Ulster Unionist leader David Trimble due to become First Minister was it, I wondered, after months of protracted negotiations and weeks of sleepless soul-searching that Seamus was appointed ahead of his party boss and peace-process architect John Hume?

'It was the First of July, a Wednesday,' he recounts. 'I arrived at Castle Buildings for a party meeting. I had a cup of coffee and read the papers.

David Trimble came to the door to arrange a meeting for later in the day. Although there was nobody else about but me, I said yes. That afternoon we had a party meeting in a Belfast hotel. I turned up an hour-and-a-quarter late. As I was walked in, John Hume told me he would not be taking the role and I would have to take it. I said: "That's all right!" That was the entire conversation on the matter!'

Within minutes his appointment was confirmed by his Social Democratic and Labour Party colleagues. By nightfall the world knew – a new dawn was breaking in Ulster politics.

The SDLP deputy leader's matter-of-factness at his high-profile appointment might, in part, stem from the fact that he never wanted to be an MP in the first place. In the early '60s the son of the principal of a Markethill primary school had himself become the principal of a Markethill primary school. Comfortably off and comfortable.

'It was the Macmillan era,' he says. 'We'd never had it so good and I was living the life of Reilly. I didn't want to be involved in politics.'

It was also the time of Martin Luther King's civil rights movement in America and, closer to his County Armagh home, there were things that Seamus could not ignore.

'There was a large family at my school who lived in a hovel – no running water, no kitchen,' he says. 'The local councillor allocated houses and his reply to a request for housing was that "no Catholic pig or its litter will ever get a house in Markethill!" The father came and told me what had happened. I told him I'd think about it and asked him to come back. I knew then I had no choice but to do something. I enlisted the help of a few others in the village, two of whom were very staunch Unionists, and took on the problem. I realised that if it was happening in Markethill it was happening elsewhere.'

Before he knew it Seamus was involved in the housing issue – and politics – on a wider scale. By 1973 he was a member of the Armagh District Council and a Social Democratic and Labour Party representative in the Northern Ireland Assembly. Was it with a sense of mission or vocation?

'Nobody should be in politics unless they are motivated. This can happen in various ways. For me it was seeing injustices around me. I wouldn't say it was out of a sense of vocation, but it certainly pricked my conscience and I had to respond.'

Seamus came from a 'very traditional rural Catholic family' learning Greek and Latin at his primary school.

'You attended mass on a Sunday, you went to confession and woe betide you if you didn't!' he says with a smile. 'That was the way it was in those days.'

Was he ever tempted to rebel?

'Not really. I have my views and certain experiences have made me look hard at my faith but I still worship on a Sunday. I'm no Holy Joe but it is a fundamental part of my life. Over the years my religious beliefs have started to gel with my belief in human nature. To me the spiritual life is a luxury if it's not rooted in my own personal relationships with people. Faith must be translated into relationships. That's the only way it can make sense.'

On the person of Jesus, Seamus has doubts and certainties.

'Given that the Gospels were written years after Jesus, I still assume he did many of the things claimed of him. But I know the way in which auras can grow up around great people. Yes I have questions about this figure called Jesus Christ. How, for instance, has he sustained his influence for so long if he was just a very impressive man? So you must conclude that he is not just a man – that he is maybe as he says he is, the Son of God. Quite honestly, if Jesus is just a man we are all wasting our time.'

Some people have interpreted the past 30 years of violence in Northern Ireland as a religious war with Christian fighting Christian. Is that the way it is?

'No. It is not a religious war. It is not about religious dogma or issues. That's one of the fundamental political mistakes that is often made. The central problem has got religious overtones – sectarian overtones even. But the conflict is a political tension between those who espouse Unionism for whatever reason and those who have sought a resolution of the problem in an all-Ireland context. Even that is too pat and too inaccurate. Back in the 1800s, for instance, Republicanism was very much a nonconformist issue. It was not a Catholic philosophy.'

Today, however, a united Ireland is the SDLP's key aspiration – the ultimate goal.

'It's clearly stated in our constitution and in our election manifesto,' he says. 'We want to see the creation of Irish unity through peaceful, democratic means. By agreement and in no other way.'

A united Ireland is also the expressed aim of Republican terrorists. Doesn't that come as an embarrassment to the SDLP?

'That analogy is wrong,' he says. 'The National Front would share some of the views of most of the leaders in Britain. But I don't see why Her Majesty the Queen or the Prime Minister should be embarrassed because the National Front shares a type of general objective. However, Republican violence has done more damage to the prospect of Irish unity than ever Unionism has done. They have given Republicanism a bad name. They have tarnished the objective, they have tarnished the type of relationships that are going to be needed if unity is ever to come.

'The strength of the SDLP is that from the minute we were formed in 1970 we clearly defined how Irish unity would be achieved.'

And isn't it the case that the Catholic community has suffered at the hands of Republican terrorism?

'It's a well-recorded fact that more Catholics have been killed by Republican paramilitary groups than by the security forces. The Catholic community has suffered grievously, directly and indirectly, from the campaign of violence. Directly in the forms of being held to ransom and intimidated (which still goes on). And indirectly from the security presence that was created to deal with paramilitarism.

'But I am very loathe to talk about this in terms of just one community. The Catholic community has suffered greatly but so has the Protestant community.'

Against the background of 30 years of mutual suffering has come overwhelming public support – north and south of the border – for the Good Friday Agreement. Will the Agreement deliver long-term peace?

'The Agreement challenges the certitudes of Unionism and Nationalism at its extremes. Each generation has a right to write its own history. One of the problems about the north of Ireland is that we have had the legacy of other people's history and the assumed necessity to fulfil the legacies of other people's times. Part of the problem in both communities, especially in paramilitary groupings, is that there's a legacy of the past and a debt to the future. There's talk of "handing on the torch".

'This Agreement is the script for this generation, based on a set of principles that are correct, fair and workable. The Agreement has succeeded in translating those principles into political reality. It will be up to future generations of Unionists and Nationalists to develop the Agreement by consensus.'

But isn't the political reality that as much as some politicians might write the script, extremists – paramilitaries and politicians – are out to wreck it. The script might never get enacted.

'That is the cynic's view. But then part of the political process is to challenge cynicism. Of course, there are those who want to wreck it, inside and outside. Yes, there are those who want to continue with violence. But this Agreement challenges everybody. Are those who want to create a better future, who want a new quality of life, who want respect not just for themselves but for others, who want to work together, are they going to capitulate to the small numbers who want to wreck and destroy? No, they are not!

'The vast majority of people in the north of Ireland on all sides want this to work. They voted for it in a referendum. They voted for it overwhelmingly in the referendum in the south of Ireland. This Agreement will work because it is based on sound principles. It is fair and just to all sections of the community. The political process itself has got to be strong enough to ensure that it works and to prevent those who want to wreck it from wrecking it. That will be the acid test.'

One of the early tests of the Trimble/Mallon partnership came days after their appointments – Drumcree.

'It was an horrific two weeks,' says Seamus. 'A baptism of fire. We worked very closely together. Perhaps I wouldn't say we solved it or settled it but I think at least we removed the crisis element from it. I cannot divulge the sequence of events but I am convinced that Drumcree would have been solved without the horrific burning to death of three young children in Ballymoney. But we got through and I am convinced we will keep going.'

With the establishing of a new administration executive, a North/South Ministerial Council and a Council of the Isles all before Stormont opens for business, Seamus knows there is much work behind the Agreement. He also has fears if the Agreement cannot be made to work.

'If that's the case then Unionism will have probably lost its last chance to negotiate a settlement here. British patience is running out. If you follow the line of thought that has been pursued by successive British governments, if you look at the attitudes of the British establishment outside politics, if you look at public opinion, especially during the time of Drumcree, there is a very distinct train of thought that the same effort will not be put into another agreement.'

So is the Agreement the last chance?

'No, I am not saying that. But we will never again get the political convergence that we have now – a Prime Minister who is prepared to give the same amount of time to this problem; an Irish Government with the same commitment; a President of the United States with the interest that President Clinton has shown. So the actual working of this agreement is a political sine qua non.'

As one who under the Agreement is responsible for putting the Agreement and its subsequent legislation into practice, Seamus knows that the early euphoria over 'peace' has to be translated into volatile issues such as the appointment of ministers, prisoner releases and decommissioning. For one who came reluctantly to politics (no childhood ambition for him), who has known first-hand the illusive search for justice and peace, and whose life has been under constant threat since doing so, why is Seamus Mallon still in politics?

'You can't walk away from problems that have got to be solved,' he says. 'It's not a luxury any of us has. I don't want this to sound sanctimonious (although it probably will) but I have one great belief – the strength of the human spirit is what overcomes problems. It is that strength and will of the human spirit that is the crucial factor in Northern Ireland throughout all communities. That sounds platitudinous but it is really the essence of politics. I've always disagreed with the old cliché that politics is the art of the possibles. To me, politics is the art of making the impossible become possible.'

And if Seamus can be instrumental in doing that, his name, surely, will go down in the history books.

Michael Mates

*Conservative MP for East Hampshire since 1983. MP for Petersfield, 1974 –
1983. Born in London in 1934. Before becoming an MP Michael was an
officer in the Queens Dragoon Guards. Minister of State, Northern Ireland
Office, 1992 –1993. Michael is a member of the Church of England. Divorced.
Has two sons and three daughters.*

The interview was conducted on 2 July 1996.

IT'S hard to imagine Michael Mates singing 'O, for the wings of a dove' but
the former King's College chorister is definitely committed to peace.

'If there were one thing I could change about the country,' says the
Conservative MP for East Hampshire, 'it would be to create a society where
people didn't feel the need to act violently, whether it's road rage, terrorism,
school bullying or armed robbery, so we could air our differences
peacefully. That would probably be a very significant improvement in all
our lives. Specifically, I'd like to be identified with being part of bringing
a permanent peace to Northern Ireland. Because that's where I've spent so
much of my military and political life.'

Michael's involvement with the province goes back further than his
spell in the early '90s as a Northern Ireland minister. A visit to the province

shortly after the civil rights marches of 1969 became a stepping-stone in his own political sojourn.

'I'd always been interested in politics but the military didn't encourage that. I'd been there before but this was a defining time for what's happened to me politically since.'

Before the IRA cease fire, the press reported that Michael had had secret talks with Sinn Fein at a time when the Government denied direct contact. Were the reports correct?

'I've had direct talks with all sorts of people in Northern Ireland,' he says. 'Since that press report I have maintained an absolute silence about it. Except to say that, yes, I will talk to anybody who thinks I can help maintain the peace.'

Does he regard Sinn Fein and the IRA as separate entities?

'No. They're one and the same. The myth they have tried to sell is that somehow they are separate, but it doesn't bear any examination. Gerry Adams and Martin McGuinness, for example, have been and are members of the IRA Army Council. Danny Morrison, who was Sinn Fein's head of publicity and public affairs, is serving 10 years for an IRA offence. Many of Northern Ireland's Sinn Fein councillors have been convicted of IRA offences. I haven't looked closely at the people who were elected in the May elections but I've no doubt many of them have seen the inside of the Maze Prison because they've been terrorists. There is no difference.

'Gerry Adams sometimes tries to distance himself in his rhetoric because he thinks he will persuade American public opinion that he is a genuine democratic politician. But then you see him carrying the coffin of the terrorist who's just killed half a dozen people in the Shankill Road for the sole reason they were of a different faith. So he is indelibly identified with the terrorists.

'I am prepared to accept that Adams and McGuinness have decided there's a better way than killing to achieve what they want.

'I have been prepared to accept they are genuine in their desire to look for a peaceful settlement. But they have only been allowed to do so on the basis that if they don't get what the IRA wants the IRA will return to a bombing campaign such as happened at Canary Wharf and Manchester. Adams has condemned neither of those incidents. If he did, he would no longer be the head of Sinn Fein. That tells you how close they are.'

Does the former Dragoon Guards colonel think the IRA has used the ceasefire to regroup?

'Certainly. They had taken a great number of casualities prior to the ceasefire. They have been retraining, regrouping, planning. However, the ceasefire is worthwhile.

'We've had very nearly two years of relative peace. I want to do everything I can to continue that because I think the longer we have a relatively peaceful situation in Northern Ireland the harder it will be for the IRA to start up. They know that resuming a campaign in Northern Ireland would alienate an awful lot of opinion north and south which at the moment tolerates what they do quietly. They fear there would be a backlash and I think they are right.'

So a resumption of an IRA campaign in the province would force the republican community to distance itself from the IRA once and for all?

'If there was a bombing, shooting, random-slaughtering campaign as we had before, a lot of them would. The Irish Government would have to take a very much stronger line. The Americans would finally switch off.'

How can peace come to the province?

'That's the $64,000 question. We have a sort of peace on which to build. The most important thing is that nobody does anything to upset it.

'It's very laudable that the Protestant paramilitaries, who are just as unpleasant and ruthless in their way, have not responded to the IRA violence. The longer we can persuade them to do that the better.

'The longer people sit around a table and talk, even if they're not agreeing, the better. That's why everybody made the most superhuman efforts to get Sinn Fein to the Stormont talks. Talks that include Sinn Fein are more likely to be fully acceptable all round than talks that don't. But they have excluded themselves by the way they behaved. I'm very sad about that.'

Over the years, people have labelled The Troubles as another example of religion causing war; this is what Christians do to each other. Is that a valid argument?

'No. Because it isn't about religion,' he says. 'There is a basic enmity which has a religious foundation in that most of the people involved on one side are Roman Catholic and most of the people involved on the other are Protestant.

'But then some of those involved in the terrible deeds of either side have not been Christians at all. The Roman Catholic Church has been getting more and more robust about this to the extent of not wanting to bury terrorists or give them last rites.

'Northern Ireland is a much more religiously orientated community than any you'll find anywhere else in Great Britain. Leaders such as Archbishop Eames and Cardinal Daly have done great work which has given the Christian religion rather a good name.'

Michael's own religious foundation started when, as an eight-year-old, he became a chorister, first at Salisbury Cathedral School and later at King's College, Cambridge.

'In those days that meant singing full matins and a full evensong every day, and full matins, full choral eucharist and full evensong every Sunday.

'Two and a half hours on a Sunday morning is a long time when you're nine or 10! But I grew to love the beauty of the architecture and church music. I have loved them ever since.'

Michael cannot say precisely when he made the Christian faith personal.

'If you start at eight years old, twice a day for an hour, it's a very dominant factor in your life and it becomes a habit. I remember the beauty of it. The loveliness of the cathedral, the wonderful words.

'I have great difficulty now with new liturgies. Because I have sung them to settings by composers like Bach, Stainer and Benjamin Britten, the words have become indelibly ingrained in my mind as part of my religious experience, and I find it very difficult to pick up these new books which have no relevance to what all my life's been about. But that's habit and that's not necessarily a good thing. But it's a very powerful thing when it goes on from the age of eight to the age of 21.

'I wouldn't have continued in the choir if behind it all there hadn't been a fundamental acceptance and belief. So I can't actually say which was chicken and which was egg.'

So there was no defining moment as such, no conversion experience?

'No, absolutely not. My faith has always been there. It's always been part of my life; a comforting thing behind everything I do. It's not something that drives me every moment of the day, as it does other people. But in a crisis when something's gone horribly wrong or when there's great unhappiness around one does stop and think.'

Might some readers be surprised that this robust, sometimes outspoken MP is a man of faith?

'It's almost impossible in public life to say anything on this subject without being misunderstood,' he says. 'There are a number of people who make it a major part of their public lives. That becomes understood and accepted. I try not to bang on about religion. I'm not a Bible-thumping politician.

'If I wanted to be a person who preached the gospel and had a vocation to do so I'd go into the Church. Incidentally, I wish some churchmen would have the same self-denying ordinance about going into politics! As an MP, I can and do help Christian causes but I try to keep a low profile and feel very uncomfortable flaunting it.'

Michael is also uncomfortable at the prospect of his personal faith being used as a potential vote-winner. Although he is prepared to meet with all manner of religious and non-religious groups, he refuses to take part in election campaign 'beauty contests' where candidates appear together to put forward their views. He also refuses to campaign on Sundays.

It is in church, amid the music and architecture, that Michael feels closest to God.

'I go into some of those places and feel a Presence there,' he says. 'This is one reason why I've found it difficult coming to terms with the dismantling of all of that. I understand the argument that the Church is out of touch and you've got to take it to people and all of that. But for me, a very important part of it all is the mystery and I think it is wrong to take mystery away.'

When, after 20 years in the army, Michael won the Petersfield seat in 1974, he could have been forgiven for looking mystified himself.

'I was totally unprepared for political life,' he confesses. 'I wasn't even a member of the party when I applied to be the candidate because service personnel didn't join political parties in those days. I was selected on 22 August, left the army on 1 September and found myself in Parliament on 11 October. It was a pretty sudden transition and the only immediate consequence was a 50 per cent pay cut!'

While military manoeuvres did not prepare him for future political battles, Michael sees similarities between life in the mess and life on the benches.

'Looking after people is very much the role of a peacetime officer. If you've got to train someone to stand beside you and possibly die in war you've got to look after them in peace. I enjoyed that part of Army life very much. I now enjoy looking after constituents who've got problems and trying to help them when they are in difficulties or when the system has let them down.'

Whichever party wins the next election, Michael reckons it will have to face the perpetual challenges of the economy, unemployment, inflation, and taxation.

'The problems are not going to change. We all want to do more for health, welfare, education, the disabled, the homeless, the old and the sick.

'The thought that one party is more interested than another in good education, good welfare and in helping the poor and the disabled, is absolute nonsense. Behind any party's rhetoric everybody wants to do all they can for disadvantaged people.

'People who say Conservatives are hard-hearted and don't care are as foolish as those who say Labour only cares about the working class and doesn't care about anything else. These are ludicrous, old-fashioned caricatures. They were never true. The argument is how we go about it. The electorate has to choose between priorities.'

Michael's priority, meanwhile, is to be instrumental in bringing lasting peace to the land that has come to mean so much to him. For that, the ex-choirboy will need more than a wing and a prayer.

Rt Hon Sir Brian Mawhinney

Conservative MP for Cambridgeshire North West since 1997. MP for Peterborough, 1979 – 1997. Born in Belfast in 1940. Before becoming an MP Brian was a university teacher in America and London. Minister of State, Northern Ireland Office, 1990 – 1992. Minister of State for Health, 1992 – 1994. Appointed a Privy Councillor, 1994. Secretary of State for Transport, 1994 – 1995. Cabinet Minister without portofolio and Conservative Party Chairman, 1995 – 1997. Knighted, 1997. Brian is a member of the Church of England. Married Betty in 1965. Has two sons, one daughter and four grandchildren.

The interview was conducted on 11 September 1996.

IF Brian Mawhinney, Conservative Party Chairman, had seen the devil in the 'demon eyes' featured on the 'New Labour – new danger' posters the Tory party's controversial campaign would have had a different look. 'At no point did I, nor do I, see them as demon eyes,' he says. 'Had the thought occurred to me, and it never did, I would not have pursued it. It's neither appropriate politics nor appropriate Christian behaviour.'

'The phrase "demon eyes" was actually dreamed up by a Labour MP who didn't like what Clare Short had said about there being people behind Tony Blair whom she called sinister. She called them people who work in the dark. She said they were dangerous, that they'd say anything to get themselves elected. 'What I did was to put her words and the picture of Mr Blair on the advertisement. We looked for some way to convey this idea, so we put eyes behind him to signify it. I took something that was on the record and sought to portray it pictorially.

'When I became chairman, one of the first rules I laid down was that if something is on the record, it is a legitimate source for comment. If it is not on the record then I am not interested. I have absolutely no intention of running a dirty campaign. The electorate doesn't want it. The party isn't comfortable with it. I'm not comfortable with it.'

Chairman since July 1995, Dr Mawhinney does not occupy a comfortable pew. There is plenty to occupy his time. He is the MP for Peterborough. A Cabinet minister without portfolio, Dr Mawhinney contributes to the development and presentation of Government policy. He sits on most Cabinet committees dealing with national issues and policy. He works closely with the Deputy Prime Minister, Michael Heseltine, in overseeing the way in which Government policy is presented to the media.

As party chairman he heads a staff of some 220 employees around the country. He liaises between Westminster MPs and grass-roots party members. He is responsible for getting his party's message across to the electorate, and helps in the recruiting, training and equipping of local party activists.

As chairman it's his job to win the election for the Conservatives.

'That's the general perception,' he says over tea (black) and biscuits in his Smith Square office. 'But I don't kid myself into believing it's a job I can do by myself. That would be great foolishness. While I am ultimately responsible for the presentation of the party, a lot of other people are involved. I take professional advice and share with senior colleagues. But to the extent that any one person in party terms has the responsibility to win the election that would be me.'

Looking for the winning formula is something to which Dr Mawhinney is well accustomed. A physics graduate from Queen's University, Belfast, in his native Northern Ireland, he gained a doctorate in radiation biology at London University. After three years of teaching at the University of Iowa Medical School, he became a lecturer at London's Royal Free Hospital Medical School.

Why did he leave a meaningful career to enter the less secure world of parliamentary politics?

'I suppose over the years I was pushed into it by other people,' he says. 'I enjoyed teaching medical students and being an academic but I was also interested in the world around me. I read lots of newspapers and magazines and, as a result, found myself better informed than my peers. It wasn't a particular virtue, it was just the sort of person I was. If my wife,

Betty, were here she would tell you that, in contrast, I'm never going to win any handyman competition. I don't have the motivation.

'I didn't have an upbringing of always being determined to be a politician, much less an MP. In fact, I didn't join the party until I was 30. Like most voluntary organisations, if you've got a little bit of talent and interest you tend to get the jobs.'

Since he was elected those jobs have included being Minister of State in the Northern Ireland Office and in the Department of Health, and Secretary of State for Transport.

Was it with a sense of mission that he left the lab bench for the back bench?

'Yes, in the sense that as a Christian I have a sense of mission. But it's a very personal thing. I don't like it when Christians try to appropriate God for their particular viewpoint. I'm not saying there should be a great divide between my Christian beliefs and how I live my life. I try to minimise that gap.'

Would it be too strong to say that he felt God calling him into politics?

'That depends on how other people wanted to interpret that remark. I could see an unfolding of opportunities in my life which in terms of my Christian beliefs fall into the category of my saying that this was God leading. But I would be cautious in terms of how I explained that, particularly to non-Christians, because you run the risk of leaving in the minds of people some presumption about God and me, or about God and Conservatism which I wouldn't necessarily want them to have.

'I opened a one-day conference once at Westminster Chapel, entitled Conservatism and Christianity. As a way of grabbing the delegates' attention I stood up and said, "God is not a Tory. Neither is he a Socialist, a Liberal or a Social Democrat. God is God. And that is where we are starting our conference this morning."

'My God transcends party politics. That's important to me. Incidentally, as I drove back to Parliament I heard the newsreader on the one o'clock news announce: "A Tory MP admitted today that God is not a Conservative."'

Speaking of Christianity and the Conservative Party, how does he answer the sometimes-voiced question, 'How can a Christian be a Tory?'

'There's a presupposition in that question that suggests it's difficult to be a Christian and a Tory. I don't understand what the difficulty is supposed to be. It's usually explained on the basis that Christians are caring people. But a large proportion of the caring that's done in this country is done by people who, in the privacy of a ballot box, vote Conservative.

'If you look at who's running the big charities, and at who's doing the likes of meals on wheels up and down the country, you will find a significant proportion of people involved would call themselves

Conservatives. They may not be party members but that's the way they vote. It is a misguided question.'

But wouldn't Tory critics also say that, good as they are, voluntary agencies shouldn't have to get involved? That people are unemployed, on the street as a direct result of uncaring Tory government policies?

'That's not sustainable because unemployment exists under all governments. It is a fact, for example, that unemployment has risen sharply under every Labour government. But I wouldn't conclude from that that if you are a Labour Party supporter you can't be a Christian. That's nonsense!

'Shortly after I was first elected, I went to an interdenominational Good Friday open-air service in Peterborough. Two women in front of me held one of those staged conversations knowing perfectly well I was standing immediately behind them. One said to the other, "I see the MP is here this morning." The other said, "Yes. I'm surprised." When her friend asks why? she says, "Well, he claims he's a Christian but he doesn't believe in the Campaign for Nuclear Disarmament!"

'Had I been invited to comment I would have said that I wasn't aware of any verse in Scripture that made membership of CND a precondition to God's forgiveness or of becoming a Christian. If people add preconditions to the gospel it is diminished.

'One of the strengths of our political system is that because it is based on Judaeo-Christian principles we have very little debate about what ought to be the general ends of policy. The debate is about the best means of achieving those ends. In that sense the mechanism of achieving good housing can't be 'Christian' or 'non-Christian'.

'I'm never particularly impressed by the sort of person who comes to me and says: "I can't understand how a Conservative can be a Christian". Frankly, though I seldom say so, that actually tells me more about their presuppositions than it does about either the Christian faith or the Conservative Party.'

Mawhinney himself was brought up in a 'loving Christian home', going to two church services and Sunday school every week.

'By today's standards I suppose it was reasonably strict. But in no sense was it stifling. I'm deeply grateful for the love, guidance, spiritual example and encouragement I was given as I grew up.

'As a teenager I came to realise that I couldn't inherit this faith from my parents. I had to do something for myself. I am a Christian because I have a personal knowledge of and relationship with Jesus Christ. The older I get the more conscious I am that a Christian is someone who is forgiven, although as a teenager I wouldn't have expressed it in those terms. That, for me, is the ultimate definition of a Christian.'

How does he describe his faith?

'Important. Growing, in the sense that one continually gets spiritual insights. I think if that were to stop happening, I'd have to sit down and ask why. My faith is an inner source of strength in the face of the pressures and demands made upon me. As I've grown older I've become increasingly aware of God's love, mercy, forgiveness and grace.'

He is also aware of the danger of Christian MPs being misunderstood or misrepresented. Media-friendly gospel sound bites, he reckons, do Christianity a disservice.

'As party chairman I try to take complex ideas and turn them into easy-to-understand concepts,' he says. 'I have always been very cautious about seeking to do that with my personal faith. The danger is that you set yourself up as some sort of example. There is no sense in which I want to set myself up as a yardstick by which others should measure themselves. I am too conscious of inadequacies and things which in spiritual terms could be improved.'

Brian is also wary of his personal faith being misused for political ends.

'Betty and I never make any secret about our Christian faith,' he says. 'But I can truthfully say we have never sought to ram it down anybody's throat. Many of our constituents know about that part of our lives. If they want to talk to me about Christianity then I am happy to talk about it. But you would be hard pressed to find anyone in Peterborough who could truthfully say that I had made an issue out of it or had tried to win votes on the basis of my faith.'

Does he reckon Christian MPs are under extra pressures compared to their non-Christian colleagues?

'I'm impressed by the standards of service that MPs of all parties and all religious persuasions give to their constituents,' he says. 'Ours is a system of which any country could be proud. MPs who are not Christians don't, on the whole, have inferior standards.'

Casting an eye to the future, what political ambitions does the prospective Conservative candidate for North-West Cambridgeshire have?

'My political ambition has always been to do the job that I happen to have at the time to the best of my ability. I hope that doesn't sound too pi. But even if it does, it is true. Doing your job to the best of your ability is the Christian way to behave. If, in my world of very ambitious people, I am asked to move on to something else then I do the new job to the best of my ability.

'I never spend time thinking about getting promotion. If I were to be asked what I wanted to do next, I truthfully couldn't say. I am preoccupied with what I have to do at the moment.

'As a Christian I am comfortable with that approach. And, besides, I'm too old to change!' he says with a twinkle in his smiling Irish eyes.

Alun Michael

Labour and Co-operative MP for Cardiff South and Penarth since 1987. Born in North Wales in 1943. Before becoming an MP Alun was a journalist and a youth and community worker. Opposition Whip, 1987 – 1988. Opposition Spokesman on Welsh Affairs, 1988 – 1992. Opposition Spokesman on Home Affairs, 1993 – 1997. At the 1997 general election Alun became Minister of State, Home Office. Alun is a member of the Church of England. Married to Mary . Has two sons and three daughters.

The interview was conducted on 28 January 1997.

IN the wake of Labour's revolutionary election victory, newly-appointed Home Office minister Alun Michael wants to turn the youth justice system from a 'vicious circle to a virtuous circle'.

'Everyone, from the courts to the schools to the police, blames each other, and the system doesn't work,' he says. 'We need to let young people know that bad behaviour will result in serious punishment. But we also have to give them hope. To see young people as only being bad is the worst thing we can do. Young people are our hope for the future. They are looking to us to get things right.

'There's been a long-running debate on whether we should be lenient on offenders and tackle the social conditions that underlie crime or whether we should punish offenders. What we need to do is get the balance right. In the words of that famous phrase, we have to be tough on crime and on the causes on crime.

'Punishing offenders shows that certain behaviour isn't tolerated. It also gives a warning signal to others. But we should also be concerned about how we can rehabilitate offenders, how we can motivate them to live a positive and useful life on their release from prison. At present, all too often, they come out to commit more offences and more serious offences. We must stop penal institutions being colleges of crime.

'I believe very strongly that when someone is sentenced we should immediately be asking, "What treatment does that person need?" As well as making them fit to return to society, we need to ask whether they need help with psychiatric problems, behavioural problems or drink or drug addiction.

'We also need to give people adequate supervision after release, because the better the standard of supervision the better the chance that they won't re-offend.'

A journalist by training, Angelsey-born Alun was a voluntary and then a full-time youth worker before winning his Cardiff South and Penarth seat in 1987.

In Opposition he moved from the whips office to become shadow minister for Home Affairs and the voluntary sector. As such he was deputy first to Tony Blair and then to Jack Straw. His new position, as deputy Home Secretary responsible for criminal justice, the police and the voluntary sector, allows Alun to indulge in a political passion.

'I've always been interested in youth offending,' says the former Chairman of the Cardiff Juvenile Bench. 'There are too many offences committed by young people. They not only ruin the lives of their victims, they also ruin their own lives. Many of the offences are unnecessary and preventable. I want to work towards preventing youth crime.'

From his time as a youth and community worker he knows that young people need to be encouraged – to be given something to live for – lest the devil finds work for idle hands.

'Many church and community-based organisations, including youth clubs, were formed in Victorian times when people recognised that you have to give opportunity to and nurture young people to be themselves in a positive and supportive environment.

'Many young people today have been abandoned on inner-city streets. If we adults don't help them grow up with a proper sense of rights and responsibilities, a sense of citizenship, then we shouldn't be surprised if things go wrong.'

Wanting to prevent things going wrong led Alun in the early '70s to become a Cardiff City councillor and set about tackling the problems of unemployment and crime among local youth. Sixteen years later he wanted to adjust the larger picture.

'I realised you couldn't get it right at a local level unless national government set the context in which things could happen. Until the national agenda was correct, people who for years had ploughed an unsung furrow couldn't get on with the job. I felt I couldn't complain about national government without offering myself for election. If you don't put yourself forward then don't blame those who do. That's why I decided to stand for Parliament.'

Alun reckons he has been on a learning curve from day one.

'I came with a sense of mission without thinking very much at all about what it would be like to be an MP,' he admits. 'Nothing can prepare you for being an MP. Every MP does the job in a different way. You do it in the way that fits your interests, your beliefs, your conscience, your life-style, and what it was that motivated you to come here in the first place.'

Describing his politics as 'mainstream Labour', Alun is a 'passionate supporter of Tony Blair'.

In the past, he reckons, Labour was punished electorally for 'failing to communicate its underlying principles and what it was doing. At other times we did not listen to the aspirations of the people we sought to represent. We had a tradition of fighting the last election but one.'

New Labour, according to Alun, is ready and radical.

'The party remains true to its main traditions and to me the first is that of democratic socialism. We must listen to those we represent. We must beware of arrogance.

'Secondly I believe there is much more to our heritage than the narrow one that was portrayed by some people in the late '70s and early '80s.

We are the party of everybody. The Labour Party is in touch with its own history, its future and with the people it seeks to represent.'

Brought up as a Welsh Presbyterian, Alun became an Anglican while a student at Keele University.

'When I first went to university I started to drift away from the Christian faith,' he says.

'Your priorities change and become dominated by your studies and friends. But it was the influence of other Christians that spoke to me. They lived out what they believed. I saw something in them which was attractive and right.

'I became an Anglican because I was attracted by the pattern of worship – the accessibility of ideas through repetition. Ideally I would like to combine the best of the free church and the best of the liturgy. I am an ecumenist by nature and background. I feel just as comfortable in chapel as in church.

'My faith gives me a starting-point for looking at life. It gives me a way of looking at individual issues as time goes on.

'What it doesn't give me is easy answers. Just because I'm a Christian doesn't mean I have all the answers to the great issues of our time. They still have to be wrestled with. I try to be consistent with my Christian beliefs when legislating for this world. But the idea that you can translate moral judgments about what an individual should do into the law of the land is absurd. We have to legislate for the world in which we live and for the things that happen in the world in which we live.

'I think if you don't recognise that, it's very difficult to reconcile your individual beliefs and your political activity.'

So the public is wrong to look to Parliament to give a moral lead?

'In some cases, yes. It is primarily the Church's responsibility to give a lead in terms of individual moral decisions. But Government should have a public morality – the way in which we treat people and the way Parliament treats people through the law.

'For example, it is morally right that our education system should be effective for all children. It's not good enough if we're letting some children down. As a society we should be giving opportunities to all school-leavers.

'The fact that some communities, like inner-city black youngsters, are being let down in this respect is unfair and wrong. It's a recipe for discontent. We are failing to encourage the requirements of citizenship – rights and responsibilities. We want to support communities, especially families.'

Have there been times when in following a Christian morality Alun has struggled in deciding which way to vote?

'Surprisingly few,' he says. 'Obvious conscience issues are, of course, left to personal conscience. For some people some of those issues, like abortion, are clear-cut. But if you look at the wider issue of how to legislate for a society in which there are so many evils you have to look much more carefully.

'The difficulty in framing the law is to balance the freedom of people to make decisions or to behave in certain ways and the good of society as a whole.

'At one extreme the argument is that there should be no constraints, people can do what they like. At the other, the proposed activity should be prohibited.

'The judgment of public morality is where you set the limits. It's difficult. You must follow your conscience but your conscience must guide you to the right public decision, not just the one you would choose for yourself, members of your family, or your church.

'We need to create a society in which people can make those choices. Many people are under pressure. They are not free to choose. Many children are brought into the world only to lead miserable lives. Some children are neglected and abandoned. That is an outrage in terms of public morality!

'Yes, the person who offends against the child must take the blame. Clearly that person is responsible for his or her actions. But society is failing if it doesn't find the best possible methods of preventing the abuse of children. Offenders need to be caught and punished, so society is protected against repetition.'

Before and during the general election campaign much was made of the Christian credentials of politicians, the Prime Minister included. How does Alun gauge the seeming spread of Christianity within his party?

'As a member of the Christian Socialist Movement I think the discussion that has gone on among Christians within the Labour Party in recent times has been of great value. Large numbers of people have joined the Christian Socialist Movement in recent years. Not because there is the building of a pressure group within the Labour Party but because people want the opportunity to exchange views about our political activities and how that grows from our individual beliefs and our beliefs as Christians together.

'For me, being a Christian, a member of the Labour Party and of the Co-operative movement has no boundaries. I can't see where one stops and the other starts. Why should I and others who are Christians and Socialists leave our Christianity outside the door when we come to a Labour Party meeting?

'In allowing people to feel comfortable about their Christianity informing their political views, Tony Blair – and John Smith before him – has done this party a great service.

'It doesn't mean you have to push Christianity down people's throats. It doesn't mean there's anything wrong with a Moslem or a Sikh Socialist or that their contribution is any the less. What it does mean is that we acknowledge the impact Christ has both on the individual believer and on society as a whole through the Christian values which have made us what we are. That is of great value to the Labour Party.'

Replacing individualism with a sense of community is, Alun reckons, the biggest issue facing the new Government.

'The Thatcherite emphasis on competition and individual success has led us astray in terms of public policy and public morality,' he says. 'I hope the new Government will be less arrogant and less confrontational.

'We need to rediscover a sense of community and of co-operation. We need to rebuild the sense of mutual responsibility – the balance between rights and responsibilities. The tackling of crime and its causes.'

If he can achieve that during his time at the Home Office, many people will consider Alun to have squared a very big circle.

Peter Pike

Labour MP for Burnley since 1983. Born in Hertfordshire in 1937. Before becoming an MP Peter was a bank clerk, Labour Party organiser, factory worker and shop steward. Member of Barnsley Borough Council, 1976 - 1984. Opposition Spokesman on Rural Affairs, 1990 – 1992. Opposition Spokesman on Local Government, 1992 – 1994. Peter is a member of the Church of England. Married Sheila in 1962. Has two daughters.

The interview was conducted on 5 December 1996.

WESTMINSTER is too full of lawyers for Peter Pike's liking. 'We're getting far too many barristers and solicitors in here,' says the Labour MP for Burnley. 'Parliament has to be a cross-section of society. That's why we have to get more women MPs and working-class people here as well.'

For some the notion of working class is outdated – old language discarded by New Labour. But not Peter. It's a language he understands.

Born in Hertfordshire, Peter moved to south London as a young child. When his father went off to war, Peter was evacuated to his mother's home-town of Burnley. By the time peace broke out Peter, aged eight, had already settled on his ambition – to be the town's Labour MP. 'Most of my mother's family were staunch Conservatives but my father was Labour,' he says. 'At election time, we put Conservative posters in the window during the day and Labour ones at night. As I grew up we had lots of arguments about politics.

'Even though I was young, I remember being struck by the differences between the modern south London suburb I'd moved from and the North, where it was smoky and dirty. People lived in houses with no proper toilets, no bath and no hot and cold running water. The majority of people went to work in clogs. It was like another world.'

It was the injustice in the contrasting lifestyles of north and south that spurred Peter into action long before the 'north-south divide' became a spin doctor's sound bite. 'I just had a feeling that Labour was going to change it all in one go,' he says. 'Clem Attlee is my hero. His government transformed this country in a way that we now take too much for granted. He is still very underrated for what he did as Deputy Prime Minister during the war and the changes he made in society after it.

'While she may have damaged some of the things he set up, not even Mrs Thatcher dared to destroy things he created such as the welfare state, the National Health Service, the changes in working conditions and a mass of things that has since become known as "consensus". They have become part of what people view as a civilised, caring society.'

By the time he had been given the key of the door, Peter had walked through the doors of the party recruiting office. He returned from National Service to help in the 1959 election campaign. Having left school at 17 to work in a bank, Peter spent two years combining work with serving on south London's Merton and Morden Urban District Council before moving back to Burnley in 1965 to become a full-time party organiser and agent.

In 1973 he went to work on a production line in a local factory.

'It was only supposed to be a temporary move until I decided what I really wanted to go for,' he says. 'I became shop steward and stayed 10 years!'

In 1976 Peter was elected to Burnley Borough Council. Four years later he became Leader of the Council, a position he held until winning his parliamentary seat in 1983.

Peter readily admits a lifetime's involvement in politics is not without its cost.

'Too often my wife and daughters have taken second place to the Labour Party,' he admits. 'While it's fashionable to talk about the disturbance to the family life of women MPs, we shouldn't lose sight of the fact that it affects men too. At times, my daughters have resented my being involved with party business. Although they are both party members, I sometimes wonder if I was too busy with politics while they were growing up.'

Ten years ago, during the height of apartheid, Peter was part of an all-party Parliamentary Christian Fellowship delegation to South Africa. The trip left a lasting impression on him.

'There were three of us - Simon Hughes, Alistair Burt and myself,' he says. 'The idea was that a group of MPs from different parties would show that Christians can be united in their faith despite their political differences.

'I discovered South Africa to be a very strongly Christian country, although it was very divided. Churches were packed on Sundays. Sadly, they were all segregated. We found it was where people were most polarised that they had the greatest faith. Some Afrikaners justified apartheid from the Bible while others sought to change apartheid. We tried to use our common faith as a way of getting people to talk to us and to each other. We were able to gain trust so that by our third visit we found whites talking to members of the ANC. The Church played a major part in bringing the people of South Africa together. Sadly, this fact has been underestimated or dismissed since.'

Peter describes his Christian faith as 'very traditional'. 'I went to Sunday school as a child and regularly attended the monthly scout church parade,' he says. 'While I was in the Royal Marines during National Service I, like many others in my squad, was confirmed. It's something I took very seriously.

'My wife, Sheila, and I regularly worship at the local parish church. We're very happy there. We're not ones who want arm-waving and the like in services. Having said that I recognise that the evangelical wing of the Church of England is the side that is growing. I've no problems with that so long as the Church realises its responsibility to care for people. Christianity in the New Testament is where Christ shows he cares for the less fortunate, whoever and whatever they happened to be. He shows us who we should care for and help.

'Among other things, my faith gives me guidance in making the right decision, personally and politically. I always hope I'm doing things for the right reasons. For me, the really difficult issues are the conscience issues.

'For example, I get a lot of criticism from Christians for not voting against abortion. The present law is about right, but it should be more rigorously enforced. Although I don't like abortion, I don't believe I can say to a woman that in certain situations an abortion shouldn't be available. But I think we should try to lessen the number of abortions through more sex education and by making birth control more widely available. It's a very difficult issue. But then the churches aren't unanimous on this subject so why expect Christian MPs to be?

'Ultimately, on conscience issues I'm not answerable to my electors. I'm not answerable to the Labour Party. I'm answerable to myself and to God. So long as I'm trying to make decisions for what I believe are the right reasons, people have no right to judge me.'

Should the Church have no say, then, in conscience issues?

'Of course it should. The Church has to be involved but not in a party political way. If the Church isn't concerned about these issues something is wrong. It has to be relevant to the times. Christ was relevant to the time in which he lived. He used things that were happening in his society to make his point. For example, he didn't dodge the issue of Roman occupation but used it to challenge his hearers about the Kingdom of God.'

Increasingly the electorate is looking to the occupants of Westminster for moral example, if not moral guidance. Is that a realistic expectation of MPs?

'No,' says Peter. 'MPs are no better people than anyone else. Although most MPs are very decent people, it is unreasonable to expect Parliament to be made up of 651 people with perfect, unblemished characters. I wouldn't claim to be a saint. I'm not all that different from the constituents I represent. I don't set myself up in any way and it's not for me to judge other people's morals.

'MPs personally need to remember that what they say and do affects a lot of other people. Parliament has a responsibility in society. But so has the Church. Often the public wants MPs to be doing what the Church should be doing and, like clergy, we get publicly hammered for our misdemeanours. But Christianity is strong on the idea that even though people have failings they can be forgiven and start again.

'If Christianity is declining in this country, the Church should address its relevance to the majority of people. We don't want a third world war to bring people back to pray in churches.'

But isn't it up to politicians to give the legislative signals to say what society will and will not tolerate?

'Absolutely. We are the legislators and we can't dodge that. We have to lay the ground rules, and certain people will disagree with any law that we make. In a civilised society you have to have laws, and change should come through legal means. Take the Poll Tax; I was never one of those who refused to pay in order to change it. You change it through the ballot box, which, in the end, was how it was changed. It wasn't the Don't Pay campaign that did it. It was that the Government were losing too many by-elections.

'We have to legislate for things which are acceptable and enforceable throughout society as a whole. An MP can't always get a clear picture of public opinion from his or her mailbag because it is always the vociferous who write and they might not represent the majority view of the constituents. On any emotive issue I will have letters both for and against the proposed legislation. I make my mind up and defend my position. People have the right to disagree. However, they might agree with me on many other issues.

'But MPs are not the only people who should face up to society's problems. Others, including the Church, also have a responsibility.'

So far as Peter's personal parliamentary responsibilities are concerned, having spent four years as a frontbench spokesman, he now serves on the Procedural Select Committee ('where we suggest ways of improving the business of the House') and the Deregulation Committee – scrapping out-of-date and out-of-touch legislation.

He describes his Christianity as 'very traditional'. Are his politics in the traditional mould?

'I would call myself old Labour, only because I don't like the term New Labour, although I understand why Tony Blair uses it. The Labour Party has changed a lot over the years. The party is much more open and democratic than it was. A lot more women are involved in it.

'In the '70s and '80s we allowed the means of achieving objectives to become more important than the objectives themselves. Once we were paternalistic – for example, insisting that every fourth council house door was painted yellow. Now we are realistic.

'In many ways, we are now closer to the original purpose of the party. Getting decent housing, employment, and health provision for people is right back at the top of the agenda. Labour was formed to put people first. If it is not about people then there is something wrong. But to be able to do anything, we have to win an election.'

For Peter, unemployment is the biggest issue facing whichever party wins the election. 'Unemployment is an evil for those who have to suffer it,' he says. 'Getting people back to work is the key to unlocking so much more. When I talk to industry I say we don't want to take a higher portion of your profits but we want you to make more profit and for our share to go up so we can put it on overseas aid and the welfare state, the National Health Service, education, housing and the like.

'Tackling the housing issue would actually do all of those things. It would get the economy going, it would reduce unemployment and it would start to tackle the major housing problem. I can't understand why the government fails to deal with housing.

'Almost every independent organisation in the country says we need about 100,000 more houses a year. Next year we are geared to building about 20,000 – way below what we need: Last year we built only about 2,000 council houses. We must do something to provide affordable decent quality housing.'

Doing that will mean a concerted effort from all members of the House – shop stewards and solicitors alike.

Bridget Prentice

Labour MP for Lewisham East since 1992. Born in Glasgow in 1952. Before becoming an MP Bridget was a teacher. Opposition Whip, 1995 – 1997. Government Whip 1997 - 1998. Bridget is a member of the Roman Catholic Church.

The interview was conducted on 8 July 1997.

TO the outsider a government whip is one who indulges in early-morning indiscretion-monitoring and late-night arm-twisting in an attempt to get MPs to toe the party line. If that stick doesn't work, perhaps the promise of frontbench promotion will induce backsliders to mend their ways.

What the onlooker does not expect is for a whip to describe their job as caring. But that is precisely how Labour London whip, Bridget Prentice, sees her role. 'There are a great many myths about whips,' says the Honourable Member for Lewisham East. I won't break them. We need them!' she adds, smiling.

'Yes, we have to deal with discipline. After all, our purpose is to get legislation through the House. Sometimes that means being fairly tough with people by saying, "You can't go home tonight, this is a crucial vote."

'But there's a pastoral role too. You cannot enforce discipline if people are deeply unhappy with what they're being asked to do. We deliberately take the view that friendship and cooperation is generally a better way of persuading someone than beating them about the head.

'When MPs are first elected they get a lot of adulation. This could turn your head if you don't keep your feet on the ground. People need to be supported. It's our job to make sure newcomers don't feel isolated. Parliament can be a very lonely place when you're away from home and missing your family. We try to help everyone get involved.'

Following the devil-finds-work-for-idle-hands school of political thought, the whips also try to keep their charges occupied.

'Everybody who becomes an MP wants to change things; they don't like what they see, think it is unfair or unjust,' says Bridget. 'Giving all our MPs some responsibility and focus within the House and encouraging them in their constituency work is a huge challenge for the whips.'

But aren't MPs confused by a whip's role? Don't members wonder if a whip is being kind because they care or because they're cynical?

'That's part of the myth of the whips,' Bridget admits. 'People do think "Why are you asking me this question?" and "If you're asking me to do this what are the consequences for me if I do or if don't do it?" That is part of the myth we're trying to break. We want people to feel they can come and talk to us about things.

'The business about the secrecy of the Whip's Office – there is truth in it. What people tell us is not for public consumption. There has to be confidentiality. We have to build people's trust. If people have confided in us and we start talking to all and sundry about it in the tearoom we wouldn't be whips for long.'

As well as being a whip Bridget has responsibility in the Department of Health and is involved in the forming of a new strategic authority for London.

Before becoming a teacher at the London Oratory School, Bridget went to her home-town university of Glasgow. In the mid-80s she became a JP and a local councillor.

'I suppose, like most MPs, I came into politics to try to do some good,' she says. 'To me politics is a vocation. I don't feel adequate enough to say I have a mission. But I feel very strongly that one should be a full-time MP and not have other jobs preventing you focusing on being an MP.'

Politically, Bridget describes herself as centre left – 'very much part of the Blair modernising progressive section of the party'.

Despite the changes that have taken place within the Labour movement, Bridget feels the things she wants to achieve for the country are the things the Labour Party is about.

'In the past we made huge mistakes by not going about things the right way. Not understanding what the people of Britain wanted us to do. We were not very good at explaining what we were trying to achieve. Following a total reassessment of the party, we now know of better ways to bring about social justice and equal opportunity for all.'

So things, in the words of Labour's election theme song, can only get better?

'Yes. We want to make Britain a better place for everyone. We want to get rid of the sleaze.

'We see education as the main plank of how we will change the way things happen; change people's attitudes.

'People should have decent jobs to go to. They should also realise that the state is not going to provide for them totally. They need to take some responsibility for their lives. At the same time we'll ensure people realise we won't be able to do it all overnight.'

In the lead-up to the General Election, Conservative advertising warned of Labour having a hidden agenda. New dangers lurking in the shadows. How does Bridget answer criticisms that the Government has a hidden agenda which is very liberal on homosexual marriage, euthanasia and abortion?

'As far as I'm aware we have no policy on homosexual marriage,' she says. 'Certainly the majority of Labour Party members voted for the age of consent to be equalised. But any issues of conscience are taken on a free vote.'

Bridget's upbringing was one of a 'fairly traditional' Catholic family.

'Shortly after I moved to London I was in a Labour Party meeting where they were discussing some moral topic. Someone said "Oh, we have to be careful because Catholics have funny views about this!"

'I was appalled. In Glasgow being a Catholic wasn't odd. But in London I felt I was being intimidated.'

At what point, did Bridget choose the Christian faith for herself?

'I'm not sure I can pinpoint a specific time,' she says. 'Not long after I came into Parliament in 1992 I became more conscious of the fact that I wanted to identify myself as a Christian. I joined the Christian Socialist Movement and I was happy to speak on platforms on that basis.

'I can't tell you why that happened, because I don't know. Perhaps it was the marrying of the two parts of what I wanted to do with my life that came home to me at that point. Having been brought up in the Catholic Church I learned from an early age about the effects of poverty, injustice and social inequality – areas the Labour Party is keen to challenge.

'One of the most important things my faith gives me is a set of beliefs, standards and principles that I can judge things against. It gives me a kind of confidence without being overconfident or blind to other people's points of view. An inner certainty that helps me explain and deliver the things I want to see happen.'

Talking of certainties, does Bridget have any doubts about her faith?

'Yes. We wouldn't be very good Christians if we didn't sometimes have doubts. The important thing about doubt is that it gives you time to reflect, to return to those fundamental beliefs and see whether you can still stand by them. If you can, then that particular doubt can go.'

Bridget reckons she's been fortunate in not having had to face major conflicts between her faith and her politics.

'Part of being a Christian is recognising there are other people with strong moral values and beliefs that should be respected,' she says.

'On the abortion issue, I don't take what is seen to be the perfect view of the Roman Catholic Church,' she confesses. 'But I equally strongly feel that the idea of wholesale abortion on demand is unacceptable.

'Abortion is the issue that stirs up the greatest emotions. Sometimes things get distorted, even quite nasty. There are threatening views about why one should take one side or the other.

'I think the Abortion Act as it presently stands is fairly satisfactory and I don't particularly want to see any changes. I know I won't please either side with my position but it is precisely because I have given it much thought that I don't accept the extremes.

'There's a bit of me that's a great compromiser. I tend to go for the middle way. But then, we all compromise.

'Divorce is another difficult area. I accept that divorce is sometimes the best solution. What I don't accept is that people can get married, have some kind of bust-up and then immediately say, "Let's get a divorce."

'People need to be more responsible than that. We need to find ways of encouraging people to be more careful about entering marriage and being sure that this is the commitment they want to make.

'We need to make sure that when things go wrong there are support mechanisms to help couples remain together if that's what they want. I would have liked to have seen more time for reconciliation incorporated into the new divorce legislation.'

When Bridget was first elected she was one of 60 women MPs, now she's one of 119. Has anything changed?

'The number of women has made an enormous difference in the atmosphere of the House. A lot of the male-dominated yah-boo politics is beginning to disappear. Women don't shout and sneer in the way men do. Women are more conciliatory. They are the great compromisers – they're used to running a home, a family and a job.

'Women look for the most practical way of achieving things because they simply haven't got the time to find some complicated system!

'I'd like to see Parliament modernised by, say, talking things through with interested parties before a bill is presented to the House. That would take away a lot of the adversarial nature of things. It would also make for better laws.

'After all, if someone comes up with a good idea, why not use it? Listening to what the Opposition says does not demean your position.'

When Labour was in opposition it had plenty to say on the question of political sleaze. Is New Labour the new broom that will sweep clean?

'I hope so. It will take some time. We're still learning what the Nolan recommendations have provided us with. To be tarnished with sleaze, as all MPs are, makes me angry and uncomfortable. It's not easy to hit back.

'MPs are not perfect, much as we might act as if we think we are. We all make mistakes and there will be some people who do things that are unacceptable. We need to ensure the electorate can have faith in us. We need them to believe we are not here to line our own pockets. People believing all politicians are corrupt is bad for democracy.

'There again, people shouldn't make moral judgments about politicians any more than any other group in society. We reflect society. We're as fallible as anyone else.'

So the public shouldn't expect higher standards of behaviour from its MPs? 'The public standards of those who make the law for their fellows should be higher than just the basics,' says the law graduate.

'Making decisions in the public forum using public money requires MPs to have higher standards. However, I would be slow to say that I judge people's private lives.'

Not surprisingly for an ex-teacher, Bridget sees education as the big issue facing the Government.

'We need to raise standards in schools and reward teachers for doing a professional job. We need to ensure our schools are such that highly qualified, highly motivated teachers inspire young people to reach their full potential. We need to encourage industry to invest in young people.

'I'd like to see a total change in the standards in schools, sending people out into the world with decent qualifications, along with a real sense of self respect and motivation which, at the moment, an awful lot of young people don't have.'

And a biblical hero or heroine?

'No. Not really. I'd be better at some of the villains,' cracks the whip.

That's one myth still intact.

Andy Reed

Labour and Co-operative MP for Loughborough since 1997. Born in Kettering in 1964. Before becoming an MP Andy was a European Officer for Leicestershire County Council. He is a member of the Church of England. Married Sarah in 1992.

The interview was conducted on 20 January 1998.

A FAVOURITE mantra of Members of Parliament is that Westminster is a cross-section of society at large. Not only do MPs formally represent their constituents, they also informally represent a host of opinions, backgrounds, weaknesses and strengths, vices and virtues.

Like the rest of us, MPs' present-day opinions are shaped by their past. None more so than Andy Reed, Labour and Co-operative MP for Loughborough.

Born in 1964 Andy was adopted when he was three months old. Three years later the Abortion Act became law. It is an issue close to his heart.

'I've often wondered what would have happened to me if abortion was legal at the time,' he says. 'It's impossible to say, of course, but somebody might have taken a different course of action. That's always at the back of my mind.

'I'm a firm believer in adoption as an alternative to abortion. Nobody likes the idea of abortion but I wouldn't want to see it abolished. I am, however, concerned that too many abortions are allowed to happen in this country each year. It is the way the law is interpreted that needs tightening, not the legislation itself.'

While many adopted children have a hankering to discover their birth parents, for Andy the natural parents/adoptive parents question is not an issue.

'I've never really understood people wanting to trace their natural parents,' he says. 'As far as I'm concerned my mum and dad are my mum and dad. Whatever happened before was just something that happened.'

As a child Andy's parents encouraged him to go to church.

'I went to Sunday school at my local Methodist church. My teenage years revolved around the Boys Brigade. I was in the band, played football, went camping, everything. It was great!

'Then, like many teenagers, I got to the stage when I thought: I don't need this. I was about 18 or 19. I started playing rugby on Sunday mornings and drifted away from church. I never lost my faith completely but I got out of the habit of going to church.

'Maybe it's harder for people who have been to church all their lives because it can become the expected thing to do. I'd like to think my faith is now stronger through my rediscovery of Christ.

'Although I made a Christian commitment as a child, it has only been in the past five years or so that I have come to a more mature understanding of the faith. My wife, Sarah, who was a very committed Christian when we met, has been a great influence in this respect. Jesus is now central to everything I do. Our marriage and our work – Sarah is my PA at Westminster – revolve around him.'

One of the first things the first-time MP did when he arrived in Parliament was to seek out like-minded believers. He now meets once a fortnight for prayer, discussion and breakfast with five other Members – Christians from different parties, different denominations. It is a much-needed lifeline.

'The hardest thing in life is trying to follow Christ's example,' he says. 'I don't take stances easily. I try to consider other people's points of view to the extent of being accused of sitting on the fence.

'Being able to share with other Christians is important because I feel that where the Bible is concerned I've a lot of catching up to do. Probably one of the reasons I left the Church was because I had a lot of rebellious-teenager questions to ask and no opportunity to ask them.'

As well as representing his constituency Andy is part of the leadership campaign team – a small group of MPs whose job it is to make sure the Government keeps in touch with the electorate. He also works for Transport Secretary Gavin Strang, ensuring transport issues receive media attention.

Here again his faith is invaluable. 'When I'm still working through my in-tray at 11 o'clock at night it's easy to lose a sense of purpose. But my faith gives me purpose and a wider perspective on all I do. Through prayer God gives me a much-needed sense of calm.'

As a Christian, does he believe the public should rightly expect all MPs to be above reproach?

'It would be nice to think that those who put themselves forward for public office have extremely high moral standards,' he says. 'But I don't think being an MP necessarily means you're saying your private life is perfect. It would be nice to think that everybody in the country had perfectly happy marriages but unfortunately that's not the case.

'If we want politicians who are human we have to accept that they will have personal difficulties the same as the rest of the population. And unless we do have MPs who have experienced divorce and the like then we can't truly reflect society.

'If an MP's private life doesn't impinge on their work then it should be outside the realms of public interest.

'With financial probity, however, the public has every right to expect high standards from MPs. That's the only way we can rebuild confidence between politicians and people.'

Before becoming an MP Andy, as a county council employee, lobbied Europe on behalf of Leicestershire. He was particularly interested in helping those who were disadvantaged in the labour market – ethnic minorities, people with disabilities, people with learning difficulties and so on.

It was a burning, driving vision against injustice, particularly in Third World development and the international arms trade, that brought him into politics.

'As a teenager I was appalled at the gross inequalities that exist in the world,' he says. 'It's not right that we are able to produce enough food to feed the world yet have a system that prevents us from doing so. OK, the issues are not as clear-cut as they seemed when I was younger, but the injustice is still there.

'On the domestic front it was seeing people locally being made redundant and losing all hope in the early '80s that got me involved in urban regeneration. It breaks my heart to see people despondent when they have so much to offer.'

Andy, a member of the Christian Socialist Movement, sees his MP role as very much God's calling for his life. But how much of a socialist is he? Does he think his party has become too up-market for the traditional working class?

'No I don't,' he says. 'Society has changed. People's views have changed and the Labour Party had to change with it. In the past we lived 10 or 15 years behind the rest of society.

'We haven't ditched our principles. We have just put them into a modern setting. We want to help the many, not just the few. As the Government we represent all parts of the country. Our aim is to build a wider consensus, not just hold power for the sake of it.'

He speaks of building consensus but doesn't the political reality of a 170-plus majority mean the Government can ignore all noises-off and do what it pleases?

'That's exactly why it's even more important to work co-operatively,' he says. 'If we're to bring about lasting change – on constitutional reform, for example – then we need cross-party support.

'It's even more important with welfare and pensions reform because they have long-term implications. It's no good doing something this year that will be torn up by political opponents five or 10 years from now.

Has his party been too harsh in some of its welfare reforms?

'The most difficult decision has been over cutting lone parent benefit,' he says. 'I am one of many backbenchers who were unhappy about it. But the Government is not out to destroy the welfare state. It wants to refocus on the poorest.

'When the welfare state was introduced in the 1940s people thought it wouldn't be needed 40 years later. Sustaining it now is very expensive.'

Government ministers talk a lot about 'tough decisions'. What will Andy do if asked to vote against his conscience?

'I wrestle with some of the issues,' he says. 'Often there is no easy yes/no solution, and I want to say "yes, but". If faced with a genuine moral dilemma, then – although I've signed up to the party whip – I'd make it clear I couldn't vote as the party required and would ask to be allowed to do otherwise. If the whips wouldn't allow that I would take the consequences.

'I have already made it very clear that if disability benefit reforms are handled in the same way as lone parent benefit then I would be prepared to say that it is not the manifesto on which I was elected and feel duty-bound to protect those most disadvantaged. Not all backbenchers are the lobby fodder some people suppose.'

How would he like his Government to respond to the Third World?

'Debt is a colossal crisis,' he says. 'Mozambique, for example, spends 33 per cent of its national wealth on debt repayment, three per cent on education and about six per cent on health. If they could spend the debt interest on health and education it would make an enormous difference.

'Writing off Third World debt is the priority. It will take a lot of persuading. But it is not the only option. I'm very interested in encouraging the setting up of micro-credit schemes – giving people basic machines rather then hi-tech computers so they can set up small-scale engineering or craft facilities in their town or village. Helping them to help themselves.

'We should also be targeting overseas aid on those countries who need it most rather than on those that will give us the best contracts in return. We must break the link between aid and trade. Also we must make sure we don't sell arms to countries with oppressive regimes. There are difficulties, of course, like deciding who is repressive, and the possibility of losing jobs in the UK arms industry. It will take time. But we must take steps in the right direction.'

If changing the world is going to take some time, what one thing about the country would Andy like to change overnight if he could – apart from captaining England at rugby, that is?

'I would end the scourge of unemployment,' he says. 'Too many people are alienated because they want to work but can't get a job. That is not good for them. It is not good for the country or for the rest of us.

'Unemployment is the essential issue this Government must deal with. Fewer people are working longer hours and under more stress. We must deal with that inequality.'

Peter Robinson

Democratic Unionist Party MP for Belfast East since 1979. Born in Belfast in 1948. Before becoming an MP Peter was an estate agent. Member of the Northern Ireland Assembly, 1982 – 1986. Deputy Leader of the Democratic Unionist Party since 1980. Member of the Northern Ireland Select Committee since 1994. Peter is a member of the Pentecostal Church. Married Iris in 1979. Has two sons and one daughter.

The interview was conducted on 17 September 1997.

'THE only hope for Northern Ireland is a spiritual revival,' says Democratic Unionist Party deputy leader Peter Robinson. 'Even though I'm a politician I don't put my trust in the political process, or in those who operate it. The problem of Northern Ireland is beyond the ability of man to resolve.'

The East Belfast MP should know. He's been involved in Northern Ireland politics since becoming a local councillor in 1977. Two years later, the former estate agent was elected to the House. Only one of Ulster's 18 MPs has held his Westminster seat longer – the Rev Ian Paisley, Peter's party leader.

It was the murder of an old school friend, Harry Beggs, at the hands of terrorists that changed the direction of Peter's life.

'Until then I was following other interests,' says Peter, 'but learning that

Harry had been killed by a bomb outside his Electricity Board office sharply concentrated my mind on the political situation in the province. It propelled me towards a political career. I was frustrated that the Government seemed to be doing nothing about the increased violence – those were the days of regular street rioting – so I decided to do something about it.'

An outspoken critic of terrorists, Peter is on their death list. An armed police escort, bullet-proof car and letter bombs in the post are matter-of-facts-of-life.

Being a target has sharpened Peter's appreciation of faith. 'Politics is a calling,' he says, in his fortified east Belfast office. 'Throughout my political life I've been aware that God has had his hand on me.

'The front line of politics in Northern Ireland is no place for an academic faith. There have been many occasions when the police have called to tell me that terrorists have plans to kill me.

'I try not to dwell on it, that would be a morose existence. But in such an everyday life-and-death struggle you have to have that assurance in your heart that, come what may, there is Somebody walking beside you and that in eternity your existence is secure.'

Peter reckons his faith also gives him compassion for those who, regardless of political persuasion, come to him for help.

'Given that I'm generally regarded by the press as a right-wing Unionist, people might think it difficult for nationalists to come to my constituency office. But I probably see proportionally more nationalists than Unionists. People in need will search out those they think are prepared to respond. It is because of my faith that I want to reach out and help others in their moment of need.'

Belfast-born Peter grew up in a committed Christian family. His father was a Presbyterian elder, his mother the president of the women's guild. At what point did he become a Christian?

'Like many people who have a Christian upbringing I went through a period of rebellion before I was eventually brought to my knees. That was on 13 July 1973. I had been under conviction for some time. But this night, alone at my bedside, I surrendered my life to Jesus.

'People who had seen me at church for years might not have noticed anything greatly different about me, but I knew Christ had put new priorities in my life, and in that sense it was very dramatic.

'Although there have been many occasions when I have wandered from the path, that is the moment I have never regretted and always rejoiced in.'

With the stridency of his faith (Peter is a member of a Pentecostal fellowship) and the numerics of the House, Peter has never faced a conflict of conscience when it comes to the vote.

'Ulster's MPs are sometimes regarded as those who have determined, "I'm voting against. Now, what's the issue?"' he grins. 'But being in a small party where all the MPs have been Christians, I have not faced a crisis of conscience.

'On abortion, I have supported David Alton's bills throughout. I consider that the unborn child is a life that has to be protected. I cannot understand how people are prepared to take away that great potential of a life. However, I accept there are circumstances, like the saving of the mother's life, where abortion is necessary.

'Euthanasia is no different. It is not up to man to determine how long another should live. That is in the providence of Almighty God. We can't step in and say that we know better than the supreme moral arbiter how long people should live. It is an issue about life and the sanctity of life.

'So far as homosexuality is concerned the Scriptures are abundantly clear. It is wrong. God has made it clear in the Scriptures that it is evil. I am prepared to accept that and don't have to question it. People may think they have a better judgment than God but I don't believe they have.'

During the past 25 years of The Troubles many people have looked to the sectarianism of Northern Ireland and accused it of giving Christianity a bad name. Does Peter think this is a fair assessment?

'I rather suspect the churchgoers on a Sunday are not the rioters of a Saturday night,' he says. 'Many societies are a mix of extremely good people and extremely evil people. We must be careful not to judge the whole society on the actions of a few individuals.

'There are tens of thousands of people in Northern Ireland who are praying for peace. But they don't want peace on the basis of giving in to terrorists. They want a peace founded on principles. It is the job of Christians to say and do things that will sometimes be extremely unpopular. Many times I have swum against the tide of public opinion, even within Unionism. But God has vindicated my stand.'

So this is not a religious war?

'Not at all. It is about identity. It is two communities looking in different directions. One of them looking towards Britain and seeing their identity in a British context. The other, a Gaelic tradition, looks towards the Republic of Ireland.

'Of course there are religious elements. The role of the Roman Catholic Church and of the Protestant community. By and large the two political communities fall into two religious communities, but it is essentially about identity.'

With Peter's frequent travelling (Westminster and Washington included) and involvement in local politics (he is a Castelreagh Borough alderman) his family has adopted something of an 'if you can't beat 'em, join 'em' policy. His wife, Iris, is also a councillor and his son Jonathan works in his constituency office.

'My wife claims she decided to stand for the council so she would see more of me,' he says, jokingly. 'It is far from a normal lifestyle but it has drawn us together as a family. During an election they are out fighting along with me. So ours is a very closely knit family, very protective of each other, and I think that often happens when one of the members of a family is under very considerable threat.

'I regret that my children, Jonathan, Gareth and Rebekah, haven't had as much of my time as they deserve. But we still go on holiday together, even though they've grown up. There are not many families who can say that.'

Despite the pleasures of the beach, the pressures of the bench have never been far away.

In December 1985 Peter, along with other Unionist MPs, resigned his seat in protest at the Anglo-Irish Agreement. He was re-elected a month later. Today he and his party are boycotting the Stormont peace talks. Why?

'I am not prepared to sit down and talk about the future constitution of Northern Ireland in the full knowledge that the only reason some people are at the table is that they have bombed and shot their way to that table.

'If you are to be involved in negotiations you must first determine who it is proper to negotiate with. In the current peace process the ground rules must be that the only people who are entitled to attend are those who are exclusively committed to peaceful and democratic means.'

Is there a difference between Sinn Fein and the IRA?

'No, they are one and the same. The membership of the Sinn Fein talks team comprises a number of convicted IRA terrorists, including Gerry Kelly, who was one of the Maze escapers.

'There are attempts to bluff the British public into thinking that some distinction should be drawn. But the Prime Minister is on record, as was John Major, as indicating that they are two sides of the one coin. The Prime Minister of the Irish Republic also recognises that Sinn Fein and the IRA are inextricably linked.'

So what would enable him to take part in all-party talks?

'The first test is time,' he says. 'If they haven't returned to violence then one can assume that they have moved away from it. For example, the Official IRA was once a substantial terrorist group but it renounced violence, broke away from the Provisionals and committed itself to political means. Its members now work through the Workers Party. They have shown they are no longer engaged in violence.

'Dismantling the network of violence is the second indicator. Have they given up the implements of violence? This is why the question of decommissioning is so important. We don't suggest the IRA disarm because we believe they couldn't get new arms; of course they could. We want decommissioning prior to any talks because it is in itself a symbol that the IRA no longer need weapons, because they don't intend to cause violence.

'The third test is that of their words and behaviour. There is no indication in any IRA statement that its members have turned their backs on violence. They congratulate the violence of their so-called volunteers. They never condemn it.'

Not only is Peter Robinson untrusting of some of the people seated around the Stormont table, he is also sceptical about the peace process itself.

'There is a great danger in peace movements and in peace processes,' he says. 'They are designed to inculcate the belief that peace is the most precious pearl.

'We should all strive for peace. My children – the eldest is 24 – have grown up knowing nothing but violence in our country. But I believe liberty and freedom are the ultimate prizes.

'Peace comes once you've established your freedom. It can't be a goal in itself – peace at any price. The current process is based upon the principle that you buy off the terrorists. You give the terrorists what they want to win the silence of their guns. Giving in to terrorism is a very dangerous policy.

'If peace had always been the priority then we would have surrendered to Hitler, to Galtieri, to Saddam Hussein and to many other dictators throughout history. But there was a recognition that it was important to fight to maintain our liberties and our freedoms.

'People are war-weary but we must have peace with principle. The political battle is the same as the battle of the Christian life. You don't accommodate evil, you overcome it. There can be no compromise.'

Andrew Rowe

Conservative MP for Faversham and Mid Kent since 1997. MP for Mid Kent, 1983 – 1997. Born in London in 1935. Before becoming an MP Andrew was a schoolmaster, civil servant, lecturer and Director of Community Affairs, Conservative Central Office. Parliamentary Private Secretary to Trade and Industry Minister, 1992 – 1995. Andrew is a member of the Church of England. Married Sheila in 1983. Has one son and two step-daughters.

The interview was conducted on 29 October 1996.

PARLIAMENT can be a very lonely place, according to Andrew Rowe, Conservative MP for Mid Kent. 'At one level it is a very gregarious place, an affable place – like a club. But, I suspect, there are very few MPs who on hearing of a colleague's misfortune do not pretty rapidly reflect on how this might affect their own career.

'If, for example, you are young and ambitious and hear that one of your colleagues with whom you may have been quite friendly has died, your first thought may be, "Gosh! How awful! I was talking to him only yesterday. His poor wife and children!" But your second thought is, "I wonder what sort of vacancy that has created."

'Many of us don't trust our personal feelings to colleagues because we are, to some extent, nervous lest some piece of information be used against us. Admitting a health problem to a colleague, for example, might result in being ruled out for promotion.'

If some relationships are, at best, superficial and, at worst, openly hostile, why did this Public Accounts Committee member become an MP?

'I often light-heartedly say it's partly out of vanity,' he says. 'When I was at university I became Librarian, which is effectively vice-chairman, of the Oxford Union. I enjoyed speaking and felt it was a shame that I was a rent-a-mouth but nobody was renting me!

'More seriously, I have always had a sense that one ought to try and do something for other people – try and make the world a better place. I am rather ashamed that I find it easier to do that at one remove rather than hands-on.'

Andrew describes himself as 'an untypical politician' in that he does not delight in the cut-and-thrust of in-House gossip and manoeuverings.

'I am interested in issues that aren't at the top of the political agenda. I am as interested in issues such as how we look after our children as in whether or not to ban knives and guns. I get a lot of satisfaction out of helping individual constituents battle their way through bureaucracy. I'm very interested in lifetime homes. New houses should be built with subsequent generations and the disabled in mind. It's crazy that we don't insist on it. I'm trying to get the rules changed.'

Andrew is also studying the problem of planning blight – the effects of road and rail schemes on house prices. This sprang from the building of the Channel Tunnel rail link through his constituency.

His own route to Westminster was hardly fast track. 'I'm a rolling stone,' says Whitechapel-born Andrew, describing his somewhat circuitous path. After university and national service he tried and failed to enter the diplomatic corps. He taught for a while at his old school, Eton – before passing the diplomat exams at the second attempt. Because of his wife's ill health he did not take up a posting but instead took a job in the Scottish Office. Then in 1974, after lecturing in Social Administration at Edinburgh University, Andrew became a voluntary organisations consultant to the Home Office.

'Around that time, I was very angry about the way the Conservative Party had fought the October election,' he says. 'There were two elections in 1974 and in the second one they didn't really try. They were spineless.'

Andrew complained to the only senior Tory he knew – Sarah Morrison. In January 1975, Andrew had a new job – Director of Community Affairs in Conservative Central Office.

When Margaret Thatcher won the 1979 election he left party headquarters and became self-employed. It was a dark time for Andrew. Not only was he 'not the world's greatest entrepreneur' but his marriage had broken up. 'With a son away at school, I was terrified I wouldn't be able to make ends meet,' he recalls.

Although denied the chance of standing in an election while on the Central Office staff, Andrew eventually stood for, and won, his present seat in 1983. He describes himself as a 'mainstream Tory' but reckons others regard him as 'well on the left of the party'.

'Mainstream' might also usefully be employed to describe Andrew's Christian faith.

'I come from a long line of vicars,' he says. 'An aunt is a retired Congregational minister. My grandfather was Archdeacon of Westminster.

'I was brought up by my father's mother. She was a firm believer and taught me to say my prayers. I went to Christian schools and I was a member of the congregation at St Aldate's at Oxford.

'It was while I was an undergraduate at Oxford that I gave my life to Christ as a result of the ministry of Cuthbert Bardsley. I was about 22 years old.'

Would Andrew describe himself as an evangelical?

'I actually have no interest in these labels,' he says. 'In fact I'm not sure that I understand them. Because every now and again when I think I know where I stand with the Church I discover that I am clearly wrong. But to the extent that I try to read my Bible and say my prayers every day, and I meet with others to study the Scriptures and pray together, I suppose I am an evangelical Christian, if that is what it means.

'Equally, I greatly enjoy choral evensong, am very happy to go to the 17th-century prose service, and have no serious difficulty in going to services where there is incense. I've often threatened my wife that I'll write into my will that I want "When the saints go marching in" at my funeral. As Christians we should enjoy ourselves and have fun. The Christian family is wonderful and where you are in it doesn't matter!'

Andrew's faith was severely challenged around the time his first marriage broke up.

'I blame myself quite a lot for the breakdown,' he says. 'We should never have got married. Our relationship fell to bits. I then went through a period when I felt my personal behaviour was such that my Christian faith was not being put very strongly into practice. It was a hard time. But I still went to church and prayed – for forgiveness really.

'I think it's possible to be conscious that you are not behaving very well and yet remain in the bonds of Christ. It didn't make me feel very good but one justifies one's behaviour to oneself on occasion.'

Although Andrew did not lose his faith during those days it was only after his marriage to Sheila in 1983 that he felt 'one could hold one's head up'.

The service of blessing at Andrew's parish church was a turning point.

'In the service, Richard, the vicar, said to the congregation, "We are not here to pretend that the past has not existed. We are not here to say that there have not been faults in the past. We are here to say that Sheila and Andrew need our prayers and come to ask for them."

'That was just right. The willingness of that congregation to accept us was undoubtedly a boost to our faith. That sense of being included is one reason why I'm very wary about pressure to exclude people from the Church. It's terribly important, if you can, to hang on to people.'

Today, Andrew's faith is further strengthened by his membership of the Parliamentary Christian Fellowship. How does the former fellowship chairman see the current media fascination in MPs' faith?

'There is a huge danger in it,' he says. 'The Parliamentary Christian Fellowship is very strict in that as a fellowship it does not take a view on political issues. It's possible for Christians to be on either side of almost all issues. The best advice that was ever given was: "Render unto Caesar the things that are Caesar's and unto God the things that are God's." MPs viewing issues from the perspective of their faith in Jesus Christ and disagreeing about policy is a good thing and is to be encouraged.'

Is he discouraged that a cynical candidate might use Christianity as a way of attracting votes, causing genuine Christians to be seen as bandwagon Christians?

'I think one should be wholly indifferent about it,' he says. 'All one can do is consider one's own relationship with Jesus Christ and try to apply what that means to the issues of the day. Just as one should have been bolder in the early days about saying one was a Christian, but didn't for fear of being derided, so one shouldn't be afraid to speak up now merely because some people might think you are trying to curry favour.'

On a personal level, Andrew's faith gives him assurance that he is not alone – that help is available – and direction to his life.

'My faith also gives me an assurance about death,' he says. 'We don't talk much about death these days. Two years ago, I had a serious cancer which needed surgery. I felt grim about the prognosis, yet confident about the next life.

'Sheila was cross with me because I'd become resigned when I ought to have been fighting. I had the operation, the cancer was removed and I am cured. I can only conclude there must be something useful for me still to do. Jesus has made sense of my life. I have a clearer understanding of what makes life work well. I feel he holds my hand every day.'

Andrew thinks it is 'wholly unrealistic' for the public to expect MPs to be above reproach. 'It is quite improper in a sense. We are here to represent the great British public. Quite honestly, the great British public instinctively knows this. If you look at what has happened to a substantial number of the people who have been publicly disgraced, you will see they are held in considerable affection by a large number of British people.

'After an initial burst of censoriousness people feel rather reassured that MPs behave in ways in which they themselves behave. The public has no right to expect MPs to be behaving much better than they do. However, the public has every right to expect the House of Commons to take a very strong view against corruption.

'Part of my contract with my electorate is that I'm not going to be bought. Any suggestion that one is being bought should be dealt with. That is exactly the same thing as expecting my bank manager not to put his fingers in the till. But I do not expect my bank manager to live a life of total moral purity in order to be my bank manager. Similarly, I don't think you can do that as an MP.

'Clearly I believe that the better a life one can lead, the more one is carrying out Christ's desire and the closer to Christ one becomes. That's the objective and it is good if you do it.'

How does Andrew react to the criticism that his party is quick to extol 'family virtues' but slow in supporting marriage?

'I believe the vast majority of young adults would prefer to have a secure long-term, exclusive relationship. They would much rather be settled parents for their children.

'We should do everything we can to support marriage. But there are a lot of women who see very little point in marrying a man who can offer poor support to her and their children because, say, it's difficult for him to get a job.

'And if a woman does enter a relationship, she often does so with the hard-headed notion that if things get rough she'll leave.

'Many young women feel they can't afford risking their career by taking time out to look after children. Promotion policies, pension arrangements and the taxation system are weighted against a woman who wants to stay at home to bring up her children. We should be altering the system to allow women genuine free choice to stay at home if they want to.'

Andrew reckons there will be three big issues facing the next government.

'Our relationship with Europe is a huge concern. Secondly, how to prepare young people for the 21st century in ways which will not only allow them to maximise what they have to offer but also allow society to rest peacefully. Thirdly, how to ensure that people who leave their principal occupations with an average of 37 years left to live have sufficient expectation of care at a level which will give them what they need.

'I'd like to remove the generation gap,' he says by way of describing one thing he would like to change about the country. 'To see the idle youth and the idle newly-retired work together would be marvellous.'

Rt Hon Gillian Shephard

Conservative MP for Norfolk South West since 1987. Born in Norfolk in 1940. Before becoming an MP Gillian was a school inspector and lecturer. Parliamentary Private Secretary to Economic Secretary to the Treasury, 1988 – 1989. Parliamentary Secretary, Department of Social Security, 1989 - 1990. Minister of State, HM Treasury, 1990 - 1992. Appointed a Privy Councillor, 1992. Secretary of State for the Employment, 1992 – 1993. Minister for Agriculture, Fisheries and Foods, 1993 – 1994. Secretary of State for Education, 1994 – 1995. Secretary of State for Education and Employment, 1995 – 1997. Shadow Leader of the House of Commons, 1997 - 1998. Shadow Secretary of State for Environment, Transport and the Regions since 1998. Gillian is an Honorary Fellow of St Hilda's College, Oxford. Gillian is a member of the Church of England. Married Thomas in 1975. Has two step-sons.

The interview was conducted on 24 September 1997.

GILLIAN SHEPHARD can be every bit as much a giggling schoolgirl as the serious-minded Secretary of State for Education and Employment she was until the election.

She is no longer in office and having come to meet me in Central Lobby she is now locked out of her office. She apologises and scours the narrow labyrinthine corridors behind the Speaker's Chair for Security to let us in.

She's relaxed. It's a bit of a laugh. Eventually the Right Honourable

Member for Norfolk South West comfies herself in her armchair, kicks off her shoes and throws herself into the interview. Giggles, laughs and fun-poking accompany. As does the straight talking.

'Why did we lose the election? I think any party that hoped to be re-elected after 18 years would be very optimistic,' she says.

'We left the economy in excellent shape and reformed the education system. There's been an explosion of opportunity, especially for young people, and an increase in prosperity and respect of Britain's position in the world. But after 18 years, I'm quite sure a boredom factor set in.

'We also made mistakes. Because we had such a tiny majority at the end we were perceived – correctly – as being obsessed with getting legislation through Parliament rather than listening to what people in the outside world were telling us.

'We should have handled things differently. We were punished at the polls. It's now up to us to rebuild the party and the public's trust in the party. It's a challenging time to be in politics.'

Listening to the electorate will, she reckons, be the key to making the Conservative Party electable. 'We have to respond to what people are telling us and help them feel more involved,' says the shadow Leader of the House. 'We have to rebuild our own vision and philosophies because in a democracy you have to have alternative philosophies from which the electorate can choose. Many of our policies have served this country well and have been adopted by the present Government.

'Above all we need to be an effective Opposition – pointing out the Government's mistakes, injustices and broken promises. Sackcloth and ashes are very important. But only up to a point. We mustn't forget the good things we delivered in government.'

Sackcloth and ashes are tokens of repentance. Of what does she feel her party needs to repent?

'I think we feel we made mistakes,' she confesses. 'We were widely perceived as not listening. We lost the election badly in terms of parliamentary seats, although not that badly in terms of votes. We must live with that defeat in appropriate humility. Having said that, we shouldn't be shackled by humility into immobility.'

For the past seven years Gillian, who also serves as shadow Public Service Minister, has been upwardly mobile.

When John Major became Prime Minister in 1990 he appointed Gillian as Minister of State to the Treasury. She was a minister throughout the Major years, becoming Secretary of State for Employment and for Education when they were separate departments and heading the merged department in 1995.

How did she adapt to being in the Cabinet one week and out of power the next?

'It isn't quite as brutal a cut-off as that,' she says. 'The position of Cabinet minister didn't exist during the six-week election campaign. At first, I was relieved that the red ministerial boxes didn't keep coming and the phone wasn't always ringing. It was great not being ordered onto radio or TV programmes. The previous 12 months had been excessively busy.

'After the initial reaction I set about facing a new set of challenges. There's no reason why this period of my life can't be as productive as any other time. It's a question of attitude.'

Born in north Norfolk, Gillian read French and Latin at Oxford before embarking on a career in education. Over the years she became a teacher, career adviser, school inspector, education administrator and lecturer. When she married in 1975 she took a part-time job with Anglia Television before becoming a county councillor in 1977. Ten years later she stood for Parliament. Why?

'It sounds very old-fashioned to say it but I saw my work in education and local government as public service,' she says. 'Becoming an MP was an extension of public service.'

Her decision to stand for the seat she has represented since 1987 was gradual rather than sudden.

'We had a lot of friends who were being selected and becoming MPs,' she recalls. 'The opportunity arose in our area. I was very keen to represent my home county. I felt I would have more conviction if I represented an area I knew well.

'As it happens I was wrong because I later discovered that MPs are enthusiastic about their constituency whether they were born in it or not. But at the time it was important to me and I am still very happy to be representing Norfolk South West.'

While the decision to stand for Parliament might have been gradual, the motivation was very clear.

'I was particularly concerned about education and agriculture. I've always wanted to see if you can apply efficiency and good management practice to government. I've since learned that it's rather more difficult than one thinks. Events, personalities and personal ambitions intervene.

'I had a wider political vision also. As a Conservative I believe very strongly in the empowering of individuals, diminishing the role of the state and increasing reliance on market forces. I believe people will do their jobs with more conviction if they feel they are part of the organisation – a hospital, school, company, or whatever.'

Describing herself as 'economically dry', by which she means she supports measures which enable the economy and individuals to flourish, Gillian says she has never felt part of a particular wing of the Conservative Party.

'I'm strongly unionist and a great believer in market forces. Unfettered public spending weakens economic output. But there are some things a Government must run and must run well, including education, health and a good benefits system for people who can't otherwise manage.'

As a child Gillian attended the parish church and was a Sunday school regular.

'I don't mind admitting it was sometimes less than enjoyable having to turn out every Sunday afternoon!' she recalls. 'I was confirmed when I was about 13 or 14 and have remained strongly involved with the Church ever since.

'At school we had a very strongly Christian headmistress. There was an excellent assembly every day and a lot of devotional activities. So we had every sort of help to get us going on the Christian path. When I went to university I was fascinated to discover there are many ways of being a Christian.'

Was there a defining moment when she discovered Christianity to be true for herself?

'For me that happens every so often,' she says with a smile. 'Certainly at different periods of my life I get the conviction over again. And that isn't because my faith has particularly lapsed in between times. Underlying everything I have a certainty in my faith.

'Every so often people say politicians shouldn't dabble in religion. But if you believe that politics is a way of achieving public service and making the world better then you can't avoid connections with religion.

'On the other hand there are some unresolvable questions with which you're faced as a politician. Questions of high ethics such as abortion, euthanasia and genetic engineering. I'm very conscious of the need for a spiritual dimension in almost all the things I do as an MP.'

How does her faith help her cast her vote on such issues?

'As far as euthanasia is concerned I have no problem at all,' she says. 'We can't have it. It's partly a faith thing but partly a practicality thing. If you say euthanasia can be justified in certain circumstances you then have to define the circumstances, the means and so on. It would be very difficult to frame law in that way.

'For me abortion is a more clouded issue. Abortion is different. It shouldn't be but it is. There are two lives at stake – the mother's and the child's – and that complicates it.

'I'm in favour of abortion under certain definable circumstances. We might need to look again at the time limit within which it can be performed. Medical technology is proceeding at such a rate that the foetus has more chance of survival.

'I know that's inconsistent with my view on euthanasia. I know it would be easier if I could say a life is a life, full stop. But everything would be very easy if one were able to be absolutist about every issue.

'There are people like that in the House. I think how awfully simple it must be for them. But I don't have that simplistic turn of mind.

'Everything that passes through the House has a moral, ethical or spiritual dimension. What ambition makes people do to one another and so on. The way in which people deal with one another in the political world is often less than Christian.

'In my worst moments I tell myself there's just as much back-biting in hospitals or in business as there is in the House of Commons. But it isn't a pretty sight to see these kinds of things paraded so very nakedly in the media.'

In the transience of politics how does it feel to be flavour of the month one minute and dumped the next?

'It's not easy. Anyone who feels betrayed by those whom previously they have trusted is likely to find it difficult to bear,' she says. 'It's important not to be vengeful. In politics everybody has some grounds for being vengeful but it's not a very healthy state of mind.'

Everybody including her?

'Ha, I sometimes think so,' she laughs. 'But I'm not. One of the fascinations of politics is that it responds to the wider world. Sometimes promises and deals aren't honoured because the circumstances have changed. You have to try very hard to maintain your own standards despite whatever else is going on.'

Should the public expect its MPs to maintain higher standards than their own in all their dealings?

'It would be nice if everybody were above reproach!' she challenges. 'In a group of 650 people you must expect to see a reflection of the strengths and weaknesses of society as a whole. In a group this size you will find from time to time somebody who falls from grace. It is totally unreasonable, and frankly ludicrous, to think it should be otherwise.

'However, what people mustn't do, whatever job they are in, is take advantage of that job for ill-gotten gains. For some MPs, being in the public eye is not the incentive to be seen to be doing things correctly that one might expect. Quite the reverse, in fact. Some have an arrogance, an air of "I'm important therefore I can do what I like and get away with it." The public is right to be impatient and unaccepting of such behaviour.'

While for Gillian the handling of the economy is the big test facing the present Government – 'without a strong economy you can do nothing' – concern for education is still close to her heart. Having benefited from a strong Christian influence during her own schooldays Gillian is keen for schools to continue teaching religious education and holding daily assembly.

'I know there are practical problems for some schools but the mere fact of bringing your school together as a community and having assembly is a valuable part of a school day. It is a legal requirement and it is a good law.'

But if it's not well done, couldn't a 'broadly Christian' assembly be a bad advert for Christianity?

'It needn't be. And besides, it shouldn't be the only advert. There's also the Church and the home. Head teachers have a duty to ensure that assembly is carried out by the most appropriate staff member. And if there's nobody suitable in the school they should invite people from the local community.'

The privatising of school assembly. Now there's an idea!

Rt Hon Chris Smith

Labour MP for Islington South and Finsbury since 1983. Born in Hertfordshire in 1951. Before becoming an MP Chris worked for Shaftesbury Society Housing Association and the Society for Co-operative Dwellings. Appointed a Privy Councillor, 1992. Shadow National Heritage Secretary, 1994 – 1995. Shadow Social Security Secretary, 1995 – 1996. Shadow Secretary of State for Health, 1996 – 1997. Secretary of State for Culture, Media and Sport since 1997. Chris is a member of the Church of England.

The interview was conducted on 11 December 1997.

A COPY of *Smash Hits Poll-Winners Party* magazine is not the sort of reading material conventionally provided for those who await an interview with one of Her Majesty's Secretaries of State. Nor is a football encyclopaedia, *The Illustrated History of British Theatre* or a book on Man United. But this is the New Labour-new title Department of Media, Culture and Sport. A department that celebrates the best of British.

'I am fascinated by this job,' says Secretary of State Chris Smith. 'With so many people's livelihoods and aspirations dependent on the decisions this department makes, it would be very difficult if the Secretary of State wasn't interested in what he was doing. There's no danger of that with me.'

Before he became Labour MP for Islington South and Finsbury in 1983

Christians in the House

Chris spent six years as a housing development officer, first for the Shaftesbury Society, later for the Society for Co-operative Dwellings. He stood for Parliament because he 'wanted to get nearer to where the decisions were made. It was important to me to try to influence them.'

Among his duties in Opposition he was Labour spokesman on – successively – national heritage, social security and, immediately prior to the election, health. He resigned from being a governor of the Sadler's Wells Theatre when he took his seat on the Government benches.

When Labour came into office, people were attributing everything from warm weather to Wimbledon success to the new Government. The minister is quick to acknowledge that his influence in this respect is decidedly limited.

'However, where sport is concerned, our job is to create the framework which enables the best sportsmen and women to have the facilities to train to the highest possible level. We're working on a UK Sports Institute which will provide a centre of excellence so our top athletes can get the best possible medical research, training and coaching facilities. At the same time we want to boost Sport For All in schools and communities.'

Chris's own athletic achievements are not on a field of play but in open fields. A keen mountaineer, he has climbed all of Scotland's 3,000-feet-plus summits – the Munros. It is in the great outdoors that he finds inner solace.

'Climbing the summit ridge of a Scottish mountain brings the presence of God and his creation to me in a powerful way,' he says. 'God gets through to me in quiet moments of prayer and reflection. Sometimes that's against a background of music, the rich language of the Bible or in worship, at other times it is not.'

As a child, Chris had 'the advantage of being brought up in a Christian household'.

'I realised there was Something There from a very early age. From the age of 10 I grew up in Scotland and started going regularly to a Church of Scotland church.

'I was confirmed when I was about 17. It just seemed the natural thing to do.

'The more I have subsequently read, thought and prayed about it the firmer that teenage conviction has become.

'There was no one particular moment when everything became blindingly clear. Rather my faith has grown gradually.

'While I was at Cambridge my faith was again confirmed and reassured. I didn't join any Christian societies at university, partly because I was throwing myself wholeheartedly into political activity, but I attended college chapel regularly.

'Doing an English degree also brings you into contact with a wide range of literature which raises major and disturbing moral questions. You begin to realise the importance of having a compass to guide you through some of those.'

With the Bible as his map and God as his compass, what is it that his faith gives him?

'A certain amount of serenity, I hope. So that when everything appears to be falling to pieces around you and there are five different crises landing on your desk all at once and the world is being terribly unfair to you and the last newspaper column you read was telling the world what a dreadful man you are, you have an assurance that there's a lot more to life than worrying too much about all of that.

'I hope also it gives me the sense of being able to judge people genuinely by what they are saying and doing rather than by a prejudice about who they are. And to enable me carefully to consider different points of view and not simply take a line because that's the way it has always been or that's the expedient answer in the circumstances.'

Has he been the subject of personal prejudice from within the Church for his well-publicised openly homosexual lifestyle?

'Not from within my own church community, no,' he says. 'I have always taken the view that it's important for politicians to be honest. The way in which I have tried to approach it is to say: yes I am gay, so what? Now let's get on with the business of being a decent MP.'

Honesty is one thing. But how does he answer the assertion of evangelical Christians that homosexual practices are incompatible with Christianity?

'It is love, commitment and faithfulness that matter,' he says. 'That applies whatever sort of expression people give to the relationships they undertake. My vision of Christianity has always been one of an inclusive religion.

'Someone once told me this story. It has always stuck. Years ago in the southern states of America a black man walked up to the doors of a church one Sunday morning. A pearly-white farmer met him at the door and asked, "Where do you think you're going?"

'The black man said, "I want to come in and join the worship in the church."

'The farmer said, "Sorry, you can't come in here. It's not for the likes of you."

'The black man turned round very sorrowfully. Halfway down the steps the Lord speaks to him and says, "Why are you so sad?" The man says, "Well, Lord, I want to go in and worship you and they won't let me in." And the Lord says to him, "Don't worry, they haven't let me in there for years either!"

Being honest about oneself is not only something Chris applies personally, he also regards honesty as a requirement of all MPs.

'Being an MP has privileges. But it also has responsibilities,' he says. 'If you put yourself up as a public representative you should expect to meet standards of financial probity. There is no justification at all, for example, for anyone selling the opportunity to ask Parliamentary questions.

'When it comes to personal relationships things are more complicated. Politicians, like anyone else, have frailties. Relationships end, other relationships form. Provided you are not being hypocritical, I'm not sure that it's necessary for the press to pry into every corner of people's private lives. Saying one thing in public and another thing in private is not the way for a public representative to operate.'

There have been, he admits, 'a very few' occasions when he has had to struggle between the public voting demands of his party and the private convictions of his conscience.

'Most of the time there is no problem because you come at things from a political perspective. Your faith has helped to inform you and what you're voting for accords completely with your faith and your politics.'

In the course of a day's work Chris might deal with anything from England's place in this year's World Cup Finals to the success of the Spice Girls or the plight of English opera.

One thing that won't go away is the millennium. Why should we be spending millions celebrating it at all?

'Because primarily it is a moment when, by accident of the calendar, people will want to pause to reflect on the past and make resolutions regarding the future. A bit like one super New Year's Eve.

'Celebrating as it does the birth of Christ, it is also a good opportunity for the Church to get the Christian message accross.'

Closely linked to the millennium celebrations is the National Lottery, also part of his departmental portfolio. As a Christian can he be happy that the Lottery is turning us into a nation of gamblers?

'I don't think it is doing that,' he says. 'It is actually doing the country some good. I'm very keen to protect the Lottery as an affordable punt rather than something which tempts people into gambling beyond their means. I am very worried about pub-based games which have draws every 10 minutes. That is an enticement to gamble excessively. I don't think the Lottery does that.'

Not even when there is a roll-over?

'That's a bit of a myth,' he says. 'If you compare the social spread of people who play the Lottery and the amounts they spend with society at large you will find that the people at the bottom end of the income scale, the Ds and Es (the people on benefit) spend slightly less on the Lottery than their percentage of the population.

'It is the middle-income group, the C1s and C2s, who are spending most. In other words those who can afford to lose.'

On a wider front how does Chris answer the accusation that his

Government's plans to cut lone-parent benefit, introduce university tuition fees and cut assisted school places for gifted children from low-income families show them to be losing touch with ordinary working people in this country?

'These are difficult decisions, but that is in the nature of government. You have to decide on priorities. Some of those priorities will marginally disadvantage one group to provide much greater advantage for another.

'Plans for the lowering of lone-parent benefits were introduced by the Tories but they made no budget provision, which is one reason why we had to go ahead and do it.

'The phasing-out of the Government's assisted places scheme is specifically so that we can raise money to reduce class sizes for all primary school kids. Similarly if we're to expand opportunities for young people to go into further or higher education then there needs to be some means of financing it. The idea is that people won't be repaying tuition fees until their post-university income reaches a certain point.'

But when Labour was in Opposition it criticised the Government for cutting the social security budget. Now it's implementing some of those Tory policies. Is that part of the game or is it hypocrisy?

'It is neither,' he says. 'We're not making benefit cuts for the sake of it. If we were just implementing a cut in lone-parent benefit and putting nothing in its place then it would be right to criticise. But as well as cutting this benefit we are introducing a major welfare to work programme.'

So backbench revolts over benefit cuts are not signs that New Labour is struggling to keep its long-cherished image of being the party for the poor?

'I don't think that's happening at all. There are vigorous debates within the party on how best to help the disadvantaged. Everyone is agreed that the best solution to poverty, whether for lone parents or anyone else, is to have a job.

'Five years ago Labour was seen as the party of the poor and dispossessed while the Tories were the party for the rest, including the ordinary citizen. We have rebuilt the party so that we're the party of the poor and the ordinary citizen. We must never abandon our commitment to the dispossessed. Nor dare we lose touch with the vast majority of people in this country.'

Health and education, reckons the man with a doctorate in English, are the big issues facing his Government.

'We need to get the education system right so that every kid has the chance of the best possible quality of education and the greatest amount of opportunity.

'If I had a magic wand I'd transform things so every school was in an absolutely prestigious building; every class had a maximum of 30 pupils; there were real opportunities and a wide variety of subjects with the most dedicated and effective teachers in the world available for our kids. It would be wonderful!

'That is what we need to aim for. That's not going to happen overnight or even in five years. But we need to lay the foundations.

'We must also re-establish the health service as something that will always be there when we need it, at the time we need it.

'The NHS is a very precious thing. It has been starved of resources for too long. It has a million very dedicated people working for it and is undoubtedly the best way of organising health care. Waiting lists are getting longer but we have an opportunity to rebuild, even though it will be a long uphill task.'

An uphill task it might be, but Chris Smith is well used to mountaineering.

Rev Martin Smyth

*Ulster Unionist MP for Belfast South since 1982. Born in Belfast in 1931.
Before becoming an MP Martin was an incumbent Presbyterian minister.
Member of the Northern Ireland Asembly, 1982 – 1986. Ulster Unionist
Party Whip and Spokesman on Health and Family Policy since 1995.
Married Kathleen in 1957. Has three daughters, one of whom is deceased.*

The interview was conducted on 11 December 1995.

WHEN terrorists murdered Belfast South MP Robert Bradford in November 1981, his friend and colleague the Reverend Martin Smyth had some hard thinking to do.

As vice-president of the Ulster Unionist Party, Martin was involved in finding a candidate for the forthcoming by-election. It was while encouraging others to stand that Martin wondered whether *he* was the man for the job.

'A couple of fellow clergymen asked me, "Don't you think this is the time to put yourself forward to represent the people?" I also asked myself whether I could ask somebody else to do a job I wasn't prepared to consider myself. So I made it a matter of prayer, and allowed my name to go forward and left it to the selection committee and the electorate to decide.'

At the time, Martin was in charge of Belfast's Alexandra Presbyterian Church, where he'd been for 19 years. In March 1982, Martin was duly elected.

Fourteen years on, he still regards his job as an MP as part of his Christian vocation. 'I believe this is where I should be at this time,' he says. 'I still continue to preach regularly, although I'm not involved in the pastoral work of the church.'

Thirty-five years earlier, it was through the influence of a fellow rugby player that Martin became a Christian. 'I was 16 years old when this lad asked, "Isn't it about time you became a Christian, Martin?" I'd been brought up to go to church and was a member of the young people's Christian Endeavour. I knew the gospel intellectually. I knew the facts but I still hadn't come to a personal knowledge of Christ, although as a young lad I had a feeling that I was going to become a minister.

'None the less, I prayed: "Lord, if I'm good to the end of the year, I'll be a Christian next year."

'But there was no difference in Martin Smyth. Later I realised the real significance. A Christian is someone who has received the gift of eternal life in Christ. Only then can they begin to live a Christian life. I didn't tell anyone of my decision at first. It was only in the following May, when I started to tell people I believed in Christ, that I had a sense of assurance I'd been forgiven.'

Although Martin had a long-seated feeling about being a minister, when the time came to make career choices he was caught between the ministry and the civil service. He told himself that if he passed his exams he would take it as a sign that he should go into the ministry. Although he had to resit one subject, Martin kept his side of the bargain.

As an Ulster MP, Martin represents a community that's had more than its fair share of suffering. His calling into parliamentary politics was against a background of violence. How does Martin feel he can represent the hurts of his constituents?

'There are times when I must reflect the hurts but not major on them. If you major on hurts you can appear lop-sided and embittered,' he reasons. 'I think I represent them best by pinpointing the basic responsibility of government to punish the evil-doer and to protect those who do right. I keep emphasising the responsibility of the Government to deal with terrorism. At times the Government has opted out of its responsibility and has not dealt purposefully with terror, allowing a mafia to develop in Northern Ireland.'

Martin views the current peace process with a 'healthy scepticism and a welcoming realism.' He's quick to point out most people want peace.

'I view it with a welcoming realism, in so far as for the past 16 months there's been a turning away from mass bombing and intensive shootings. For that we are thankful. I view the process with a healthy scepticism in so far as in the housing estates there are individuals who, night after night, live in terror of being beaten into subjection by masked men. It's horrendous.

'I do not believe the peace process will necessarily do away with the ideas and aspirations of those who aspire to what they conceive to be Irish nationalism. That is an honourable pursuit. But if they want to have a nation with their fellow citizens then they must pursue it rationally and democratically.'

Martin has long felt that religious revival is the answer to the conflict. What does he say to those people who think that religion and politics shouldn't mix?

'That view is based on a misunderstanding. Firstly, the state cannot curb the independence of the individual conscience. Secondly, the word "politics" literally means "in the city". The Bible teaches that civilisation began in the Garden of Eden and ends in the city – the new Jerusalem, a redeemed community.

'Christians cannot escape from the realities of politics. Representatives of God have a responsibility to care for the underdog, to care for people. We are commanded to pray for our rulers. We are to pray against tyranny. We are commanded to pay our taxes. Christians cannot opt out of the real world. We are called to be the salt of the earth.'

Martin describes himself as a 'Christian capitalist'.

'While we're at liberty to pool our resources for a common purpose, I believe God has given us rights of property. We're all equal in one sense – before the Lord in judgment. I find it difficult to see any equality anywhere else. We've all got different gifts to be used in the purpose of God for the common good.'

What happens when Martin has to choose between supporting the party line and following his conscience?

'On issues of morality there's always been an open vote in our party, so there's been no problem in following my conscience. But on other issues I've had to tell myself to be careful that I did not make them matters of conscience just because I disagreed with the majority. Is it *really* conscience or am I just being awkward? But where it's clearly something that goes against my conscience, I would go against the party. Most parties tolerate that, as long as it doesn't become a habit.'

How is a Christian MP different from his or her non-Christian colleagues?

'He or she is not necessarily better at the job but should be different in the breadth of understanding; in the way a case is presented; and above all he or she should be doing everything to the best of his or her ability.'

If the way in which MPs perform their duties is important, what does Martin feel about the public's lack of respect in the light of political sleaze?

'MPs reflect the society from which they come,' he says. 'Perhaps those who keep indicting the MPs should begin to examine their own lives and the society in which they live. Because that's the society that produces MPs.

It's a scandal that a corrupt press seeks to demean the work of MPs by suggesting they're being paid about £100,000 a year. It's also a challenge. The quality of service the British public gets from their MPs is by far and away greater than the average service in any other community in the world.'

For Martin, serving his constituents rates as his greatest political achievement. 'I'm pleased that as a backbench MP I was able to co-sponsor the Disabled Person's Act in 1989, which provided consultation and advice facilities to the people of Northern Ireland.'

Despite, or maybe because of, his demanding workload, Martin safeguards Sunday lunchtime as a time for his family. He and his wife Kathleen have two married daughters and four grandchildren. 'I try to be home each weekend. We normally have a family gathering after church. They all join us for lunch and we spend Sunday afternoons together,' he says.

So far as political ambitions are concerned, Martin aims to 'serve God faithfully and fulfil my calling fully, which at the moment is to represent the people of south Belfast to the best of my ability.' Martin hopes to stand in the next general election. If selected, it will be his last.

One can only hope that his leaving of Westminster will be in happier circumstances than his entry into parliamentary politics.

Caroline Spelman

Conservative MP for Meriden since 1997. Born in Bishops Stortford in 1958. Before becoming an MP Caroline was a director of a food biotechnology consultancy. Opposition Whip since 1998. Caroline is a member of the Church of England. Married Mark in 1987. Has two sons and one daughter. The interview was conducted on 6 November 1997.

MOTHER-of-three Caroline Spelman has her hands full at the House and at home. Selected just 11 weeks before May's general election, Caroline survived two recounts to hold the Midlands seat of Meriden for the Conservatives. One of the selection committee conditions was that her children should be educated in the constituency. As she, husband Mark and their children – all of whom are under seven – lived in Kent at the time, victory at the polls meant a major upheaval.

'Despite the 130-mile distance and having to move if I won, I felt very strongly I should apply for selection,' she says. 'I told myself, "If you are going to get this seat then this is where God wants you to be, and if you don't then it's not."

'God doesn't favour one side of the House more than the other. Christianity is much larger than any political ideology. But to me the fact that not only did I win but also that we found a suitable house and a good school and church within a matter of weeks is evidence that I am where God wants me.'

How does Caroline answer those who say abandoning young children to be an MP is no example of Christian motherhood?

'Of course I feel guilty and torn at times because of my children,' she says. 'That's when I remind myself that I'm sure God wants me in Parliament for a reason. When I consider how he provides for me and helps me, then the guilt gives way to peace.

'"Abandoning children" is a very emotive phrase. Mark and I discussed very carefully how it would impact on the children before I applied to stand in the election. In reality my time is split fifty-fifty between Westminster and the constituency. I usually get home on a Thursday teatime and leave on a Monday lunchtime. During parliamentary recess constituency work goes on, of course. But like any other working mum I fit work in around the children. If I have a constituency engagement such as visiting a library I take my children with me.

'It isn't easy but there are benefits. Our marriage has unquestionably benefited from us sharing the parenting of our children. And having happily married parents who are both fulfilled in their work is worth an awful lot to children.'

Caroline met Mark in a Paris church in 1984 while she was working as a linguist for the European Farming Union (she is fluent in French and German). It was while working in Europe that she became interested in politics. By the time they married, three years later, Mark knew of his wife's ambition. Today Caroline would find it impossible to be an MP without management-consultant Mark's commitment to her career and the children.

It would also be impossible for her without the assurance that this is what God requires of her, for now.

'Although I realise some people will think I'm a religious fanatic to say so, being a politician is my calling. But my faith is an integrated part of the way I live. I have seen plenty of guidance to show me I'm meant to be here. Barely a day goes by when I don't see things sign-posting that I am on the right track.'

Unlike many of her parliamentary colleagues Caroline was not attracted to student union politics while she was at university. Was there anything specific that made her decide to be an MP?

'My involvement was probably shaped by the fact that my education was very much affected by the bad days of Britain's disastrous industrial relations.

'I can remember doing my O-levels while the school could open only three days a week because we didn't have heating oil. To a young person this is coming very close to anarchy. It was frightening and you have to hold to account governments that allow those sorts of things to happen.

'I felt very passionately that I didn't want to see that degree of mismanagement by government, of whatever political party, again. That's something I find unacceptable.

'I also feel passionately about people achieving their potential. I'm concerned about the growing disparity in Britain between those who succeed and those for whom the system is failing. I want to help everyone fulfil their potential. That sounds idealistic, I know, but then many MPs are idealists.'

Might not some people be surprised to hear a Tory speak of healing divisions in society?

'The observation that society has divisions is not exclusively Socialist or Conservative,' she says. 'It is a statement of fact. This is the position of Britain today. The question is how a Conservative or a Socialist might try to solve this.

'My experience as a youngster was that education enabled me to achieve ambitions far beyond my wildest dreams. I certainly didn't wake up in my pram thinking I wanted to be an MP! My parents didn't have the money to send me to private school, had they even wanted to. In my day there was less concern about the state educational system and I went to an excellent local grammar school.

'Everyone has a creative spark. If you can ignite it by whatever means – a supportive parent, an inspiring teacher – then people can achieve their real potential and make a difference. I am a bit sceptical of a heavy-handed state being able to deliver this.'

Caroline was brought up in a Christian family and went to a 'typical parish church' where her father was a churchwarden.

'I was a bit rebellious in my teens,' she confesses. 'I questioned all sorts of things. My parents were good enough not to force me to go to church. I resisted getting confirmed while I was living at home because I wanted to be sure for myself.

'When I went to university I made friends with two girls who were Christians. We went to church regularly and a spiritual hunger grew in me. When I realised Christianity was real for me, I decided to be confirmed.

'There was no defining moment as such. When I was about 11 or 12 I started reading the Bible and Scripture Union notes. I had probably just about attained a maturity of understanding the complicated messages about eternal life and eternal death and the end of the world.

'As a teenager I went into a period of grappling with some of these things. I remember working out for myself that the truth is very simply Jesus, and that I would die for ever if I failed to recognise who he is and what he did. It was a very private commitment.

'Later, while I was working in France, I attended St Michael's, the English-speaking church in Paris. I found living by myself in a foreign country very lonely. At St Michael's the worship was more challenging than anything I had experienced before. For the first time I encountered modern church music and the biblically-based preaching and teaching were outstanding. It was a key time in helping my relationship with God.'

Today Caroline worships at a 'very lively' parish church and freely confesses to living off the weekly 'meaty' sermon and 'excellent' worship.

'Being an MP is extremely challenging – more challenging than I realised,' she says. 'It's good to be able to ask God for wisdom and strength. It makes such a difference to have the armoury of prayer at my disposal.

'At the beginning of the day I always commit what lies ahead and my family to God. I quite often pray before I speak in the House. I usually pray before, during and after committee meetings. Keeping in touch with God is the only way I can get through the most difficult times.

'One of the greatest things my faith gives me is the strength to carry on. When I am tired I am reminded by a verse that I hold on to tremendously that those who wait on the Lord will renew their strength and will rise up like eagles.

'It's good to be reminded that the strength that comes from God is supernatural. The more I depend on him, the more strength he gives me.'

How does Caroline's faith help her decide on difficult moral issues that come before Parliament? How, for example, would she vote on the question of abortion?

'The basic spiritual principle underlying the question of abortion is the sanctity of life,' she says. 'I've had a number of miscarriages. It is a dreadful experience for any woman to go through. When I finally did have a pregnancy that went beyond 16 weeks we were told that the baby had a brain tumour.

'Deciding what we should do was the hardest decision of our lives. With the help of God, Mark and I decided we would not opt for an abortion. We would carry on with the pregnancy. As it happened the tumour reabsorbed itself and Eleanor was born perfectly healthy.

'Parents do face very difficult decisions. You can't be black and white over it, but to me the sanctity of life principle is most important. Abortion being used as a form of contraception is totally unacceptable.

'It's certainly something Parliament should be constantly monitoring because medical technology advances at such a pace that life is sustainable at a much earlier stage now than in 1967 when the Act was introduced.'

Caroline describes herself as 'very unhappy' at the prospect of the lowering of the age of consent for homosexual activity.

'I am also dismayed to see the Church coming out in favour of it,' she says. 'Sexuality takes time to establish itself. To lower the age of homosexuality makes it even more difficult for young people whose sexuality isn't properly established to cope.

'Some sections of the media have dubbed me old-fashioned but I go back to the basic principles of God-given creation. The heterosexual relationship is for the procreation of mankind. And, as the Bible says, the correct relationship for the continuation of humanity is lifelong marriage.'

The sexual behaviour of MPs continues to attract media attention. Is it right to expect MPs to maintain higher standards?

'The public should be able to expect MPs to conduct themselves in accordance with good standards of morality and conduct in public life. I was asked at selection whether there was anything in my past that would embarrass the party. If you enter public life you have to make an extra effort to make sure you abide by the rule of law. I would also include abiding by a moral law.

'Of course, we are all capable of mistakes – MPs or not. But by entering public life you accept the privileges and the responsibilities. And the public should be able to expect high standards from public servants.'

Some commentators have suggested that the Tories lost the election partly because of the misbehaviour of MPs. Now in opposition after 18 years in office, what will it take to make the Conservatives electable again?

'It's a well-established fact that governments lose elections rather than oppositions win them,' she says. 'Our party is in a very contrite mood at the moment. There is ready acknowledgement that we were regarded as arrogant, sleazy and out of touch, all of which was probably absolutely true.

'We have to clean up. We have to re-organise ourselves with better discipline. We need to listen to the electorate and shape our policies accordingly. In time, people will be dissatisfied with Labour's handling of the country and will have confidence that the Conservative Party is credible and ready to take power again.'

Caroline reckons health care and welfare reform will be the big issues facing the Government.

'I wish them much success in trying to tackle these,' she says. 'We cannot afford to let health care and welfare spending continue unchecked.'

Were she able to change one thing about the country overnight Caroline would opt for a change of attitude.

'I would like to do something about the ignorance that abounds regarding the way different parts of British society live. If you live in a wealthy community it's possible to be ignorant of poorer ones. This leads to prejudice.

'Greater understanding of each other would lead to greater appreciation, tolerance and a greater sense of community,' she says, with the experience that comes from managing to get three young children to play happily together.

Gary Streeter

Conservative MP for Devon South West since 1997. MP for Plymouth Sutton, 1992 – 1997. Born in Portsmouth in 1955. Before becoming an MP Gary was a solicitor. Parliamentary Private Secretary to Solicitor General, 1993 – 1995. Parliamentary Private Secretary to Attorney General, 1994 – 1995. Government Whip, Lord Chancellor's Department, 1995 - 1996. Junior Minister, Lord Chancellor's Department, 1996 – 1997. Shadow Secretary of State, International Development since 1998. He is Vice-Chairman of the Christian Fellowship All Party Group. Gary is a member of a house church. Married Janet in 1978. Has one son and one daughter.

The interview was conducted on 17 December 1996.

WHEN law student Gary Streeter first sat down to read the Bible he set out to prove it was wrong. As Parliamentary Secretary to the Lord Chancellor, the Conservative Members for Plymouth Sutton is responsible for the running of the British legal system.

'My wife, Janet, was a believer when we married,' he says. 'I wasn't. I didn't think it important. When we moved to London for me to do my articles, I went to church to keep her company. One day, with my lawyer's eye, I set out to disprove Christianity. In three months I studied most of the New Testament and a dozen books on the evidence for Christianity. I came to the conclusion that the historical evidence for the life, death and resurrection of Jesus was overwhelming. Two weeks after this intellectual conversion I gave my life to Jesus Christ. It was June 1979 and I've been involved in the house church movement ever since.

'It's one thing to have a head knowledge of the Christian faith and to be convinced that Christianity is true. We then need to give our life to the Lord Jesus Christ, make this deeper step of being born again. That's when we're transformed and become a new creation. That's the fundamental fact of the gospel.'

How different a person is Gary?

'I used to swear a lot,' says the former school rugby captain. 'I was converted and baptised. Once I came out of the waters of baptism I stopped swearing. Less dramatically, I had been extremely arrogant and self-contained. Gradually the Lord has broken me over those characteristics. Hopefully, I'm a lot different to the 20-year-old upstart who thought he knew it all and had the world at his feet.'

By the time he was 25 Gary had a first-class honours degree in law, his articles and a job with a Plymouth law firm. Why, 17 years later, did he leave the security of the practice to stand for Parliament?

'Throughout the '80s I became aware of a calling on my life,' he says. 'In December 1985, I spent a day in prayer and fasting. That night I said to my wife, "I believe the Lord's calling us into politics." In the office the next morning I told my partners I felt it was right to go into politics but didn't know which party I should join.'

Once his partners' laughter died down Gary joined the SDP. Eighteen months later he switched to the Tories.

'Like many Christians, I knew nothing about politics,' he says. 'To my shame I'd never thought about it. I was too busy concentrating on my legal career, my local church life and my family. As I learnt more I realised that if you're serious about changing government policy under a two-party system you've either got to be Labour or Conservative.'

It would, he reckons, be an overstatement to say that God called him into the Conservative Party.

'Once I started thinking more closely, I discovered I am a natural Conservative. All my instincts run in that direction; individual responsibility, strong defence, sovereignty of the nation, the family, enterprise – the key planks of the Conservative Party are the things I believe in.'

The former Tiverton Grammar School head boy is a man with a mission.

'I want government policy to reflect traditional biblical values, particularly things like individual responsibility and the importance of traditional family life. Many of society's problems would be solved if we could see strong, stable families. A commitment to finding policies which can deliver on loving one's neighbour. If we can make progress in these key areas, I'll consider my mission accomplished.'

The Lord Chancellor's right-hand man readily admits that loving one's neighbour is beyond the capabilities of the rule of law. He is also well aware of the limitations of the law- makers.

'We can't change human nature by legislation,' he says. 'If we want to see significant moral and social changes in this country we need a spiritual revival. Parliament must set the standard for the nation. People look to MPs to lead by example. We can't legislate for morality but we can give leadership. If you seek public office you should seek to live up to higher standards of personal morality and integrity. The public, while realising there will be mistakes, expect that of us.

'MPs will fall short and we need to make allowances for that. MPs who make mistakes shouldn't be hounded out of office. The cardinal sin is hypocrisy. We shouldn't present ourselves as one sort of person, then say and do something different behind the scenes. That's where people lose trust and confidence in their leaders.'

Have there been times when Gary's faith has conflicted with others' expectations of how he should vote?

'There have been moments when I've voted for things with a heavy heart,' he admits. 'But compromise doesn't have to be a dirty word. One reason why Christians have abdicated from politics for so long is that they think politics is a dirty business. There will be tough decisions, we might feel we're sailing close to the wind as to what our faith and conscience can stand. But it's only by being involved that we can make a difference. It is tough, nobody pretends otherwise. But it is doable.'

So the Church is right to get involved in politics?

'Yes, but it shouldn't be a case of church leaders speaking out from the pulpit without knowing much about government policy. Every church leader has the right to speak out on any subject he or she chooses. But it would be more helpful if Christians as a whole became politically aware and got involved in every party, at every level – school governors, local authorities, Westminster.

'Mrs Jones acting responsibly as a school governor is making a better Christian contribution to politics than a bishop speaking out from the pulpit. If the Church could get its act together and show its love, unity and commitment of purpose it would make an awesome impact on the world. Christians getting involved in politics, the media, education and science would transform society.'

Gary describes his own politics as 'centre-right', then rapidly admits,

'These labels are increasingly meaningless, having just labelled myself! I am fiercely patriotic, which positions me to the right in terms of the European debate,' he explains. 'But I recognise there are people for whom we don't do enough and could do more. It would be a mistake to try to live their lives for them or to dish out more welfare cheques, but we should encourage them to stand on their own two feet by creating more meaningful jobs.

'Some people grow up in inner cities with no knowledge of traditional family life, the work culture or anything positive. It's almost impossible to know what to do with such people. But I know we should penetrate their lives in some way to help them to live more meaningfully.'

Being 'fiercely patriotic', Gary sees Europe as one of the big issues facing the next government.

'We are going to have to make a fundamental decision as to whether we sign up for the first wave of the single currency.

'We also need to do more to support the family. Twenty to 30 per cent of kids don't have positive role models. They don't have stable family backgrounds. They haven't seen Mum and Dad get on together. They may not have seen Dad at all. They may never have seen Mum.'

Traditionally the Conservative Party has been seen as the party of the family, but could it do more to support marriage?

'Yes. We could do more through our tax structures to support marriage. In this department we have tendered out services to groups which provide specialist marriage support services, including Relate, Care for the Family and Christian Care. We're asking them to come forward with new ideas as to how to support couples in their early years, maybe by offering pre-marriage counselling.'

Gary does not believe there are particular 'Christian' issues. God, he reckons, is 'as concerned about unemployment and the Third World as he is about abortion and homosexuality'.

On most issues there is not an obvious Christian perspective, he reckons. 'Christian MPs look at issues according to their background, their understanding of Scripture, and their political outlook,' he says. 'This is how Christians of different parties can disagree over policy.'

So Christians opposing each other is just part of healthy debate?

'Yes. It is a reflection of what Christians do in the big wide world. We should not be afraid of different points of view and arguing a different case in trying to achieve a healthy objective. It is healthy and creative and brings forward good ideas. People should realise that just because you're a Christian MP it doesn't mean you'll come up with the same policy package as all the other Christian MPs, although it's disappointing if the objectives are not similar.'

Media interest in MPs' faith is something which Gary considers both helpful and dangerous.

'Ten years ago it was probably unpopular to say you were a Christian,' he says. 'Certainly in the Labour Party, they would tell you it was almost impossible to live as a Christian in the Labour Party. That has changed now, thank goodness! The important thing is that people are genuine. The Christian faith should never be seen as a bandwagon on which people should jump for electoral purposes.

'It is very healthy that there should be a debate about biblical values, our Christian faith and so on, so long as people don't think it is going to deliver solutions to all of our problems. We need a mighty revival. But even then we will not see perfect solutions, because we are talking about a world that is predominantly fallen. I hope the Christianity debate causes more people to think about what they believe in and come to the conclusion that God is real. He is alive and it is time that everyone woke up to that fact.

'I would not like to see election candidates required to declare their faith. People should present themselves as closely to who they are as they possibly can. It is important not to hide or overstate things.'

When it comes to picking a biblical role model, it's Daniel who gets Gary's vote. 'Daniel was a great spiritual man who put his faith and calling first. He stood up for what he believed. He's an example of how a God-fearing man can make a difference in a secular age. I love the passage which says Daniel was neither negligent nor corrupt and was promoted because of his exceptional qualities. Although I fail, that's something I try to emulate.'

The one thing about the country Gary would like to change if he could would be to see a 'big strong thriving Church in this nation'.

'A united, Bible-based, dynamic Church which gave leadership and a clear moral example setting a moral agenda would have a great impact on the nation. I believe we will see it over the next 20 years. But I am hungry to see it now.

'One of my favourite Bible readings is in Deuteronomy where the Lord identifies and lists blessings and curses and then says, "Now choose life!" That's the key decision for each of us. We've all got to make that personal choice. The offer of life is the heart of the gospel.'

So, 18 years on, the lawyer still studies the Bible's law books. The difference now is that he's proved their message to be true.

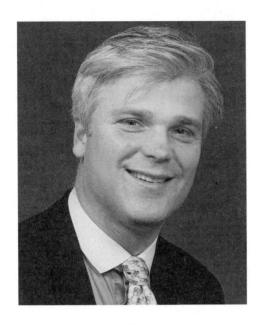

Desmond Swayne

Conservative MP for New Forest West since 1997. Born in Berne,
Switzerland in 1956. Before becoming an MP Desmond was a systems
manager at the Royal Bank of Scotland. Desmond is a member of the
Church of England. Married Moira in 1987. Has one son and two daughters
  The interview was conducted on 9 June 1998.

DECIDING which way to vote on contentious moral issues is the easy bit,
says MP Desmond Swayne, the Conservative Member for New Forest West.
'We can all pontificate. We can all say this is morally wrong and that is
morally wrong. Standing up and being counted is easy. The difficult bit is
the challenge which faces every Christian, wherever they work – living out
a Christian life. That's much more difficult.

'If we are Christians we are all effectively God's ministers. It is through
us that his word will be known. People should be able to look at us and
ask, "What is it about his life that's special?" and then say, "I want some
too!" That's an awful responsibility because most of the time we are
concerned about our own prospects not God's.

'It would be nice if I could say I must remain a politician because it is
my calling, but the reality is that I know every day I am not as concerned
with God's Kingdom as I should be and it deeply troubles me.

'It's very difficult for me to say God has called me to this because I spend so little of my time concerned about his concerns.

'I often get to the end of the day and wonder whether I've assisted in building God's Kingdom that day. How many people would look at my behaviour today and say that I'm a Christian? That to me is the difficulty. Voting's the easy part!'

In his navigation of the moral maze there is one issue for Desmond that stands out as the touchstone of public morality – abortion.

'How can people wonder at the state of society when at its heart we have a cancer – the scandal of abortion?' he says.

'Our whole attitude to life is so pervaded by abortion. The existing law is an outrage. The clear intention was that there would be no abortion on demand. That, in practice, is not the case. It's scandalous that the existing law is not enforced. Furthermore there's no legal protection at all for those physicians who refuse on principle to take part in abortions. Their careers are sidelined.

'On a wider scale people are reluctant to look at the question of what constitutes life and under what circumstances it is proper to take human life. If we have such a cavalier attitude to the value of human life can we be surprised that our attitude on so many other moral issues is defective?'

The answer, he reckons, is not just in a tightening up of the way the Act is interpreted. He wants to see it abolished.

'I would like to see the abortion law removed,' he says. 'We don't want a return to back-street abortions and we would need to look at alternatives. But we also need to step back from some of the procedures – like partial-birth abortion – which are now taking place. We need to look at the number of weeks during which abortion is permitted. Basically we need to step back from the precipice.'

Before he became an MP Desmond was a teacher (A-level Economics at Charterhouse and Wrekin College) and, more latterly, a manager with the Royal Bank of Scotland ('I never saw a customer, I was responsible for dealing room technology'). The 1997 election was his third attempt to fulfil his childhood ambition.

'Ever since I was a schoolboy I can remember wanting to be an MP,' he says. 'I suppose I was attracted by the self-importance and the enjoyment of getting up in front of an audience and giving them a piece of my mind.

'Over the years I've discovered I have very strong views. It was increasingly frustrating to read the papers, agree with things politicians were saying and yet not be able to do anything about it.'

At one time Desmond, who has a theology degree from St Andrew's University, wondered whether God was calling him into the Anglican priesthood. Even now he does not rule out the possibility. He has, he says, a 'sneaking suspicion' that he has been called to the ministry.

'I keep telling myself not yet, which is partly me trying to avoid the issue and partly wanting more experience.'

How, then, does the man who is reconciling the demands of the spiritual and the temporal in his own life see the conflicting interplay between Church and State in society at large?

'It's a healthy conflict,' he says. 'The Church has a duty to challenge politicians. But it also has a duty to challenge the public at large. The Church is wrong to criticise MPs if it does not have the moral courage to challenge members of its own congregations.

'It is right for the Church to draw attention to the correctness of political ends but the Church shouldn't be commenting on the political means. So far as Christianity is concerned – as the story of the widow's mite tells us – motives are more important than results.'

Conflicts between MPs in the chamber of the House are, Desmond reckons, similarly healthy occasions.

'I think the yah boo is very important,' he says. 'It is by adversarial politics that you challenge other people's opinions, make them think and make them come up with answers. The destructive criticism is ultimately creative. There's nothing more disastrous than a generally agreed policy – where the two parties come up with some rushed-through legislation to solve a particular problem. The Dangerous Dogs Act, for example, is awful because it didn't go through the critical process.

'Political systems that promote a consensus and force politicians to work together in perpetual coalitions are disastrous for democracy because they take choice away from the electorate.'

As a child, Desmond, who was born in Switzerland, moved around the world with his parents. Whether in Singapore or the Middle East there were two focuses of expats' attention – the golf club and church.

'I come from a long Christian tradition,' says Desmond. 'My mother's and father's families were churchgoers and I've always gone to church. I've always had trouble answering people who asked me when I was born again because I can never put a time and place on it. I've never known a time when I didn't know Christ and I am grateful for that.'

There was, he says, no typical teenage overthrowing of family faith when he left home.

'My great rebellion was not playing golf!' he says. 'Wherever I've been I've always joined a church community. I find it very difficult without that. I know some people criticise Christianity and say it's a crutch. Yes it is! The thought that we live on a dying planet in the middle of a vast and meaningless universe is such an awful prospect that I can't imagine living without the crutch of belief in Christianity. But of course just because people need Christianity doesn't mean to say that it isn't true.'

How does the theologian-turned-politician see the person of Jesus?

'Jesus was an historical figure. He has to have been a real person otherwise you're left with some sort of refined essence – a blob of cosmic glup. You've got to be able to pray to something identifiable and the only identifiable thing we have is Jesus Christ.

'I certainly don't see him as a politician. He treated politics with the contempt it deserves – give unto Caesar that which is Caesar's and to God the important things. He didn't campaign politically – not even against the scandal of crucifixion – which is why the zealous Judas saw him as a disappointment and betrayed him.

'As for the popular notion that Jesus was just a good man – a useful figure in teaching us moral truths but not the Son of God – it's a nonsense. Jesus can't just have been a good man because if you look at his claims to be the Son of God he must have been either a lunatic, a charlatan or who he said he was.'

It would be good to think, Desmond acknowledges, that MPs could set high standards of personal morality in the course of their public service. But the truth, he says, is 'we get what we deserve'.

'We elect these people and if we don't like them we can get rid of them. That's something we should treasure because there are voting systems on offer where that is taken away from people.

'In the last election a large number of people voted against a particular rascal to see the back of him. That is an entirely proper and healthy political phenomenon. One of the ways to ensure that MPs do set an example is by taking our vengeance at the ballot box when they don't.

'I think we're right to expect MPs to be above reproach but we should also expect to be disappointed. After all, none of us is above temptation.'

The 'rascal' was not the only one to lose his seat. Many of Desmond's fellow Tories did so, too. And Desmond knows why.

'We deserved to,' he says. 'We had given the impression of arrogance, of sleaze, and of being a thoroughly unpleasant bunch who were more concerned about prosecuting our differences with one another than pursuing a common agenda. People were thoroughly fed up with what they perceived was an arrogant, tired and fractious administration. And in many ways it was.

'The Tories will need two things to win a future election. We need to be electable and we need some help from the Government. People vote against governments rather than for oppositions. Labour have got to screw up. They haven't been very obliging in that respect so far but there's still plenty of time to go.'

The big issue facing the Government according to Desmond is welfare reform.

'The dependency culture has a widespread corrosive effect on society. People think it's not worthwhile to go out and work. That in turn affects discipline in schools.

'It all stems from the fact that with a budget of some £90 billion, welfare has become part of the problem rather than part of the solution. The difficulty for the Conservatives was that nobody trusted us with the welfare state. Labour now has a huge opportunity to push through an agenda of reform. Although so far what they've come forward with has been pretty piecemeal and counter-productive.

'I'm also concerned about Labour's plans for the upper chamber. The House of Lords is not something that anyone would have designed but it works. It's nonsense to think of it as a place where the will of an elected government is overturned. It doesn't do that. It is very much a revising chamber – to make the Commons think again. That's very healthy. If something works don't mess with it.

'However, as Labour have said, if you are going to reform the House of Lords by doing away with hereditary peerages and making it more democratic then MPs must realise that for the Lords to become more powerful the Commons must give up some of its power.

'If Lords are elected they won't want a Cinderella job. They'll want some of the action. If we really want that conflict in our political system then we should think hard about it before pushing through reforms.

'Labour isn't proposing to do that. Labour is proposing to say let's get rid of one element of the House of Lords – the hereditary element – now, and then at some stage in the future we will think through a reform. In the meantime they will have created the most enormous quango, placing huge patronage powers in the hands of the Prime Minister. That would be a disaster.'

Where Desmond would like to see radical change, of the magic-wand variety, is in getting people to listen.

'It's very difficult to get people's attention,' he says. 'If I could I'd make people listen or spend 10 minutes a day in rational thought. I can be entirely reconciled to the fact that people reject a message. But it is very frustrating if they never hear it, never listen to it. Looking at the popular press, the majority of people aren't receptive to any message unless it is dumbed down and robbed of any facual content. For politicians and clergymen that's disastrous.'

And, presumably, pretty devastating for someone who might end up having been both.

Stephen Timms

Labour MP for East Ham since 1997. MP for Newham North East, 1994 –
1997. Born in 1955. Brought up in Farnborough, Hants. Before becoming an
MP Stephen was a mathematical analyst. Vice-Chairman, Christian
Socalist Movement since 1996. Parliamentary Private Secretary, Minister of
State for Employment, 1997 - 1998. Parliamentary Private Secretary,
Secretary for State for Northern Ireland, 1998. Parliamentary Under-
Secretary of State, Department of Social Security since 1998. Stephen is a
member of the Plaistow Christian Fellowship. Married Hui-Leng in 1986.
The interview was conducted on 22 October 1996.

DON'T vote for a candidate just because he or she is a Christian. That's the
somewhat surprising pre-election message from Labour's Stephen Timms.
'Whether or not somebody is a Christian is not particularly important in
determining whether or not to vote for them at a general election,' he says. 'It
should be a question of what their party policies are, how they're going to set
about doing the job, and how available to their constituents they're going to be.'

Born in Oldham to Labour-supporting parents, Stephen grew up in
Hampshire before reading mathematics at Cambridge University. While on
a mission at a Forest Gate church with his college Christian Union he fell
in love with East London.

When in 1979 – the year he joined the Labour Party – he was offered a job with a telecommunications firm in London he happily settled in the East End and joined the Plaistow Christian Fellowship, where he met and married his Singaporean wife, Hui-Leng.

In 1984 Stephen was elected to Newham Borough Council, becoming its leader in 1990 until he entered Westminster in a 1994 by-election.

'Being leader of Newham Council and therefore able to make a contribution to the area was consistent with what I perceive as my calling to East London,' he says. 'When, on the death of our MP, people suggested I ought to stand for the candidacy it seemed the right thing to do.

'According to Government figures, Newham is the most deprived local authority area in the country. There is a great deal that needs to change and I've enjoyed contributing to some of the changes in recent years. I see it as my vocation to continue doing that as part of my Christian service.'

Stephen, a self-confessed Blairite ('If that's what you call somebody who supported Tony Blair since he stood for the leadership'), admits to having had the politics bug before he became a Christian. Now joint vice-chair of the Christian Socialist Movement, he sees his membership of the Labour Party as the natural political expression of his faith. He discounts the notion of a separate Christian party as 'unhelpful'.

'I don't like separatist Christian initiatives,' he says. 'Our calling is to be salt and light in the world and not to hive off into our own private world. Jesus was God become man. Our calling is to be in the world, working alongside those of Christian faith, other faiths or no faith. It's a wrong understanding of Christian calling to think that we can work only with other Christians. That's a denial of the gospel. A Christian's place is in the workplace, on the street, in the community – alongside people and not retreating into a narrow religious party, world or group.'

Stephen became a Christian as a result of attending a Crusaders Bible class.

'I went along because I thought it was a respectable, sensible thing to do. Gradually I found that what I heard there made sense and provided me with the basis of something I could believe in for the rest of my life. So, as a 16-year-old, I decided to make a commitment. After much thought, I came to the conclusion that this was true and right.

'The point of decision – the culmination of a lengthy listening, reading and discussing process – came while I was on a Crusader camp in the New Forest. It took quite a while until I was fully sure that my life had changed and that I was indeed a Christian. Having made that initial step I can remember talking to a number of people before I was confident it was for real.'

Sharing a house at university with someone who was 'extremely negative and hostile towards Christianity' provoked Stephen to research the basis of his faith and conclude that 'Christianity was right'.

'When I joined the Labour Party I thought I was going to find the same sort of hostility I'd sometimes found at college. But I didn't. People accepted Christians as maybe a little bit eccentric, but there had always been Christians in the party. It wasn't an issue. I'm glad to say I've formed many friendships with people in the party who aren't Christians.'

Seventeen years later, how does he react to current media interest in MPs' faith?

'It's a remarkable phenomenon,' he says. 'When I joined the party I was very nervous that I was quickly going to be unmasked as a Holy Joe and not taken very seriously. That wasn't the case. In fact I soon became secretary of my local party and was quickly accepted. Shortly after that I joined the Christian Socialist Movement. I was conscious that Christians in the Labour Party were small in number and insignificant in terms of party profile.

'Suddenly that's changed! It's very exciting. It means there's a space being created in the Labour Party for people whose beliefs and world view is the same as mine. It's a window of opportunity to develop ideas and thinking. The CSM has quadrupled in size over the past three years.

'But there is a danger. If we get to the point that because you're a politician you must be a Christian we're going to get nominal professions of Christian faith of the kind familiar in previous generations, that we've grown out of recently. Prospective MPs putting on a veneer of churchgoing as a way of winning over the voters is something I don't have time for.

'Far be it from me to pass judgment on any individual but if people are lying because it's expedient to claim some Christian allegiance then it's certainly bad and damaging. But if, in reality, some people have always prayed and have been believers but have been a bit shy about saying it, that's all to the good.'

What does Stephen's faith give him?

'The most important thing is that Jesus is the truth,' he says. 'I can think of many benefits I've enjoyed as a result of being a Christian, but in the end that's not the issue. The question is "Is it true?" The conviction that my life ultimately rests on assumptions that are true is the thing I would be most keen to commend to other people.'

Stephen finds comfort in the words of Jeremiah, a prophet more commonly associated with doom and gloom.

'There's a passage in Jeremiah 10 which talks about God sending the wind from his storehouse. It reminds me that God has ultimate power. It puts my life into perspective and helps me reorientate my horizons and priorities when they get out of kilter.'

How does the writer of books on information technology read the national debate on morality?

'It's an exciting time!' he says. 'If anything is going to change, MPs have to get involved. The most far-reaching changes we may wish to see will be the result of individuals changing. People, by and large, will be changed by forces other than politicians. But there will have to be a changing legal framework as well, and it is MPs who are responsible for that. The tidal wave of public revulsion at what's happening in society is an opportunity to sort out some things which have been unpleasant for a long time.'

With the public looking to Parliament to give a moral lead, are they right to expect individual MPs to be above reproach?

'Yes. In becoming an MP you take on a position of public trust. You're there to serve your constituents, not to feather your own nest. If you're not interested in doing that, don't take the job. MPs who are not above reproach should be made accountable. There should be no cover-ups.'

Nor is political comment the sole preserve of politicians. The Church pronouncing on matters temporal is, according to Stephen, part of healthy, democratic debate.

'At times during the '80s it seemed as though it was the bishops who were the only people speaking up for justice and for the poor in an effective way – capable of embarrassing the government. However, I have no doubt that were Labour elected the Church would find things it needed to say which wouldn't please a Labour government. That's a wholly appropriate role for the Church to play.'

Is it appropriate for a church to advise its members to vote for one particular party, as happened following the publication of the Roman Catholic Church's document *The Common Good?*

'The Roman Catholic Church has been clear,' he says. 'They haven't been urging people to vote Labour. As I understand it, the document is presenting well-established Catholic social teaching, bringing a moral spotlight on political issues. If the implicit conclusion inclines people towards Labour rather than Conservatives, then that's a reflection of the consequence of 17 years of Conservative government.'

A criticism sometimes levelled at the Labour Party is that it is weak on pro-life issues. What is Stephen's personal stance?

'Like many of my Labour colleagues, I'm strongly opposed to euthanasia,' he says. 'On abortion, I'm much more agnostic. The thought of abortion is repugnant, but I'm not convinced that changing the law, thereby making it harder for women to get abortions, would improve things. It is people who need to change. When people have regard for the life of a child they will not want a baby aborted. If society regarded children more highly there would be fewer abortions. I'd rather it came that way round rather than through changes in the law.

'The fact is, 17 years of Conservative culture has contributed substantially to a moral environment in which abortion is seen as all right – an aspect of consumerism. Abortion figures have rocketed under the Tory Government's obsession with individualism. People have been told it's a good thing to be selfish.'

In the forthcoming election battle, how will Stephen's faith influence his campaign style?

'I won't be castigating any personal failings of my opponents. I'm not interested in doing that,' he says. 'However, I will be fiercely critical of the consequences of Conservative policies on Britain. I don't see any reason in my Christian faith for any hesitancy on that score, but I will also be positive about the alternatives the Labour Party proposes.

'For me, it's summed up in the words of Jesus when he calls us to be as wise as serpents and as innocent as doves. The challenge to Christians in politics is to be wise and shrewd, and to understand what's happening in the world (not a simplistic superficial understanding, which is often associated with a Christian interpretation), but not to compromise what we believe.'

In Stephen's opinion, dealing with long-term youth unemployment will be the big issue facing the next government.

'There are a quarter of a million young people under 25 who have never had a job and who have no prospect of getting one. The longer this goes on the more damage it's going to do right across the spectrum of British life. The next government must successfully tackle this. Youth unemployment is a waste of resources. Huge amounts of money are being shovelled out of the social security budget to people who could be contributing to the economy.

'What sort of generation is growing up now with no prospect of being able to keep their family in decent conditions? Youth unemployment is a big contributor to the growth of crime. If this problem isn't addressed, all of us will pay the resulting increasing price of this massive failure.'

For Stephen, it would appear, faith without work is dead.

Paul Tyler

*Liberal Democrat MP for Cornwall North since 1992. MP for Bodmin, 1974
(Feb to Oct). Born in South Devon in 1941. Before becoming an MP Paul was
a public relations director and managing director of a newspaper group.
Chairman of the Liberal Party, 1983 – 1986. Liberal Democrat Spokesman
on Agriculture and Rural Affairs, 1992 – 1997. Liberal Democrat Chief
Whip and Shadow Leader of the House since 1997. Paul is a member of a
Methodist congregation. Married Nicola in 1970. Has one son and one
daughter.*

The interview was conducted on 14 May 1996.

WHEN you're up early enough to give a 6.15 am interview on Radio 4's
Farming Today, as Liberal Democrat rural affairs spokesman Paul Tyler had
been the day I interviewed him, a second breakfast at half-ten is more than
forgivable. It's essential.

Although beef is not on the Commons breakfast menu, it still tops
his agenda.

'The BSE scare is very frightening,' says the Member for Cornwall North,
over toast and cappuccino. 'I have great respect for farmers' commitment
to looking after their land and livestock.

'Farmers feel they've been unfairly picked on by the Government, by fate.
I've had farmers on the phone and in my surgery in tears, not just because they

see their livelihood going up in smoke, literally, but because their professional care of livestock is being called into question. Some of the initial stunned resentment is turning into anger and frustration. And I can't blame them.

'I've been very struck by the way in which people from all parts of the rural economy have stuck together. Something which could easily have been divisive in the rural community – especially between different types of farmers – has, in fact, united people. People are showing a lot of true Christian charity.

'One of the problems Government has is that as life gets increasingly complex, it is more difficult for people to decide whose judgment to trust. Many of the experts who say whether a product or practice is safe have come through industry and have a commercial interest. A team of experts may be only slightly converted poachers. They may not be very good gamekeepers. In the future, farmers are going to be much more suspicious about what "experts" tell them.'

Paul's own expertise is in the public relations field, where he spent most of his pre-Westminster working life.

Although born on the Devon side of the Tamar, Paul delights in being a part of the constituency he represents.

'I'm very proud of my long family connection with the area,' he says. 'My family originally came to Cornwall in 1066. One of my ancestors was Bishop Jonathan Trelawney, the great Cornish national folk-hero. My mother emigrated from Cornwall to marry a Devonian. If I wasn't involved in Cornish politics, I wouldn't be involved in politics at all.'

Paul won his first seat in Cornwall – Bodmin – in February 1974, the year of two elections. With a majority of just nine, that parliamentary career lasted just eight months.

'The 18-year gap between my first arrival at Westminster and my reappearance in 1992 makes me a prize retread,' he says.

Paul became 'seriously interested' in politics on the night of the Suez invasion in 1956. He was 15 at the time.

'I don't regard it as a calling in the way others might regard their Christian calling. But I felt that in my name and the name of the British citizen, the Government was doing something morally wrong. In my limited way, I felt I wanted to be involved.'

In between parliamentary sittings he became involved at a national and local level with the housing charity Shelter.

'Being the mainstay of a desperate family with nowhere to go, and appearing at tribunals on their behalf, was a very important experience,' he says. 'Sadly, the situation is even more desperate in Devon and Cornwall now than it was 20 years ago.'

Whereas homelessness used to be confined to the urban centres of

Plymouth and Exeter, Paul reckons he now has to deal with housing problems from even the most rural parts of his constituency.

'It's a vicious circle. There's a lack of reasonable jobs. Housing is expensive – artificially exaggerated in the West Country by people retiring or buying second homes. Transport is a problem. A person might find the accommodation they can afford, but can't find the public transport to get to work. It's affecting people of all ages and walks of life.'

Paul sees his days with Shelter as instrumental in the development of his Christian faith.

'That work gave me a broader view of life, and it was then my faith went up a notch.'

Paul needs only one word to describe his faith – 'Christian'.

'I come from a long line of Anglicans,' he explains. 'My grandfather was a Cornish parson. Although there is an Anglican tradition in my family, increasingly the denomination has meant much less than the commitment to Christ. I am just as much at home in a Methodist church, which is where I worship most often, as in an Anglican one. I have friends who are Roman Catholic. I have Baptist and Anglican friends. I don't see the labels as being terribly important.

'I've always regarded The Salvation Army as an extraordinarily important vehicle for the Christian message, because it doesn't carry the burden of a history of division, divisiveness and slight elitism that many denominations have. That's extremely important in terms of today's mission to those who are not within the Church.

'The most important development within the Church over the past two decades has been the breaking down of denominational barriers.'

Is his a blinding-light breakthrough experience similar to his Biblical namesake?

'No. All my life I've been a committed and active Christian,' he says. 'Certainly a practising Christian, in the sense of not getting it right, yet!

'I'm rather jealous of, and very much respect and admire, those who have had that blinding flash of faith.

'Very often my wife, Nicky, and I feel very humble when we've met somebody like that. I also respect those whose faith has developed over the years without the emotional boost. I console myself that those whose faith is a bit more rocky can still survive.

'As a young person I greatly admired Trevor Huddleston and Donald Soper, who both said their faith was built by being tested, and that doubts were as important as convictions.'

Paul's faith gives him a 'reservoir of encouragement and support and something to fall back on.

Christians in the House

'Whatever one's daily work, it's absolutely vital to stop and switch off from the day-to-day routine and think about why we're here and what we should be doing. I value the opportunity each week in my village chapel to be still before God – cut off from pagers, phones and faxes. I also appreciate the monthly MPs' Communion service.

'But an awareness of God can come at any time, not just in church,' he says. 'There isn't a day when I draw back the curtains at home and look out at Bodmin Moor without wondering, who made this? Why are we here? It's vital to find space every day for those moments.

'Faith's important not only in the trying times, but also afterwards when you realise you've slipped back a bit. It's just as important in the tiresome times as when the adrenalin's flowing in moments of crisis.'

Can the Church and State peacefully coexist?

'No. Because if we're not concerned about our fellow men we're not following Christ's teaching. Every Christian must be concerned about the way society is run. Church leaders should challenge whoever's in power, nationally, internationally, or locally if they think things are going in the wrong direction. If they don't, they're not doing their job.'

How does Paul feel about the idea that Christians shouldn't get directly involved in politics because politics is about compromise?

'If Christians don't get involved in politics how can we ever expect society to be run on Christian lines? Politics, just like everything else, will always be as good or as bad as the people involved in it. It's a human organisation.

'We humans are agents of our Lord. If we're not prepared to give public service based on our Christian faith, then there's going to be a lot of other people without Christian commitment to take our place.'

Is politics a case of having to choose which is the lesser of two evils?

'Life is all about choices and compromises. Another way to look at it is to say that politicians have to decide between the better of two choices.'

Has Paul ever had to choose between his conscience and the party whip?

'Never the party whip, because Liberal Democrats believe every vote should be a free vote. As a party we look at each issue on its merit. Sometimes we vote with the Government, sometimes against. There are occasions when I think the majority of my constituents might have wanted me to go in one direction and, having wrestled with my conscience and my judgment, I've gone in the other. But that's what we're elected to do in Britain. We're not delegates. We're not told how we must vote. We're elected on a broad range of issues, according to what people think our judgment will be. They put their trust in us. That's a considerable and awesome responsibility.'

If Paul could change one thing about the country it would be to dispose of the confrontational attitude of modern politics – emphasised by the two-drawn-swords-length that separates Government and Opposition benches in the House of Commons.

'MPs going hammer and tongs at each other across the floor of the chamber is artificial. It doesn't reflect life outside the House. In fact the protagonists have more to agree about than disagree. Issues such as poverty, unemployment and housing shouldn't divide people but unite them.'

Paul applies the same non-sectarian approach to his politics as he does to his religion. He founded the all-party coastal group and is a member of the all-party tourism and water groups – affairs close to the heart of Cornishmen.

'I pride myself on not being just a party hack,' he says. 'I like working with members of all parties. We have more elected representatives at every level of government – MPs, MEPs and local councillors – than the Conservative party. In town halls and county halls all over the country, we're working with other parties, sometimes with a formal arrangement, sometimes issue by issue. This seems a much more mature approach than the way Parliament behaves.'

The future of the welfare state should be at the top of the agenda in the next Parliament, he reckons.

'As a student, one of my heroes was Beveridge. The safety net of social care that he devised has been holed. The electorate expects the welfare state to be protected and improved.'

The electorate also expects something of its MPs. Will the publishing of the Register of MPs' Interests as a result of the Nolan inquiry calm public disquiet regarding the behaviour of MPs?

'I doubt it. It would be wrong if there were rules which prevented MPs doing any other work, but the register doesn't give people all the information they need. I believe that being completely open and honest is critically important. There should be total disclosure of members' interests and then the electorate should be left to decide whether or not they want X to be their MP. If constituents are happy with what their MP is doing as a journalist or orchestra conductor, that's fine. But what's important is that they know what is happening.'

As well as letting his electorate know what he's doing, Paul works hard at keeping in touch with his family – his daughter lives in Brussels, his son in London.

'Sunday is our family day, which we spend together as often as possible,' he says.

'My wife is a magistrate and school governor, as well as my case work manager. When I'm in the constituency, it's a rare day when we aren't doing things together. I couldn't manage without her!'

Jim Wallace

Liberal Democrat MP for Orkney and Shetland since 1983. Born in Annan in 1954. Before becoming an MP Jim was an advocate. Leader of the Scottish Liberal Democrats since 1992. Liberal Democrat Convenor on Scottish Affairs since 1992. Liberal Democrat Spokesman on Energy, Fisheries and Maritime Transport 1994 - 1997. Jim is a member of the Church of Scotland. Married Rosemary in 1983. Has two daughters.

The interview was conducted on 13 November 1996.

NO MP travels further to work than Jim Wallace. But for people living in the country's farthest-flung constituency – oil-rich Orkney and Shetland – the leader of Scotland's Liberal Democrats is a local hero.

With the island groups separated by a 100-mile plane journey, Jim reckons it's like having two constituencies. With some 33 inhabited islands to cover he faces a constant transport battle. But then so do his fellow islanders. 'Transport links are absolutely critical for the economic and social life of the islands. Because they are islands *and* remote, transport is at the heart of all other issues,' says the softly-spoken Scot who has represented his ain folk since 1983.

The construction of North Sea oil terminals on Flotta and at Sullom Voe during the 1970s transformed the islands' economies. Was it for better or for worse?

'On the whole, the islands have benefited from the additional resources the oil industry has brought in. While the flow has passed its peak, it has lasted longer than many people predicted. There are new developments in the Atlantic Province, so it's possible there's more oil to be found.'

For him, the fact that most oil revenue goes south of the border does not stir up nationalist feelings. It's the wasted opportunity that makes him angry.

'I'm not a nationalist,' says Jim. 'I'm an internationalist. Scotland has had its fair share of oil revenue. I don't think we can expect to scoop the pool. The point is, much of the oil revenue has been frittered away. We've had a tremendous opportunity – a bonus – in terms of the revenue which North Sea oil has brought into the Treasury but the UK has precious little to show for it. We should have invested in the infrastructure. That opportunity was not taken. Now the revenue is on a downward path. By contrast, both Orkney and Shetland have quite a lot to show for local oil revenue, through investing in industries which are going to be around long after the oil has run dry.'

The internationalist would, however, like to see the establishment of a Scottish parliament.

'Scotland should have its own democratically-elected parliament within the United Kingdom to deal with our own domestic issues such as education, health, transport and a whole range of issues which are currently dealt with by the Scottish Office,' says the LibDems' Scottish Affairs spokesman.

'Government policies are being applied to Scotland at a time when the Conservatives have only one eighth of the Scottish seats. That is not democratic. A future Scottish parliament should have tax-raising powers. Tax-raising power is what links the representative to the electorate. It creates accountability. It would allow Scots to make their own decisions on local issues.

'Not that a tax-raising assembly would solve everything. But, at least, if the decision was taken not to refurbish a school in Arbroath, say, then members of a Scottish parliament would have to answer to a local electorate.

'Even if there is no Scottish parliament, I don't see why Scotland shouldn't be allowed to raise taxes in Scotland to provide for the likes of Scottish education. At the very least, Scottish people should be given a choice.'

Jim's first career choice was law. Called to the Scottish Bar in 1979, he ceased practising when he won his seat. What made him switch to the bar of the House?

'Being an MP is less secure and less remunerative,' he says. 'But, having been fascinated by politics since childhood, it's something I've always wanted to do. It's a very rewarding job, even though much of my work will never make the headlines. Being of use to people – helping them overcome a problem with red tape, tax, social security and so on – is very satisfying.'

Mission, he reckons, is too strong a word to describe his work.

'Although, if you come in as a Liberal, you're not expecting to get into government next week. Maybe *that* is a sense of mission. It's certainly an act of faith!' He smiles.

While the Liberal Democrats share similar ground with Labour over Scottish devolution, under what circumstances should Jim's party accommodate Labour on a wider scale in the event of a hung parliament?

'I'm very wary about discussing what might happen after the next election,' he says. 'Politicians do that too often, forgetting the task in hand is to fight and win the election. We will be in a position to exercise any meaningful influence in the next parliament only if we are in Westminster in sizeable numbers. Our task is to ensure that we are here in force.

'We want to ensure there's investment in education, that the health service is secure, that we tackle crime effectively. There's a raft of constitutional changes including proportional representation (or at the very least a referendum on it), a Scottish parliament, a Welsh senate. The more of us there are, the more likely these things will happen in greater measure. But we will not get drawn into speculating our terms of agreement because it may never happen.

'However, we will not do any deal with the Conservative Party. By the election, the country will have had almost 18 years of Conservative government. The country needs a change.'

On a personal level, has Jim's coming to faith been characterised by change?

'I was born into a Christian family,' he says. 'My father was a Kirk elder. The Christian faith was part and parcel of home life. I've sat through a few boring sermons, of course, but on the whole it was enjoyable. It was never thrust down my throat.'

When the time came for a number of his school friends to be confirmed, Jim resisted. The faith, he says, had been fed to him on a plate. He wanted to wait until he left home to be sure his faith was real.

'My faith came alive when I was at Cambridge,' he confirms. 'I would never claim anything like a Damascus Road conversion. Mine was more of a growing awareness of God. I couldn't put a date or time to it. I didn't join the Church until I was certain for myself that I wanted to. I wasn't going to do it just to please my parents or anyone else.

'In my final year, I went on a mission to Immingham. It was one of the most ghastly experiences of my life. Things got out of hand. It was "All those who want to give their lives to the Lord come to the front or stand up in your place". Interestingly enough, the two of us who didn't were both Church of Scotland members. All this carry-on must have gone against the Presbyterian grain!

'I learned then that you *can* have a personal faith without such public demonstrations. It wasn't a turning-point, but it was a milestone.'

A few milestones later, Jim is now an elder of St Magnus's Cathedral in Orkney and has been a Commissioner to the General Assembly of the Church of Scotland. What does his faith give him?

'My faith gives me a deep-down sense of stability,' says the man with a 5,003 majority. 'It's a bedrock, a framework, a benchmark against which you can gauge policy issues.'

Does that mean there are issues that a Christian cannot vote for?

'That's difficult. MPs have debated many issues where there have been people of profound Christian faith on both sides. I wouldn't be so judgmental as to say the other fellow has got it wrong and I've always got it right.

'Issues like abortion are not easy. I cannot take an absolutely hard line against all abortion, principally because although you might abolish the law – making it illegal – you won't abolish abortion. The least we should do is bring it within a proper medical and legal framework.

'However, I think we've gone too far. Current legislation is far too lax. An unborn child has rights and Parliament has a responsibility to the most vulnerable. What's more vulnerable than an unborn child?

'What to do when it is discovered that an unborn child is suffering from disability is particularly difficult. I don't know what I would do if I were ever in that position. I would like to think I would say, "Yes, we'll have the child and do whatever we can."

'But it's easy to say that when you aren't faced with the dilemma. When I had to vote on abortion, I took the view that I wouldn't impose my solution on other parents who at some stage would have to grapple with that dilemma for real.

'On a less emotive issue, I find it difficult to vote in favour of cutting back the overseas aid programme. It's obscene to cut back on our overseas aid. Britain may have had economic difficulties over the years but compared with the difficulties facing some countries, we're immensely rich. The fact we have retreated so much from our UN commitments is a blot on this country's reputation.'

So the Bible does not give simplistic voting instructions or policy statements?

'The ultimate policy statement in the Bible is "Love!" Love the Lord your God and love your neighbour as yourself. Trying to translate love into party policy statements isn't easy. Martin Luther King said that you can't necessarily legislate to change the heart but you can legislate to restrain the heartless. I don't always accept that. You can legislate to change the heart. For example, over the years legislation on racial discrimination has affected race relations in our society. You can't force people to change overnight, but you can put forward policies which can change the climate.'

The climate of public opinion regarding morality seems to be undergoing changes – concern about violence, the misuse of political power and so on. How does Jim read the morality debate?

'I'm quite cynical about it,' he says. 'I'm not cynical about the Dunblane parents, many of whom I have met. They have argued their case with considerable dignity. I'm not cynical about Frances Lawrence. She's made a very valuable contribution. But I am somewhat cynical about politicians jumping on the bandwagon. The public *should* challenge MPs about the way they respond to issues. MPs should not hijack public concern and turn it to their own ends.'

Does his cynicism extend to MPs who speak out about their Christian faith?

'Anyone who goes on about it too much will make people wonder whether they are genuine,' he says. 'But generally, it is to be welcomed. It is positive for Christian MPs to be identified as such. We shouldn't be hiding our lights under bushels. There is a balance, of course. Some of Christ's harshest comments were reserved for those who wore their faith on their sleeves.

'I'm not sure there are votes in just saying you're a Christian. Policy positions are far more important to the electorate. The electorate judges us on our policies rather than on our declarations of faith.'

And does the public have a right to expect those MPs, whatever their beliefs, to be above reproach?

'If you have 651 people, who by definition of wanting to be elected to Parliament are slightly odd, you're not going to have 651 saints. It's strange that the sin of lust – and I'm not defending it – attracts great media coverage and outrage, yet no one seems to get worked up about the sins of greed or envy. Yet these might be much more damaging in terms of what an MP does.

'But then I'd like to see a country that was more concerned about other people and the community. We have been too selfish for too long.

'I'd like to think we could change and instil a sense of civic responsibility. It's about loving your neighbour and about Jesus' idea of loving your enemy. That is the most radical political statement that's ever been made. Far more radical than anything I've heard from any MP in my 13 years in Westminster.'

It is developments in Brussels, however, which Jim reckons to be a major issue facing the new government.

'The European Union is one of the crowning successes of the second half of the 20th century,' he says. 'Unlike my parents' and grandparents' generations, my generation has not been involved in a European conflict.

That's an achievement for which we ought to be extremely thankful. We must constantly be refreshing it.

'I'm not in favour of a uniform Europe. Countries should maintain their distinctive identities and traditions. I don't believe we'd necessarily lose our national identity by having closer integration within Europe. But then, as a Scot, I've been part of a union with a single market and single currency for 290 years and I haven't lost my national identity!'

Nor his determination to go the extra airmile for his fellow Scots.

Steve Webb

Liberal Democrat MP for Northavon since 1997. Born in Birmingham in 1965. Before becoming an MP Steve was a Professor of Social Policy at Bath University. Liberal Democrat Social Security and Welfare Spokesman since 1987. Steve is a member of the Church of England. Married Helen in 1993. Has one son and one daughter.

The interview was conducted on 9 June 1998.

'I DIDN'T expect to be here in the first place!' is how Steve Webb views the prospect that his first term as an MP could be his last. 'But being in a small party with a small majority is a great incentive to make sure I work hard and stay in touch with my people.'

In the 1997 General Election the Northavon LibDems turned an 11,000 deficit into a 2,000 majority. It was, says Steve, a surprise and a bonus. Since then he has relished every opportunity being an MP has thrown at him. Even if he hasn't always had the public recognition he might have expected.

'Last December the House was debating the cutting of lone-parent benefit,' says the LibDem spokesman on social security and welfare. 'At the time no one else was available so I proposed the motion and led the debate attacking the cuts. It produced the biggest Labour rebellion of this Parliament. But all the media were interested in were the Labour rebels. Nobody came up to me and said, "Gosh! You were the one who did it!"'

Such frustrations, however, are outweighed by a sense of rightness at being

228

able to blend his long-held political fascination with his academic abilities.

On leaving Oxford University – First Class (Honours) in Philosophy, Politics and Economics – Steve worked as an economist with the Institute for Fiscal Studies – an independent research institute specialising in tax and benefit issues. That brought him into contact with politicians. Then came the 1992 general election.

'I was depressed at the outcome and thought it was time I did something about it,' he says. 'So I joined the LibDems. After a while I was fed up with just being on the outside commenting on political issues. I wanted to be influencing and changing things. I resigned from the Institute, moved near Bristol, where my wife had got a hospital chaplaincy post, and became Professor of Social Policy at Bath University.

'Looking back it seems obvious, but I believe God guided me to where I am now. Because of my previous experience I can talk with constituents about benefit claims, and with government ministers about economic theory, and understand what both are saying. I feel like a square peg in a square hole.'

Steve's wife Helen is an Anglican priest. Their daughter, Charlotte, is two-and-a-half and their son, Dominic, was born in May. Steve met Helen when she was a deacon in the days before the ordination of women. Steve had already been a Christian for six or seven years.

'I became a Christian at university,' he says. 'I was never very interested in Christianity before. I had a vague awareness of what it was about and was fairly sceptical. At university I joined the college chapel choir because I enjoy music. People talked to me about the Christian faith and started telling me how great it was to be a Christian. I went to a service to hear this great evangelical preacher Michael Green. But I wasn't impressed.

'However, the Christian Union didn't give up on me. I went along to a few more gatherings and then went to St Aldate's – a church very popular with students – and heard a chap called Bruce Gillingham. He quoted the verse from the Bible where Jesus says: "He who is not for me is against me." I thought, well I am not against you so I want to be for you. I signed up for what they called a beginners group and things developed from there.

'I was 18 when I was converted. My lifestyle probably didn't change much because I was never a wild child. But my values certainly did. I became more concerned about things like world poverty and valuing people on the margins of society.

'I believe the gospel because it's true, coherent and radical. It tells me how the world ought to be and I try in my own feeble way to put it into practice. To me Jesus is someone who gives me a pattern. He gives me a picture of how things could be. I actually feel hesitant about approaching him because I feel I let him down.

'Above all Jesus gives me a sense of coherence. As Del Boy might say, "You know it makes sense." Jesus makes all the pieces fit. If I look at the times when I have felt contented and fulfilled they have usually been the occasions when I am following him as I should.'

For a number of years Steve worked as a volunteer at a drop-in centre for the homeless at St Botolph's in London's East End. The stripping away of status and education was, he says, a sobering experience. For a while he considered whether he should become an ordained minister.

His dad told him it would be a waste of a good brain. Intensive discussions with clergy recruiters eventually led Steve to a not-too-dissimilar conclusion.

'In a very contented sort of way I became convinced that it wasn't actually right,' he says, 'that perhaps the particular skills I had weren't best used in that sort of way.'

As someone trying to live out Christian values in politics how easy is it for Steve to decide on the moral issues that come before the House?

'The hardest things I have had to vote on have been Iraq (would we back the Government if it took military action?), banning hand guns, outlawing fox hunting and the lowering of the age of homosexual consent.

'On most issues I'm broadly happy to go along with the party line – I wouldn't be in the party if I wasn't broadly happy with it!

'Quite honestly, unless you know a lot about the subject, which often you don't, you trust your colleagues because you assume you are coming from broadly the same place. So it is only the free vote issues that are difficult. On the age of consent issue, for example, there is a preferred party line, but I shall probably abstain or vote against.'

Why?

'To me the law can and should take account of the fact that teenagers are facing all sorts of changes in their lives. They are expected to be more and more responsible at earlier and earlier ages. There are all sorts of pressures on them. Teenagers deciding about their sexuality, particularly if they seem to be homosexual or indulge in homosexual acts, is very far reaching, more so than for heterosexuals.

'The age of consent is by any accounts a crude legal device. But keeping the age limit at 18 might give youngsters a little more breathing space to work out who and what they are.

'I am not criminalising a 17-year-old gay couple under the present law. If they choose to break the law they are criminalising themselves. It is a very tough one and it is not a very Liberal position.'

And is it Christian not to allow the same human rights of sexual expression to homosexuals as to heterosexuals?

'As a society we have a duty to protect vulnerable people. We try, for instance, to protect young children from all sexual abuse. What I'm arguing is that for the sake of an immature 16-year-old boy who needs protection, the age limit – given that it is a crude measure – should not be lowered.

'In a nutshell, what's the rush? They have got the rest of their lives to have sexual relationships if they want to. Actually, if I thought it was feasible I would vote to raise the age of heterosexual consent to 18 as well.'

[Two weeks after this interview the Commons voted in favour of lowering the age of consent. Steve abstained on the grounds that criminalising 16 and 17-year-olds would mean they would be less likely to avail themselves of medical help.]

Steve's streetwise enough to know that just because something is illegal it doesn't mean nobody's doing it – or getting found out. So what is the point in Parliament trying to legislate for people's morality?

'The question isn't, "Does it happen?"' he says. 'The question is, "Would it happen more if there weren't those rules in place?" In one sense you can't legislate for morality but the law does set boundaries and give signals to society. Unless you set some sort of boundaries anything goes. And few people want that.'

Should our lawmakers themselves be paragons of virtue?

'MPs should be consistent in public utterances and private morality. If, for example, an MP publically condemns adultery while cheating on his or her spouse, they should be called to task.

'MPs should also be examples of financial probity. Part of the prayer which commences the day's proceedings in Parliament includes the idea that the decisions we make will be for the good of the nation as a whole – that we put aside personal interest. People certainly have a right to expect that.

'Beyond that I don't think there's any evidence that saints make good laws. Indeed, a bit of understanding of human nature probably wouldn't go amiss.'

There are, he reckons, no issues on which a Christian voice should not be heard. Similarly there is no issue where there is a unique Christian position.

'My approach,' he says, 'has been not to stand up and say I am saying this because I am a Christian. That is not to disown what I believe in, but I try to bring others on board.'

Before the election, LibDems were full of being able to come to a deal with Labour in the event of a hung parliament. One of the ideas floated was that in exchange for putting Labour into power the LibDems would realise their long-cherished dream – a change in the voting system to proportional representation. As Labour came to power with a majority of 179, is the PR dream well and truly shattered?

'I never subscribed to that idea,' Steve says. 'Once the Conservative vote had collapsed enough for us to get 50 seats there was never going to be a hung parliament.

'The hope for proportional representation is still very much alive. Liberal Democrat Lord Jenkins is chairing the commission on electoral reform set up by Tony Blair, which is looking at viable alternatives to the first-past-the-post system. The Prime Minister has promised a referendum based on the commission's findings.

'The big question is which way will the Government tilt on the referendum? I think Tony Blair might back some reform, although possibly not the reform we would want, because he is someone who looks past the next election. He knows that only 18 months ago the Conservatives were a majority government and that landslide victories can be overturned.

'I think he wants to establish some sort of reforming coalition. And in that he has more in common with the LibDems than with a significant part of his own party.'

Steve reckons that welfare rather than electoral reform is one of the key issues the Government must get right.

'But they've made a complete pig's ear of it so far,' he says. 'They were wrong on lone parent benefits. They were wrong on telling people to get out of their wheelchairs and walk across their living room to see if they're entitled to disability benefits. They were wrong to try and take money off poor people in big houses who have got big council tax bills.

'Those measures have been reversed but only after huge pressure. Above all they are wrong in making niggling little cuts instead of telling us their big picture.

'The Government must also deliver on health and education,' says the former professor. 'There are too many 11-year-olds who can't read and write properly. If things don't change they too will be on benefits.

'The big issue in my constituency is green fields being used for housing developments. Houses are being built like there's no tomorrow. Masses of people are moving into the area.

'I'm not against development. Only about where it happens. Instead of ploughing up fields and building four-bedroom executive houses why is nobody investing in city-centre housing, especially for young people?'

The one thing Steve would change about the country overnight if he could would be to 'change the Church – starting with myself. I stress starting with myself because it is very easy to say everyone else in the Church is sleepy and lacking commitment.

'I'd love to see the Church being faithful to Christ's teachings – particularly on being counter-cultural; on loving the outcast; on being inclusive rather than exclusive; and on giving the impression that something earth-shattering has gone on in their lives.'

Andrew Welsh

Andrew Welsh. Scottish National Party MP for Angus since 1997. MP for South Angus, 1974 - 1979. MP for Angus East, 1987 – 1997. Born in Glasgow in 1944. Before becoming an MP Andrew was a senior lecturer in business & administration studies. Member of Angus District Council, 1984 - 1987. Provost of Angus, 1984 - 1987. Scottish National Party Vice-President since 1987. Scottish National Party Chief Whip and Trade and Industry Spokesman, 1987 – 1997. Andrew is a member of the Church of Scotland. Married Sheena in 1971. Has one daughter

The interview was conducted on 12 December 1996.

UNTIL Scotland is free, Andrew Welsh, Scottish Nationalist MP for Angus East, has unfinished business. Boosted by a massively increased personal majority and the doubling of SNP seats in the general election earlier this month, the struggle for independence continues.

But isn't all this talk of a free Scotland rather emotive?

'If you are a Scot it is a very emotive subject,' the SNP vice-president asserts. 'Ever since Scotland lost her sovereignty in 1707 there has been a desire to restore the Scottish Parliament. So far as we're concerned that parliament was never wiped out. It was merely adjourned.

'With an independent Scotland, England would have a sister nation in the wider European Community instead of a disgruntled lodger in London.

'I'm not anti-English. I'm pro-Scottish. I believe that Scotland with our culture and history has something positive to offer the world, which we cannot do at present. We are more than a region of Britain. We are an equal partner within the United Kingdom. We want to be a part of the growing, changing Europe.

'Take the BSE crisis, for example. There's no reason why Europeans shouldn't know that Scotland is in a different situation. Most of our cattle are beef herds. BSE is basically within the dairy herds. Yet our exports are being punished.

'Similarly with fishing, Europeans should be in no doubt that Europe has fishing grounds in Scottish territorial waters. Yet tiny Luxembourg, without an inch of coastline, has more say in the Common Fisheries Policy than Scotland! It's not good enough for us to be represented by the UK fishing ministry. Scotland should be there in her own right.'

Against such logic, he reckons, 'nationalism' needn't be a dirty word. 'Nationalism is a very inefficient word to describe what we are doing,' he says. 'It can mean anything from Adolf Hitler and Idi Amin at one end of the spectrum to Winston Churchill and William Tell at the other.

'We are a modern democratic political party. We believe in the peaceful use of the ballot box. Thankfully, the violence that characterises nationalist movements in some parts of the world does not apply in Scotland.

'We are inclusive not exclusive. We welcome all who are in Scotland. To us a Scot is anyone who lives and works in Scotland and loves Scotland. It doesn't matter where you came from originally. But you cannot serve two masters. Either you put Scotland first or you don't.'

Given his all-or-nothing approach, how does Andrew react to the Government's plans for Scottish devolution?

'Devolution is an unhappy half-way house,' he says. 'With devolution you will have the same old problems. The Scottish Office budget is pocket money. We send our taxes to Westminster and get pocket money back.

'With independence, all of Scotland's revenue would be available for Scotland. If we're to tackle our poor housing and unemployment and ensure that Scottish education actually deserves the title of "The Best in Europe", then we have got to have all the resources available.

'When I see wasted potential, poor housing, unemployment, I am ashamed. We could do so much more for our people. If all the North Sea oil revenue came to Scotland we would be the eighth wealthiest per-capita country in the world.

'According to Government figures, 8.8 per cent of the UK's population lives in Scotland. We produce 9.2 per cent of government revenues. We're subsidising London. That's money that would be available to the Scottish people under independence but not under devolution. Devolution will never be enough.'

Andrew's passion springs from a lifetime in politics. Or maybe it's the other way round. He joined the SNP when he was just 12, formed local branches in his teens and was a party agent at 19 – two years before he had the vote!

He became a local councillor before winning the South Angus seat in 1974. When he lost the 1979 election he returned to teaching and local government, becoming Provost of Angus until 1987 when he won his present parliamentary seat.

Andrew readily admits politics can be all-consuming. He also knows it can be transient.

'Being an MP is an ephemeral trade,' he says. 'I often ask myself, what was yesterday's crisis? A great crisis can take all your energy and effort and then, suddenly, you're on to the next.

'This is where my Christian faith comes in. It's good on a Sunday to be reminded of eternal values. It puts what was bothering you into perspective. It gives me an anchor to hold on to in a business which changes on a whim. It's a shield against what the world throws at you.'

Andrew inherited his churchgoing from his parents but he clearly holds the Christian faith for himself. 'My Christian faith has always been a part of my life,' he says. 'If there was a defining moment of inspiration it was when I was in a Salvation Army meeting in Arbroath.

'It was the 100th birthday of a Brigadier Fraser. The Webster Theatre was packed with 650 people. The Territorial Commander asked the brigadier to say a few words. She grabbed the microphone and testified about her life and her faith. As she spoke there was a presence that I had never experienced before or since.

'I hope my faith informs and educates whatever I do. It certainly gives me stability and a reference point. I particularly like what Ecclesiastes says about there being a season for everything and a time for every purpose under heaven. That reminds me to take things as they come. That there are other values, eternal values, besides the political issues of the day.

'I'd love to see a return to the fundamental gospel. To strip away the peripherals and concentrate on the essentials. The idea of the Resurrection is mind-blowing!'

Before and during the election campaign much was made of political sleaze. Does Andrew think the electorate has a right to expect their MPs to be above reproach?

'MPs are human,' he says. 'We reflect society. We are no better or no worse than society at large. But we should expect a reasonable standard of conduct, without MPs demanding and getting £1,000 a question. MPs are sent to Westminster on behalf of their constituents, not to take backhanders from anybody or to take on directorships. We should be as open and transparent as possible. We are here to do a job of work not to feather our own nests. Such conduct is unacceptable.'

According to Andrew, so is the using of religion for political gain.

'Christ belongs to no political party,' he says. 'He belongs to everybody. If an MP says he or she is a Christian I would hope they would be seen to be Christian by what they do and not just by what they say.'

So we shouldn't be looking to MPs for moral example?

'MPs are under tremendous pressure in trying to represent a cross-section of opinion on any particular issue. There's a high casualty rate in Westminster. Scottish MPs, for example, have to travel 500 to 600 miles to be there. Family life, for many, has its problems. There's a high incidence of alcoholism and divorce. These are the things they don't tell MPs in the recruiting posters. People of all faiths should be praying for their MPs.'

Abortion is easily the most difficult moral issue with which Andrew has to deal.

'I sometimes wish I held one of the extreme views – abortion on demand or no abortion at all. Once you move from either of those positions, where do you draw the line? There is no one single Christian viewpoint on this issue. But Scripture has to influence and guide. The life of Christ has to give you an indication of what should be right in coming to a conclusion.

'I have talked to many who are involved with the practicalities of abortion. Many people seem to think that once an abortion has taken place that's the end of it. But it is not. The woman has had a most traumatic experience. There should be more post-operative counselling and help. That seems to be forgotten.

'When deciding on moral issues all I can do is to talk to people, think it through and come to a conclusion. The question is what informs my decisions and those of my parliamentary colleagues.

'I would hope that they would pray about such issues. That's where being a member of the All-Party Parliamentary Christian Fellowship helps. We pray with one another, read the Bible and talk things through.'

For a biblical hero, Andrew is clear. 'There can only be one person in the Bible for me – Christ. My failure as a Christian is that I do not always live up to the standards he set. But we must always try.'

For Andrew the question of poverty is the big issue facing the new government. 'I am a Nationalist because I want to get rid of poor housing, people living in damp conditions, overcrowding, people sleeping rough. Scotland has one of the worst health records in Europe. If you get the people right – healthy, well-educated – and if the morality is correct, all else follows.'

There is also, he reckons, a moral poverty that needs to be addressed.

'The biggest test for Parliament is to restore its tattered morale and its tattered image,' he says. 'We need to focus not on the few who were wrong but on the many of every party who work hard for their constituents. There are many hard-working, conscientious MPs who never hit the headlines.'

What one thing, above all, would Andrew like to change about the nation, north or south of the border?

'I want people to discover Christ,' he says. 'He is the standard we should all aim for. The question is: What are our lives for? What is the direction of our lives? We are on this earth for a short period of time. How are we going to use that stewardship? If Christ is your teacher and your guide, life begins to make sense.

'Sadly we live in a pagan society where the majority do not go to church. The Church has difficulty in relating the gospel to modern society. If we talk about sheep and shepherds the language turns people off. Many church services turn people off.

'Yet people are wandering around looking for something to believe in. The thing is, the truth is right under their noses. As Christians we must make our faith more meaningful to society at large.'

In the past, Scotland has produced visionaries like David Livingstone and John Knox. It was the home of St Ninian and St Columba. So should we look again to Scotland for revival?

'People who share these traditional beliefs and values are still there,' says Andrew. 'Indeed, before Scottish independence can happen there must be a spiritual revival, because independence means taking responsibility, not blaming someone else.

'But the potential for revival is in all of us, if we seek the values that outlast time and fashion. Look within yourself. Don't look to Scotland.'

Rt Hon Ann Widdecombe

Conservative MP for Maidstone and The Weald since 1997. MP for Maidstone, 1987 – 1997. Born in Bath in 1947. Before becoming an MP Ann was a university adminstrator. Minister of State for Employment, 1994 – 1995. Minister of State at the Home Office 1995 – 1997. Appointed a Privy Councillor, 1997. Shadow Health Secretary since 1998. Ann is a member of the Roman Catholic Church.

The interview was conducted on 26 September 1996.

WHEN the media wanted sound-bite reaction to erring bishop Roderick Wright's revelations in a Sunday tabloid, they turned not to the Church but to Ann Widdecombe. As though the prisons minister held the key to the solution!

The Times went so far as to put her name in the same sentence as 'called for' and 'excommunication.' Was that really the way it happened?

'No, I certainly didn't call for him to be excommunicated,' she says. 'I actually said I thought his spiritual superiors should consider his position within the Catholic communion. Unfortunately, the word excommunication appeals to the press because it conjures up medieval rituals. That is not what I suggested.

'The sort of thing I had in mind was if you are a lay Catholic who has divorced and remarried you are not allowed to take Communion, although you are still considered part of the Church. But here we have somebody accepting a bishopric knowing he is in a particular state of sin.

'It appears that when Roderick Wright was morally examined by his superiors he concealed his sin. The most damaging thing wasn't that he fell into sexual temptation – that, frankly, is no worse than falling into other temptations – it was the lack of truthfulness. The sustained deceit. And that he should seek to profit from it.

'Supposing, for instance, when he was a bishop, a young priest had come to him and said, "Father, it's no good, I'm not suited for the celibate life. I've got a lover. I must leave the Church." He would have suggested a period for reflection, told the priest to abstain, and, if the priest were sure he had to leave, put church procedures into motion. He would not have said, "My son, run off with the woman and sell your story to *The News of the World!*"

'One can't just brush behaviour like that under the carpet and say it doesn't matter. Nobody has the right to judge the sin itself except his spiritual superiors. But the conduct surrounding it is wholly unbecoming of a bishop. The Church must be seen to take a very strong stand.'

A strong stand is a familiar stance for the Conservative MP for Maidstone. She votes for the reintroduction of capital punishment. She is convinced prison works. She is against abortion on demand. She is against the ordination of women.

'I'm not interested in capital punishment as a means of retribution, but I do believe it saves lives. Between the experimental abolition of the death penalty in 1965 and its actual abolition in 1970 the number of murders which would have attracted the death penalty rose by 125 per cent. However, capital punishment should be restricted to premeditated murder and the murder of police and prison officers.'

As prisons minister, Ann is responsible for Government policy on issues including the length of sentences, release of prisoners, and educational and work facilities in prisons. She wants that policy to be geared towards taking away the public's fear of crime.

What evidence does she have to say that is happening?

'Firstly, the crime rate is 10 per cent lower than it was three years ago. Secondly, the reconviction rates for people leaving prison are lower than the reconviction rates of people doing community sentences. Bearing in mind that prisoners are either more persistent or more dangerous offenders than those doing community sentences, our job must be the harder. Yet we are getting the better results. Prison works.'

As a backbencher, Ann led a campaign for changes to the Abortion Act. Now a Home Office minister – following spells as pensions minister and in the Department of Employment – she is prevented by collective responsibility from campaigning on health issues. 'However,' she says, 'I still think that, except in instances where a mother's life is in danger, the life of an unborn child must be paramount.'

The support Ann received from the Roman Catholic Church during her campaign proved critical in her own pilgrimage of faith.

Brought up and confirmed in the Church of England, Ann attended a Roman Catholic school 'at a time when there were still very sharp divisions between the two denominations. When Roman Catholics did not go into Anglican churches. When Anglicans were taught to believe that much of Roman Catholicism was idolatrous and possibly even blasphemous.'

At university she joined the Christian Union. She took part in Billy Graham crusades and then, in her 30s, became an agnostic.

'I've always described becoming an agnostic as the erosion of faith,' she says. 'Having been brought up in a consistently religious background, I'd never had the space to question my faith because nobody around me would have been sympathetic. I needed that space. Similarly, the return from agnosticism wasn't a Damascus Road conversion. It was a gradual erosion of unbelief.

'When I came back I made a very conscious decision between Rome and the Church of England. I had greatly admired the Roman Church from afar when I was looking at Christianity from the outside. I greatly admired its consistency, its refusal to compromise, its standard that if something is true that's it. It says "We don't change the rules just because they are hard to live up to." Not changing the rules to accommodate people is the Catholic Church's real strength.

'I was becoming increasingly disillusioned with the Anglican church, which had a senior bishop questioning the virgin birth and the Resurrection and saying that perhaps blasphemy was all right. And he was not rebuked!

'Although I was very attracted to Rome, I had the doctrinal baggage of my upbringing and wasn't able to face Rome at that stage. That was my big error. I rejoined the Anglican Church and speedily wished I hadn't.

'Everybody thinks I stomped out over the ordination of women. But it wasn't just that. That was the last straw. I did not immediately go to Rome. At the time I said I had a spiritual problem and had to move on. Deep down inside I probably recognised Rome as an inevitability at that point. But there was a tremendous resolution of doctrine. I didn't believe in transubstantiation. I didn't believe in the doctrine concerning the Virgin Mary. I didn't believe in purgatory. I was willing to be convinced but I wasn't prepared to pretend to be convinced.

'What Catholic converts have to do which no cradle Catholic ever has to is affirm "I believe all the Church teaches to be revealed truth". Unless you're prepared to perjure yourself, you can't say that unless you are four-square behind it. That took some time.

'In March 1993, five months after I left the Anglican Church, I went to see Cardinal Hume about what could be done for the hundreds of Anglican priests who were distressed about the ordination of women. While we were talking the conversation turned to my own situation. In a conversation, which I have always kept private and will forever keep private, the cardinal resolved my outstanding doubts.' Some conversation!

'Add to this the support I'd received from the cardinal during the pro-life campaign, and Rome, for me, is the rock of faith in a crazy world.'

Describing herself as 'a traditional Roman Catholic with evangelical sympathies', what does Ann's rediscovered faith give her?

'Peace and a great deal of confidence,' she confesses. 'Although for me God is a rock in times of trouble, people are wrong to regard him merely as a refuge in times of trouble. Our first duty is duty to God – to seek and do his will.'

At the age of 16 Ann sensed that God's will for her included being a politician. After two failed attempts – Burnley in 1979 and Plymouth, Devonport in 1983 – the university administrator graduated to the House in 1987.

'I can't remember wanting to do anything else,' she says. 'For me, public service is a vocation and a mission to change things. I get huge satisfaction from helping my constituents through seemingly insoluble problems and, at national level, from being able to influence the course of events, to shape the country's future.'

Can the MP who lists Sir Winston Churchill and Protestant martyr Bishop Hugh Latimer among her heroes (she took the name Hugh as her Roman baptismal name) readily identify with any particular biblical character?

'I love Simon Peter because he desperately wanted to get things right but occasionally blundered. He was impetuous. He was weak. He told Christ he would never deny him and then denied him three times. I can sympathise with him. Likewise Thomas. I don't suppose any of us have ever been completely without doubt. I'm encouraged by the fact that one of the apostles had his doubts.

'My favourite story from the Gospels is the account of Christ making breakfast by the lakeside. His disciples had been out in the boats. They were cold. Christ made them breakfast. It's a seemingly insignificant thing, yet very practical.'

With MPs' religious beliefs gaining increasing coverage in the secular press, should a candidate's faith or non-faith become an election issue?

'No. It should not become an election issue. Render unto Caesar that which is Caesar's and unto God that which is God's. Anything that is an election issue becomes a party political issue. No party has the monopoly of Christians.

'While it shouldn't become an election issue, I do think it is right that Christians who enter public life shouldn't hide their light under a bushel. We should be prepared to say why it is and how it is that our Christianity influences our politics.'

How does Ann's Christianity affect her politics?

'I believe very strongly in Christian capitalism. If you want to share your goods, you first have to make them. Free enterprise is about the common good, not just about individual enterprise. To have good health, education and social services you need to create wealth. The more wealth a society has, the more it can put to good use.

'The big difference between the Conservative and Labour parties is a difference of emphasis between the individual and the state. The exhortation in the Gospels to individual responsibility draws me to Conservatism. The Good Samaritan, for example, didn't ring up the social services, he got on with it and cared for the victim himself. But I don't believe the individual can do it all. Equally, the state can't do it all.'

It comes as no surprise to Ann to hear that in recent weeks her own party chairman and a Labour frontbencher have said they don't want a dirty election campaign.

'Everybody is against negative campaigning,' she says. 'But there's a difference between destructive, negative campaigning and quite rightly pointing out to the electorate what the dangers are. There is nothing at all wrong in pointing out the dangers and weaknesses of your opponents' policies. That is perfectly fair. But where campaigning gets personal, that's when it gets unacceptable.'

Is there a big issue facing the next government of whatever persuasion?

'The fundamental issue facing most Western democracies is the breakdown of law and order and of social stability. There has been a huge growth of single-parent families. We have a high incidence of family breakdown. There's indiscipline in schools and a high level of youth crime. No political party has a magic wand. But once crime is off the streets, once people feel secure, we will be a safer and more productive society. My ideal world would be where we had the stability of the Britain of the 1950s combined with the prosperity and tolerance of the Britain of today.'

Strange how those views have never made national news headlines!

David Wilshire

Conservative MP for Spelthorne since 1987. Born in Bristol in 1943. Before becoming an MP David was a businessman, teacher and political consultant. Parliamentary Private Secretary to Minister of State for Defence Procurement, 1991-1992. Parliamentary Private Secretary to Minister of State at the Home Office, 1992-1994. David is a member of the Foreign Affairs Select Committee and Secretary to the All-Party Methodist Parliamentary Group. David is a member of the Methodist Church. Married Margaret in 1967. Has one son. His daughter, Sarah, died when she was 12.

The interview was conducted on 4 April 1998.

THE day politics ceases to be fun is the day David Wilshire will quit. 'I vowed on my very first day at Westminster that if I ceased to find it fun I'd get out,' says the Conservative Member for the Middlesex constituency of Spelthorne.

'The worst sort of politician,' he continues, 'is the one who is earnest from the moment they get up to the moment they go to bed; full of self-importance and who hasn't got a sense of humour. If you take yourself too seriously you're not going to be of use to anybody.'

A teacher and businessman before he was elected to his present seat in 1987, David has served as parliamentary private secretary to the Minister for Defence Procurement and to the Minister of State at the Home Office. Today he sits on the Foreign Affairs Select Committee.

Anyone, he insists, could be an MP. 'The essence of democracy is ordinary people governed by ordinary people. Representing people is about being ordinary. To make ourselves out as being special doesn't do any service to democracy. I'm doing a job I enjoy to the best of my ability in, it so happens, a fancy-looking building. But there are millions of others who could do it just as well.

'Like any other job, being an MP is 90 per cent tedium. But I'm grateful that every so often I have the satisfaction of knowing that I have helped somebody.'

It was a clash with the unions that brought David into front-line politics. He had borrowed heavily and remortgaged his house to get a business venture off the ground. 'I realised that if people were playing games with my future it was time to stand up and be counted. I didn't set out to be an MP, I just became increasingly involved.

'I helped in the February 1974 election and was then asked if I'd start a local Conservative branch. I stood in a district council election just to give the people of the Somerset coalfield the chance to vote Conservative. I won and was hooked.'

After 11 years in local government David moved to the big league. While he is convinced he's in the right job he hesitates to describe it as a calling. 'There's no evidence of a calling as such,' he says. 'Politics is a great privilege but it's not a calling.'

Once in Parliament David did not carry the anti-union fight to the Goliaths of the TUC. To have done so, he says, would have given him a very narrow outlook. Instead he describes himself politically as an 'old-fashioned 19th-century Liberal'.

Born into a Methodist family David was educated at a Methodist school. When he became a teenager rejection set in. 'I was just fed up with it,' he says. 'Christianity didn't mean anything to me so I said "Blow it" and left. I came back to it subsequently of my own choice and I think I'm more committed as a result. I quite envy people who haven't had to do it that way.

'I'm not sure that there was any specific event that triggered my rediscovery of the faith. My beliefs don't extend to that sort of divine intervention. It seems illogical to me. After all if we are people of free will able to choose our own futures it doesn't really make sense if life is all mapped out and we don't have any choice.'

David did, however, go through what he calls the 'born-again process'.

'I don't think I've ever fully worked out what happened,' he says. 'I'd been going out with the woman who is now my wife for some time and one evening I ended up listening to somebody bang on about his faith. I found myself thinking that's a load of rubbish, then hearing a voice saying, "It's not rubbish."

'I said, "Go away, you don't exist." But he did exist!

'It would be overstating it to say that it was a Damascus Road experience. It was just something that happened. I can't deny it, I can't escape it. There is no point asking me to prove it really happened. There's no point in asking me how and why, I can just tell you it did happen. It is beyond debate. Nobody will convince me my experience of God is untrue.'

David acknowledges that some people regard being both a Tory and a Christian as a contradiction. What is his answer?

'"How dare you!" is my usual reply,' he says. 'I've even been told that by a Church of England clergyman! My Christian faith led me to conclude that I shouldn't judge your beliefs nor your sincerity. If you have worked out for yourself your relationship with Jesus then that is for you. It is deeply presumptuous of me to put a value on it. Equally I find it presumptuous of anybody to tell me whether I'm a Christian or not. Nobody is in a position to make that judgment. I find it very hurtful.

'I do find myself wondering, however, whether somebody who is prepared to make that kind of judgment has actually grasped the New Testament clearly. It is monstrous to presume to tell somebody else they are misguided, lying and insincere. There is nothing more hurtful for a Christian than to be told your faith is a mockery. It's something I've had to put up with, and I protest!'

Perhaps surprisingly for one so strident, David is reluctant to list the personal benefits of his faith. His lack of enthusiasm is not without reason, however.

'I don't want to end up sounding holier than thou,' he says. 'The last thing I've ever wanted to do is suggest that anybody should look to me as an example of anything. It's not a politician's job to preach. If I had wanted to preach I would have gone into the ministry. My instincts are not to talk religion but to leave people to work out for themselves what makes me tick.

'I am a Christian. But I'm hopeless at it. I don't do any of the things properly that I ought to do. But I can't escape the basic commitment. I can choose to ignore it but I can't eliminate something that happened. So to that extent I am stuck with it. And I'm delighted to be stuck with it.'

When it comes to voting on moral issues David does not see it as his political role to take one specific definitive 'Christian' line. He is aware of his own contradictions.

'I don't go round day-in, day-out calculating how I should handle this issue or that decision as a Christian.

'On the issue of abortion, for example, I always vote in favour but the older I get the more I become opposed to it. My wife and I have never personally had to confront the issue so anything I say is by way of theory rather than practical experience. But I still vote in favour because I believe in giving people the chance to make up their own minds. It's not for me to deny other people the opportunity to think it through for themselves.

'Politics is about compromise. That's why it conflicts with the absolutes of theology. Anyone who translates the certainties of their Christian faith into absolute certainties about politics is going to have trouble.'

So there are no definitive Christian answers to issues that come before the House?

'Oh there are! But only God knows what they are. MPs are not elected to have those kind of moral certainties. I don't feel able to insert my faith into my politics in that direct way. The best we can do is try to reason what we believe to be the Christian response and reflect on it alongside all the other pressures. I was elected primarily as a Conservative candidate, not because I am a Christian.'

Why, at the last general election, did so few of his colleagues get elected and his party lose power?

'There were so many reasons and every reason I have heard is correct in some form or other,' he says. 'After 18 years in office you become stale – you can become out of touch – you can seem arrogant. Whether or not you are sleazy the image sticks. Whether or not our policies were working they were hurting people. British people seem to like a change every so often. Basically our time was up and we were silly enough not to see it coming and take steps to prevent it happening.'

How does an MP cope with being in office one day and out of power the next?

'I'm probably the wrong person to ask,' he says, 'because I had only my seat to lose. I knew we were going to lose and told myself that providing I managed to retain my seat it would be relatively straightforward. It wasn't! It was a very levelling, humbling experience. I'm now a great deal wiser.'

David is adamant that politics and politicians should be above board. But he reckons it is not realistic for voters to expect their MPs to be above reproach.

'It is wrong to put MPs on pedestals. If you go down to the local supermarket and round up 659 people at random you will have a cross-section of society. I'm pleased we have a cross-section of society in Parliament. In any such group there is going to be the odd crook, it's the law of statistics.

'It doesn't excuse them and if you find out who they are you should get rid of them, but one shouldn't be amazed that ordinary human beings inhabit the House of Commons and we all have our failings. The difficulty with being in the public eye is not just that you have to be honest, you have to be able to prove that you are honest.'

Some people, MPs included, want to make a distinction between financial and personal improprieties. But David can't. 'By an act of financial impropriety somebody is being deprived of what is rightfully theirs, and that is wrong. The disapproval is in the fact that somebody is getting hurt. Hurt is the key. When a man leaves his wife for another woman there is once again hurt. Both types of hurt tell us a lot about the character of the man.'

Britain's relationship with her European partners is, David reckons, going to be the definitive issue for the Government.

'Europe will determine whether or not New Labour's concept of Britain as a region within a federal Europe comes about or whether we reassert our sense of separate identity.

'Everywhere else in the world countries are breaking up into smaller states. But Europe is trying to become a super state. Europe isn't just about economics. It's about personal and national identity.

'I am really rather proud and grateful that I am British rather than something else. As a nation we have made positive contributions to the world and have a distinctive way of life.

'Some people find identity through religious faith, while for others it lies in the history, traditions and culture of their country. Many people in Britain have grown up in a Christian tradition. We shouldn't give it up just like that.

'I long for the day when this country returns to its Christian roots. I'd love to see a return to a godly society through people being brought back to faith. I'd die content if I saw that happening.'

Ann Winterton

Conservative MP for Congleton since 1983. Born in Sutton Coldfield in 1941. Before becoming an MP Ann was a company executive and a full-time wife and mother assisting her MP husband, Nicholas. Chairman of the All Party Parliamentary Pro-Life Group since 1992. Ann is a member of the Church of England. Married Nicholas (MP for Macclesfield) in 1960. Has two sons, one daughter and seven grandchildren.

The interview was conducted on 24 July 1996.

ANN WINTERTON, Conservative MP for Congleton, succeeded where all others failed. As chairman of the Parliamentary All-Party Pro-Life Group she managed to get all the Northern Ireland parties to sit down together and agree. The subject for discussion was not peace, however, but how to prevent abortions becoming available in the province.

'It was a unique occasion,' she says. 'All parties supported the proposal. As a result, abortion is still illegal in Northern Ireland.'

Mother-of-three Ann 'never thought much about pro-life issues before standing for Parliament'. Shortly after she was elected in 1983 she joined the group, replacing outgoing chairman Sir Bernard Braine eight years later.

The pro-life group is one of the largest in the House of Commons. Because some of its members could face de-selection by pro-choice constituency committees, the group does not publicise the identity of those within its ranks.

'We do not seek to embarrass pro-life colleagues,' she says. 'But we do have members of all parties from both Houses. We are an independent group and represent a wide range of pro-life opinion. While organisations such as the Society for the Protection of Unborn Children provide us with expert medical opinion and technical advice, we are not a wing of any pro-life campaign group. We are free to accept or reject advice. I, personally, am not a member of SPUC or any similar pro-life organisation.'

The Parliamentary group promotes pro-life views when new legislation is going through Parliament, campaigns to get existing legislation amended and highlights the legal and moral implications of the introduction of new medical techniques.

It is currently campaigning to outlaw partial-birth abortion – an American technique whereby a baby is delivered feet first and killed before the head is delivered.

'We have successfully outlawed the use of eggs from aborted foetuses,' says Ann. 'We have raised in Private Members' Time the issue of coercive abortion and sterilisation in countries such as China, and deplore the way in which public money is being used through some overseas aid agencies to assist these practices.'

Is the group's ultimate aim to abolish all abortion in this country?

'All members of the group will have a slightly different answer. We know we can't outlaw all abortion in one go. We have to campaign issue by issue. Our recently-published *Fetal Sentience* report contains medical evidence suggesting that foetuses as young as 10 weeks old have the ability to feel pain. As people become more aware of this they'll increasingly see the unborn child as human and realise it should be treated as such.'

The climate of public opinion – the oxygen of MPs' fiery campaigns – for whole-scale change does not currently exist. Department of Health figures reveal that more than 167,000 abortions were carried out in the UK in 1994. According to some estimates, 44 per cent of women will have at least one abortion in their lifetime. Ann, however, is undaunted.

'We keep chipping away. As we keep tackling abortion issues, bit by bit public opinion will change. We will eventually get to the ideal situation where abortion is carried out only in very extreme circumstances – to save the life of a mother.'

Following events at Queen Charlotte's Hospital, west London, where surgeons performed an abortion of a healthy twin foetus because a single mother couldn't cope with the addition of two new babies, Ann wrote to the Secretary of State for Health, Stephen Dorrell, demanding an investigation into the circumstances of the case and for the report of its findings to be made public.

'Abortion on the grounds of the mental health of the mother is a catch-all,' she says.

'Money worries are not grounds enough. The intentions of the 1967 Abortion Act have been hijacked and are being implemented in a way that was never intended. It is being too widely interpreted. It has become virtually meaningless. We have abortion on demand. This cannot be a good thing. It is anti-women.

'It is both ethical and moral that we should protect human life. Millions of people agree with me that life begins at conception. Sadly, in the past 30 years we have seen an explosion in sexual activity without responsibility. I am pro-choice in that I believe people should be responsible before and after conception takes place. In this day and age there should be no need for social abortion. You can't change human nature, there will be unwanted pregnancies, but I want people to recognise their responsibilities and to have respect for each other.'

For Ann, that includes respect for the dying as well as for the unborn. She is clear she does not want to see legislation introduced that legitimises euthanasia. But does she have sympathy with those who want to help someone who is in great pain to die?

'The most important aspect, for me, is the motivation of the person caring for his or her patient. Doctors should not strive to prolong a patient's life if that patient is dying. They should seek to allow patients to die in their own time and alleviate the pain, if possible. Patients should not be pumped full of drugs to prolong life for no reason.

'The question arises, if in administering that pain relief the patient dies, is that euthanasia? I would say no, because the doctor's motivation was to relieve pain, not to kill the patient. We see this principle being applied in hospices, where people are cared for, supported and loved and where the emphasis is on trying to control and alleviate pain.

'With an ever-increasing elderly population this issue is not going to go away. Parliament cannot allow legislation which effectively says "Do away with them, it'll cost us less!" That would be completely un-Christian. If the day ever comes when we fail to look after the most vulnerable members of society – the unborn, the handicapped, the elderly – we will truly have ceased to be a Christian country.'

Speaking of which, how would Ann describe her own faith?

'Being a fairly introverted person, I find it difficult to talk about my faith,' she confesses. 'I was baptised into the Methodist Church. At the age of 11 my parents bought me a Bible but for many years I went to church only occasionally, even though my husband, Nicholas, and I had our children baptised in the Church of England. Although I may not have been an active, practising Christian all the time, Christian principles and philosophy have underpinned my whole life.

'It was later in life that I started going to church regularly with my daughter, Sarah. As I did so I became more interested in spiritual matters and my faith began to grow. Because I'd never been confirmed I wasn't allowed to take Holy Communion. The idea of going forward for a blessing felt second-best. Eventually, I took my courage in both hands and was prepared for confirmation. That was six years ago, when I was 50. So I'm a late convert.'

Would that be 'late convert' as in 'conversion experience'?

'No. There was not a blinding moment when I decided I must turn to God. Rather there was a slow, growing process. Mine was a growing awareness of God rather than a sudden discovery of him.'

While, like many others, she may struggle to put her spiritual experiences into words, Ann unhesitatingly knows what her faith gives her.

'Strength. Conviction–' she rattles off with the air of a stumbling *Mastermind* contestant who's suddenly found herself with an easy question. 'Strength to face life and its daily demands. Conviction in trying to follow a path that you know in your heart of hearts is right. My faith has also focused my political interests in pro-life issues and helps me do that work.'

Surprisingly, for one who joined a select sisterhood – women MPs – at a time when there was a woman prime minister, Ann does not believe women should be priests.

'It's not a case of women not being good enough,' she asserts. 'Of course women are good enough and capable enough. But Jesus was a radical. Everything he did was calculated, purposeful. He chose men as his disciples and entrusted those male disciples to carry his word. He chose a special role for women. We see that in the likes of Mary, his mother, and Mary Magdalene. Women have a very special role, the most important being that of motherhood.'

The bringing up of her own children (two sons, one daughter) was something Ann found 'immensely satisfying'. It was not until they were more independent that she started to consider a Parliamentary career. Her husband, Nicholas, had been MP for Macclesfield since 1971. Due to boundary changes the new seat of Congleton was created which included a third of the old Macclesfield constituency.

'I would never have tried to go into Parliament when my children were young,' she says. 'I believe the time you give to your children is very valuable in giving them stability and a sense of identity. The most valuable thing parents can give to their children is time.

'When Nicholas entered Westminster, I supported his career – looking after things in the constituency when he was in London. That gave me a flavour of what people require from their MP. Once the children needed me less, I realised I had to find something else in life to make a contribution to society.

'I applied to be a magistrate but was turned down. I was considering standing for county council elections when, by a fluke, the new Congleton seat was available. When I was approached, my first reaction was to say no. I didn't have much personal confidence. I was frightened. I didn't think I had the experience. I didn't think I was articulate enough. We discussed it as a family and, given that this would mean representing the area in which we lived, I decided I should try.'

Six months after agreeing to stand, Ann joined her husband on the back benches. The Conservative Party's first Commons husband-and-wife pairing. Today there are 61 woman MPs. Does Ann think there should be more?

'I want to see more women in public life,' she says. 'But positive discrimination in favour of women is quite unnecessary in this day and age. It's an insult to women and their capabilities. It's the quality of the individual that's important, not whether they are male or female.

'Some women are put off going into Parliament because it is not a nine-to-five existence. You have to operate in your constituency and in Westminster. If your husband has a separate career it may not be possible for him to uproot and live in your constituency. Therefore you have to operate in three places. You cannot easily plan to have weekends or evenings free. There are domestic as well as political crises to handle. If you have young children, child care has to be organised. You don't get to see your children very often.

'Traditionally, selection committees of all parties have recognised these difficulties. They realise that if you select a man and he's got a nice wife and two-point-four children, then not only are they going to get the man as their MP, but they'll also get the wife as an unpaid assistant!'

Which is, after all, what the old Macclesfield constituency had in Ann Winterton before she stopped being a housewife and became a House wife.

Nicholas Winterton

Conservative MP for Macclesfield since 1971. Born in Leamington Spa in 1938. Before becoming an MP Nicholas was a sales manager. Nicholas is a member of the Church of England. Married Ann (MP for Congleton) in 1960. Has two sons, one daughter and seven grandchildren.

The interview was conducted on 31 October 1996.

FOR millions of viewers, Anne and Nick were daytime TV's top sofa team. On Westminster's back benches, however, Ann and Nick are the component parts of Team Winterton. While Ann has represented Congleton since 1983, her husband Nicholas is now in his 26th year as the Conservative Honourable Member for Macclesfield.

It was while gardening one day that Nicholas found his political career taking root.

'I was mowing the lawn when somebody called to say they were forming a local Conservative Association and would we come to the inaugural meeting,' he recalls. 'Ann and I had been married for about three years and were fairly new to the village. I was concerned about Britain's image in the world – the way in which the country was being run. I expressed my views at this meeting and, as a result of opening my mouth, was elected chairman of the new branch. This automatically put me on the executive of the whole Conservative Association.'

Mowing the lawn, however, was no short-cut to Westminster. It took eight years of local politics, including six as a county councillor while he ran a construction machinery company, and two failed election attempts, before Nicholas took his seat in 1971.

Although he has wide Parliamentary experience (he has chaired legislative committees for 10 years and is chairman of the influential All Party Media Group), Nicholas has never been promoted. Why not?

'Because God gave me a mouth and I have used it,' he says. 'That hasn't always made me very popular with the establishment. People are my motivation. I am there to promote my constituency – to help the people I represent.

'If you see an injustice you want to get it put right, even if you have to overcome a great deal of opposition from the establishment. Departments of State and local government don't like an MP going to the press criticising them. Therefore you can use your position to get better service, attention or justice for somebody you believe is not being fairly treated.

'I have more black marks to my name than fingers and toes. Clearly those black marks follow from one leader to another. "The establishment" isn't just the leader of the moment. It is there from one leader to the next.

'When I came into politics I wanted to restore people's trust and respect for the role of MPs and for the institution of Parliament. I've tried to match my actions to my voice. That has from time to time put me at loggerheads with my party. It has been done sincerely and not with the intention of upsetting my party. But I do think you should have a loyalty to your constituents.'

As if to prove the point, shortly after this interview Nicholas threatened to withdraw his support for the Budget and other key votes unless the Government reversed its decision to axe two agreed road improvement schemes in his Cheshire constituency. In the light of his 'strong and persuasive representations', as the roads minister's letter to Nicholas put it, the Poynton Bypass scheme was saved.

But how long will a party put up with somebody who is seen as a maverick?

'It's sad there aren't more MPs in all parties who are prepared to take an independent stand in accordance with their instinct, experience and knowledge,' he says. 'If they did, it might make government more difficult but it would create better government.

'When I entered Parliament the vast majority of MPs came to serve – to do the job for the sheer challenge, joy and satisfaction. They didn't come believing they should be ministers or Prime Minister. Today, however, Parliament is dominated by career politicians. That's a pity.'

Winterton is not afraid to speak out on moral issues. He fully supports his wife, who is chair of the All Party Parliamentary Pro-Life Group.

'You can't mess about with the sanctity of life,' he says. 'Life starts at the moment of conception.

'I am totally opposed to abortion on demand. On those occasions when the mother's life might be in danger if a pregnancy went full-term I would say the mother's life must be considered more important than the child's and that a termination should go ahead. But that would be the exception rather than the rule.

'Some people wonder how I can be opposed to abortion on demand yet be in favour of capital punishment. I don't like the idea of taking life in any situation. But I support capital punishment because as a deterrent it can save life.

'I am strongly opposed to euthanasia. It is open to abuse by unscrupulous relatives. It would destroy people's respect for the medical profession. Life is precious and while doctors have a duty to minimise discomfort and pain where people are terminally ill – and I don't think they should keep people alive abnormally – I do believe that to bring about death in any way prematurely is wrong, and unethical and unchristian. Allowing people to die with dignity is one thing, putting them down as you would a dog is quite another.'

Should moral issues become part of party politics?

'No, they should remain separate. Sadly, there is a very strong driving force within the Labour Party for women to be pro-choice – that if a woman wants an abortion she should be able to have one. I believe Tony Blair is not in favour of abortion on demand. But he is heading a party that is. At times he has felt obliged to vote according to the majority view within his own party on abortion. Had it truly been a free vote I suspect he would have voted against. But these issues don't divide tidily and comfortably along party political lines.'

As a child, Nicholas worshipped in the Church of England. Life at school – Rugby School – was also 'very Christian orientated' with daily chapel to attend and Scripture prep to attend to.

'That became very much part of my life and established a firm trusting belief in the Bible,' he says. 'I'm a traditionalist. I learnt the Lord's Prayer, the Nicene Creed etc, and I don't want to change those words which to me are romantic and moving.

'I don't like the way the Church is moving away from biblical example and leadership. I believe very strongly in basic biblical teaching. The Bible is life. I know that sounds bland but it is. You can read the Bible and get advice, experience, support and encouragement from it.'

Was there anything in particular which persuaded him towards Christianity?

'I think I was persuaded by the fact that the Bible means something,' he says. 'My faith provides me with a strong element of certainty. I think one of the great problems of life is instability, which occurs because there is increasing uncertainty and doubt. Even the Church has contributed to that doubt by seeding doubt about some of the fundamentals in the Bible and in the Prayer Book. That is sad.

'My Christian faith gives me strength, support and encouragement for some of the difficult things I have to do. Some of the things Jesus Christ himself did were not easy. His example encourages me. Doing things that people don't necessarily want you to do is not necessarily wrong.'

'–like speaking out' is left unsaid.

Nicholas is strongly in favour of the current morality debate.

'I want a move back to discipline, morality, marriage, the family, and personal responsibility. Progress – economic and moral – can be made only from a position of stability. People are concerned with the way morality has deteriorated. There has been, for example, an increasing number of single mothers. At one time society frowned on such behaviour, I think quite rightly, because marriage was sent and meant for procreation and the bringing into the world of children.'

While accepting that no one party holds the monopoly on morality, Nicholas believes MPs should set a good example.

'The Prime Minister's back-to-basics speech was a genuine attempt to address these things,' he says. 'But the behaviour of some of his ministers made a mockery of what he had said. It wasn't that he was wrong to make that speech. It was their behaviour that made him look stupid.'

Corporately, the Government, he reckons, must also takes some blame. 'My Government has sought to improve the quality of life for everybody in Britain,' he says. 'But some policies have led to an increase in materialism. (Maybe that would have happened under any other party anyway.) Community service and voluntary work has deteriorated as a result. That's a great pity. We're in a much more materialistic world. While the material quality of some people's lives has improved, the social and moral quality of life has not. Materialism has taken far too great a hold.'

Might some people be surprised to hear a 'traditionalist' Conservative MP saying that?

'I don't think so,' he says. 'I don't discourage wealth creation. Far from it. But when people are fortunate enough to make lots of money, they should put some of the benefits of that back into the community. That's not happening as it used to. Business is now run by accountants who are only interested in the bottom line and short-termism. Materialism is too powerful. Everything is driven by the bottom line. Surely there is more to life than money!'

Speaking of ministers who let the back-to-basics campaign down, does the public have a right to expect MPs to be above reproach?

'People should be able to look to Parliament as an example, and respect not only the institution of Parliament but also the position of MPs,' he says. 'Of course, there are times when it doesn't and when human weakness dominates. However, Parliament is merely a representation of the general public. If there are evil people out there, you will probably find one or two in Parliament. If there are philanderers in the country you will find one or two in Parliament. You will find homosexuals in Parliament. You will find lesbians in Parliament. You will, sadly, find a very limited number of people who are less than honest because inevitably Parliament has to, and does, reflect the population of the country as a whole.

'But I believe very fervently that MPs should set an example. When an MP betrays people's trust, that MP is letting down Parliament. Those who come to Parliament should accept that it is an important office. An office that can be used for good and not an office which should be abused. Abusing one's position undermines public confidence in the institution of Parliament. People look to MPs to be honourable.

'If you say something to somebody or a group in your constituency – 'I agree with you on this, I think this is wrong, it should be put right' – then when the matter is debated in Parliament and a vote takes place you must match your vote to your word. Practise what you preach. Quite simply, if you want to do things that are less than ethical, don't do the job!'

How does Nicholas react when he hears of a colleague's 'human weakness' through the newspapers?

'In some cases there's a measure of understanding,' he confesses. 'A person can make a mistake. If they accept they have made a mistake and make a proper apology then they can live it down and be forgiven. MPs are happy to forgive if they feel someone has genuinely apologised. Unfortunately, errant MPs are, on some occasions, not prepared to apologise for what they've done. That is a mistake.'

The one thing Nicholas would change about the country if he could would be to restore the role of the family.

'If we did that we would have a happier and healthier country. The breakdown of society stems from the disintegration of the family. The Church should stress the importance of marriage and the family. And the state should support by positively discriminating in favour of families through taxation.'

Maybe, for once, Nicholas's outspokenness will not get him into trouble. In the House. Or at home. But, rest assured, Ann will be the first to tell him if it does.

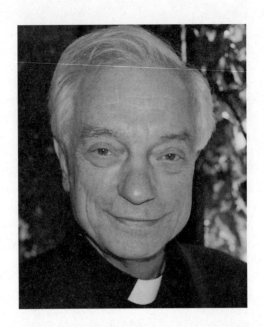

Rev Canon Donald Gray

Chaplain to the Speaker, House of Commons, 1987 - 1998. Chaplain to HM The Queen since 1982. Born in Manchester in 1930. Before ordination Donald was a laboratory assistant. Curate, Leigh Parish Church, 1956 - 1960. Vicar, St Peter's, Westleigh, 1960 - 1967. Vicar, All Saints', Elton Bury, 1967 - 1974. Rector of Liverpool, 1974 - 1987. Canon of Westminster and Rector of St Margaret's, Westminster Abbey 1987 - 1998. Appointed Commander of the British Empire, 1998. Married Joyce in 1955. Has one son and two daughters.

The interview was conducted on 4 August 1998.

ON the walls of Donald Gray's book-lined study in the cloisters of Westminster Abbey hangs, alongside the Howatch novels and Hansards, a photograph of his Parliamentary baptism. The inscription reads, 'I hope this will be the first of many Parliaments for you and that your service as Chaplain to the Speaker and to the House will always be fruitful and happy.' It is dated 25 June 1987. It is signed 'Jack' – Speaker Bernard Weatherill.

On 21 October 1998 Canon Dr Donald Gray, CBE opens the proceedings of the Commons with prayer for the last time. After 42 years in the Anglican ministry Donald enters retirement and is off to Lincolnshire with wife, Joyce, to write a few books. As one who has seen close-up the rise and fall of MPs, ministers and Prime Ministers, will he be indulging in a bless-and-tell expose?

'That would certainly be a good title for it,' he laughs, with characteristic chuckle. '*Bless and Tell*. My, my. No, a number of people have suggested that I ought to write my memoirs. But if it is to be at all interesting it would have to be indiscreet and that is the last thing I want to be. I couldn't do that.

'I hadn't been here long when I realised that I could make an awful lot of money from the things I had heard from MPs. But that of course would have been the end of the job. The job depends on integrity and discretion.'

And not only *his* job.

'Nowadays it seems that to be told something in confidence means you don't tell more than two people. That is a great fault of the age. Part of Christian ministry is to be able to share somebody else's troubles – their deepest thoughts. If I feel I cannot trust you to keep what I tell you to yourself then a valuable ministry is lost. That's sad because more people would be helped if they knew that in the Christian context they could bare their souls to somebody else in complete confidence.

'Never ever telling another soul what you've heard isn't easy but it's part of the pastoral role of a priest and it's something Christians should understand.

This chaplaincy (and any chaplaincy) is based on absolute trust. When you first arrive people are weighing you up. Can I trust him? Is he professional enough to keep his mouth shut?'

One of the books that is on Donald's agenda does, however, stem from his time as Speaker's Chaplain – *How to Conduct a Memorial Service*.

'I have composed and conducted over 150 memorial services since I've been at Westminster,' he says, 'so I probably know most of the mistakes!'

As well as conducting memorial services for MPs and members of staff, the Speaker's Chaplain is available for conducting Members' weddings (Donald officiated at William and Ffion Hague's in the House's subterranean St Mary Undercroft,) and baptisms for their children and grandchildren. As Rector of St Margaret's – the MPs' church opposite the House, next door to the Abbey – Donald has also conducted communion services for MPs both in St Margaret's and in St Mary Undercroft.

The most high-profile face of the Speaker's Chaplain is in opening each day's Parliamentary proceedings in prayer. He is one of only two non-Members who are in the Chamber at the time. By the time the TV cameras are switched on and the press and public galleries fill up the Chaplain is long gone. More privately he makes himself known and available to all who work in the House.

Christians in the House

Does Donald think Christianity has become higher profile during his 11 years in office.

'It's true to say that you don't need to keep quiet about it any more. There is no shame or embarrassment in betraying the fact that you are a Christian. There are those (I think quite rightly) who would be suspicious of people using their Christianity for political purposes. That's one of the great things of having a Christian witness across the parties. Christian Socialists and Christian Conservatives have Christianity in common yet are interpreting their Christianity in different ways politically. That is very healthy.'

Over the years there have been occasional attempts in Westminster to engender support for a Christian political party. Is that a starter in Donald's book?

'No. Christianity is not a social or political programme. Christianity does need to be worked in terms of politics. Jesus doesn't provide us with the political programmes – the manifesto – but he does give us the principles.

'Whatever my personal political points of view might be I'm convinced they're rooted in Christianity,' he says with another of those Jimmy Savile-reminiscent chuckle. 'I hope every politician would be able to do the same.'

And are some MPs misusing the label of 'Christian'?

'I wouldn't accuse anybody of doing that,' he says. 'But there is always the danger (and I think most Christians would acknowledge this) that an individual could go over the top and suggest that there is only one way to be Christian. And I don't believe that's right.'

Donald's own Christian heritage is from the Catholic side of the Anglican Church. Ordained in 1956 he had parish appointments in Leigh, Westleigh, Bury and Liverpool before moving to Westminster. In 1980 he started taking his week's turn as one of 36 Chaplains to Her Majesty The Queen. A job he is pleased to be continuing in retirement.

'It is only one week each because the Court is not in session for parts of the year. We preach on our duty Sunday at St James's Palace and are technically "in waiting" for the rest of the week.'

And does Her Majesty avail herself of her Chaplains' spiritual counsel?

'The Queen is very much a Christian and a church woman,' says the Commander of the British Empire, 'I am sure she takes advantage of the services of the clergy as the need arises.'

As do MPs. What sort of stresses are our politicians under?

'The worst thing for many of them is that they are separated from their families, either because of financial restraint or their children's education. The sheer responsibility of having to decide various issues – how are they going to vote, are they going to toe the party line, how far can they influence things? – is also stressful. MPs want to do their job properly. To do that they need to be structured people and this place is often chaotic!'

This Speaker's Chaplain has no time for the argument that says politics is no place for Christianity.

'The whole of Jerusalem didn't come to a stop when Jesus was crucified. The Roman soldiers would have pushed through the crowds of shoppers and traders to get Jesus to the place of execution. People, went about their daily business. Many of them would not have taken a blind bit of notice. That's where Christians should be. In the market place. In public view. Not apologising. Let people see what Christians are about and let them take it or leave it.'

Should we then be looking to MPs to provide the country with a moral lead? Should they be setting us a good example?

'I would hope that all MPs would be paragons of virtue and examples to us all, says Donald. 'But I wouldn't say a politician is necessarily a person to look up to. That is a misunderstanding of what a politician is. A politician is a person who works in politics. They might or might not be someone to admire and emulate. Politicians are empowered by God to work in politics just as doctors are in medicine or teachers in teaching. Some doctors and teachers might be people you want to look up to but not all of them. It is wrong, therefore, to give to MPs this high profile, this high expectation.

'If the democratic system is working properly and MPs are truly representative of the people then there's going to have to be a fair proportion of rogues. Rogues or not they are still God's agents because 2,000 years ago humanity assumed a new dignity by the incarnation of our Lord. That act showed how important humanity is. How you order the world and the affairs of people, therefore, is an important ministry. And politicians are very much part of that. Consequently MPs are, whether they acknowledge it or not, ministers of God. That's why I always rate politicians.

'To me being an MP is a high vocation – part of God's purpose. One of my tasks as Chaplain has been to affirm what politicians are doing. It's not just any old world they are dealing with. They are dealing with God's world in the same human flesh that the Lord Jesus shared.'

Which must come as a surprise to some of the chosen 659?

'Possibly but that's been part of my teaching role here – to help people see their responsibilities under God. Those who have ears to hear have heard.'

So even those married MPs who run off with secretaries or who are involved in sleaze are God's instruments?

"Yes, they are! There is a wonderful phrase that says that the effectiveness of the sacrament does not depend upon the worthiness of the minister. That God works just the same however much we might ourselves misuse our opportunities. We have the gift, but it is breakable pottery.'

261

And under what circumstances should a tarnished instrument resign?

'Talking hypothetically and bearing in mind human fallibility, if a public figure is guilty of a criminal offence I think they should resign. But then there is no gradation of sin. There are no big sins and little sins. Sin is sin. That's why the decision to resign is always political and never based on morality.'

The fact that many MPs regard abortion as the most difficult moral issue they are called to decide upon comes as no surprise to Donald.

'It is a very difficult issue. I am not an absolutionist but I am also very moved by some of the things I hear. Certainly the idea that abortion should be the ultimate form of contraception is quite wrong.

'There is no definitive Christian view on this. Some say abortion under any circumstance is wrong. Others say that the foetus does not become a human person until a certain stage. And others who that abortion is allowable if the mother's life is in danger. I don't think there is any Christian principle which covers all these circumstances. There are those who say "thou shalt not kill", but that is to misread the command, " thou shalt do no murder" and murder, as we know, is a defined legal term. But there is not a Christian in the House who doesn't come to a decision on matters like this without a lot of careful thought and prayer.'

It is, he says, the people – his people – that Donald will miss most after 11 'happy and fruitful' years as the Speaker's Chaplain.

'I can live without pointing them out on the TV and saying "I know him!", he says. 'But so many of those dedicated professionals – MPs and staff – have become my friends.'

And that probably tells us more about the affections of MPs than a bless-and-tell story ever would.

Appendix

THE CHURCH AND WESTMINSTER

There has been a Palace of Westminster since pre-Conquest times. Edward the Confessor (1043-1066) built a chapel within the palace grounds and King Stephen (1135-1154) is believed to have commissioned a chapel to St Stephen.

In 1292 during the reign of Edward I work began on a newly designed St Stephen's chapel. The lower floor of the split-level church was dedicated to St Mary.

The Commons took over the Collegiate Church of St Stephen in 1547 and for many years the site of the former church was the chamber of the House of Commons. The Speaker's chair was positioned at the bottom of the altar steps.

Following the disastrous fire of 1834, the Palace was redesigned by Charles Barry. In the new building the Commons chamber was moved from its ancient site, but the church-like shape was consciously retained. The custom of bowing to the chair when MPs enter or leave the chamber is not too dissimilar to the respect shown by many Christians to an altar in a church. The facing benches have a choir stall feel about them and follow the seating arrangements for worship in the old church.

Beneath the chamber St Mary Undercroft (St Stephen's old Lady Chapel) still functions as a place of worship. It is here MPs receive communion. It is here they and their dependents are married, their children are baptised and their memorial services are held under the careful administrations of the Speaker's Chaplain.

SPEAKER'S CHAPLAIN

The first Chaplain was appointed by the Speaker in 1660. The Chaplain has three main duties: the conducting of worship and special ceremonies, the pastoral care of all who work in the House and the saying of prayers to commence the day's parliamentary session. Historically the Chaplain's efforts were directed solely towards MPs. In recent years the role has expanded to include all employees, regardless of party or denominational affiliation. The present 'parish' consists of more than 2,000 souls.

DAILY PRAYER

It is something of a standing joke in Parliament that at the commencement of each day's business the Chaplain enters the chamber with the Speaker, looks at the members and prays for the country. Given that the practice has continued for over 400 years – and that as much time is spent in prayer as in Prime Minister's Question Time – it is likely that members appreciate such supplications.

Prayers start with the Chaplain reading Psalm 67. He then greets members with 'The Lord be with you', to which they reply 'And also with you'. On the Chaplain's 'Let us pray' members turn to face their seat. This is not so much a turning of one's back on the members opposite but a throw-back to the days when sword-bearing members knelt on the benches to pray.

The response 'Lord, have mercy', 'Christ, have mercy','Lord, have mercy' is followed by the Lord's Prayer, prayers for the Sovereign and for the Royal Family. There then follows this prayer for the day's business:

'Almighty God, by whom alone Kings reign, and Princes decree justice; and from whom alone cometh all counsel, wisdom, and understanding; We thine unworthy servants, here gathered together in thy Name, do most humbly beseech thee to send down thy Heavenly Wisdom from above, to direct and guide us in all our consultations: And grant that, we having thy fear always before our eyes, and laying aside all private interests, prejudices, and partial affections, the result of all our counsels may be to the glory of thy blessed Name, the maintenance of true Religion and Justice, the safety, honour and happiness of the Queen, the public wealth, peace, and tranquillity of the Realm, and the uniting and knitting together of the hearts of all persons and estates within the same, in true Christian Love and Charity one towards another, through Jesus Christ our Lord And Saviour. Amen.'

The service concludes with the Chaplain and MPs uniting in the Grace (2 Corinthians 13:14).

Prayers is the only part of regular parliamentary life that is not open to televisual scrutiny. Indeed the Chaplain and the Serjeant at Arms are the only non-members allowed in the Chamber at this time. Clerks, journalists and the general public are admitted only after prayers. The Grace said, the Chaplain leaves before the first debate.

The biggest regular turnout for prayers is on Budget Day. Without being judgmental it is unlikely that this is so MPs can make last-minute supplication to the Almighty to intervene on proposed duty increases. The more prosaic truth is that by completing and posting a prayer attendance card (and attending prayers) members can reserve a place on the benches for the day's proceedings in what traditionally is a full house.

GROUPINGS

There are a number of semi-formal Christian groups in the House of Commons. Some attend a monthly early-morning communion service in nearby St Margaret's. Some belong to pan-denominational groups such as the Christian Socialist Movement, the Conservative Christian Fellowship or the Parliamentary Christian Fellowship. Less formally people gather in prayer and discussion groups. One such comprises MPs of at least four political parties. To those who attend, such gatherings are a lifeline in keeping their Christian experience alive and informed.

Conclusion

It was never intended for the *War Cry* series to take the form of a survey. It is, however, perhaps inevitable that after many hours spent on and off the record with MPs some general conclusions can be drawn on the subject of Christian MPs in particular and all MPs in general.

TYPICAL
Perhaps the most important is that there is no such thing as a typical MP!

There is no one definitive route to Westminster. Some, like Peter Luff, were initially back-room assistants to serving MPs. Others, like Tony Colman, are in Parliament having had very successful business careers. Many have arrived after years in local government. While others, like Michael Mates and Caroline Spelman, were selected by their party just weeks before an election. Some even are 'retreads' – MPs who were defeated only to be re-elected at a later date.

There are no educational requirements for becoming an MP. Thirty-six of the series interviewees (76%) hold at least one degree. Seventeen (36%) went to either Oxford or Cambridge. But approximately a quarter of the contributors did not have a university education.

MOTIVE
Why should anyone want to be an MP? Collectively MPs are often perceived by the electorate as self-seeking and/or hypocritical, and rated for trustworthiness alongside second-hand car salesmen and journalists.

For their part MPs are quick to point out that trudging through the rain canvassing only to be met on the doorstep with a cynical, 'You lot are only in it for yourselves!' has a certain irony.

Regardless of party, MPs express their reasons for seeking office in terms such as 'wanting to do something for society', 'wanting to be of public service,' or, rather idealistically of 'wanting to change the world'.

While wanting to improve society is not a monopoly held by men and women of faith, all Christians recognise the necessity for them to discover God's will for their lives and the possibility of God being able to guide them into the right career.

The question of whether being an MP is part of God's vocation for a person draws either an enthusiastic yes or a reluctance from not wanting to appear presumptuous. It is not a notion that gets dismissed out of hand.

Most, in common with all Christians, acknowledge that God's will is most clearly recognised in hindsight and that it is often difficult to discern between God's will and personal ambition.

The answer as to where this yearning for public service originates depends on who you ask. Some have wanted to be MPs since they were children. For others it's often a particular incident that fired them into action, sometimes following a period of growing frustration with the political status quo. Andrew Rowe, for instance, wrote to Conservative Central Office complaining about the way the party fought the 1974 elections. Within weeks he was director of community affairs in Central Office. For Joan Humble it was the arrival of a National Front leaflet through her letter box that spurred her to put an election poster in her window. The nearest available was a Labour poster borrowed from a neighbour. For a 15-year-old Paul Tyler it was what he saw as the Government's inept handling of the Suez Crisis. For social worker Tessa Jowell it was feeling inadequate at not being able to radically change her clients lives. For Ulster MPs Peter Robinson and the Rev Martin Smyth it was the terrorist murder of close personal friends that made them enter what for all Ulster MPs has been a life-threatening career.

CONVICTIONS

Christian MPs, like Christians in any other job, are not lily-livered door mats. They have convictions, they have strong opinions and they are prepared to fight for them. In his interview in *The War Cry*, for instance, David Alton (now Lord Alton of Liverpool) maintained that if MPs were not in Westminster with a mission, they had no right being there.

Christian MPs do not want to appear pious or holier-than-thou. When they speak from Christian conviction they do so with a respect for the feelings and viewpoints of others. They are quick to point out that Christian insights should not be forced on others. They do not claim a monopoly of the truth. They are unanimous in denouncing the notion of using one's faith – Christian or otherwise – to win friends, arguments or votes.

They do not treat the Bible as not a political textbook, manifesto or mandate. Typically a Christian MP regards the Bible as providing principles of personal and communal behaviour which they must then interpret into today's society. This provides intellectual challenge and, on occasions, not a little heart-searching.

For them all, God is bigger than politics.

Generally there is more that unites Christians of opposite parties than divides them.

When it comes to political issues Christian MPs of opposing parties agree in principle on many issues. They agree, for example, on the evils of mass unemployment. Where they differ is over the solution to the problems. So for somebody like Stephen Timms the answer is in a subsided job-creation scheme funded by a windfall tax on privatised utilities – the New Deal. For Conservative MPs the solution is in letting free-market forces rule, creating wealth (and jobs) in the process. Neither the free-marketeer nor the interventionist likes the idea of an idle work force. It is in nobody's interest. Where they argue is over the merits of possible solutions, which is, of course, the very essence of politics and is not restricted to those who are informed by a Christian faith.

ONE CHRISTIAN PARTY?

As Christians – there is no all-inclusive umbrella group – Christian MPs do not purport to have the monopoly on the truth. Insight and political nous are not the sole prerogative of Christian MPs. Most interviewees agree that an exclusively Christian party would be a disaster. Better, they say, to stay as they are – true to their Christian convictions and their political perspectives.

If Christian MPs collectively are no more politically qualified because of their faith, so too MPs – as the then Conservative Party Chairman, Brian Mawhinney, said in his interview – cannot claim God to be exclusively on their side.

In the run-up to the 1997 General Election *The War Cry* received much correspondence on the lines of: 'How can so-and-so call himself a Christian, he's a Tory!' Hopefully the mere fact that *Christians in the House* features MPs from eight parliamentary parties will help to address such uniformed opinion.

One of the results of the series has been to realise not only how Christians can belong to different democratic parties but also the similarities of Christian experience and expression that exists among members of various parties.

Formally 10 denominations are represented in this book. More personally 47 individuals give their insights into the impact of personal faith on the public pursuance of politics.

There is also unanimous agreement – a rare thing in politics – that claiming God to be on your side on a debate or single issue is dangerous and erroneous. There are dangers also, they say, in reading partisan perspectives into the words of Jesus. Again, they agree, this is where spiritual and temporal cannot mix.

ONE CHRISTIAN VOICE?

What happens when those spiritual and temporal worlds collide? Do all Christian MPs come to the same political conclusions on the basis of shared Christian belief? No, they don't.

Just as MPs unanimously dismiss the idea of a Christian party so they agree that there is no one definitive Christian voice on any one subject. Again their inability to be united in the specifics of any one area reflects the diversity of opinion among Christians at large. It is perfectly possible, reasonable even, that people who share a common faith, even a common political allegiance, can disagree about how to interpret faith into politics.

Interviewees acknowledge the impossibility of fitting eternal values into the limited aspirations of earthly politics (and politicians). They recognise their limitations, fallibilities, motives and ambitions. They know they are not perfect – no matter how often spin doctors tell them otherwise.

They admit that even though televisual appearances and interview sound bites make them appear confident and all-knowing, they do *not* have all the answers.

MORAL ISSUES

Perhaps the area in which MPs feel their most vulnerable in terms of not having black-and-white sound-bite answers is in dealing with moral issues. Although most pieces of legislation have moral consequences – by virtue of them dealing with people's behaviour – the term 'moral issues' or 'conscience issues' is reserved for matters such as abortion, capital punishment, euthanasia and age of consent. Traditionally there are no whips in these debates and members vote according to personal conscience.

It is debatable, however, whether freedom from having to toe the party line makes decision-making easier.

One recurring theme in the interviews was the limitations in trying to legislate for public morality. While MPs are keen to point to anti-racist legislation as a prime example of how legislation can affect people's morality, the law is limited. True, anti-discriminatory legislation has brought about changes in the likes of employment and housing practice, but of itself it still cannot change people's attitudes. It doesn't touch their hearts. What is true of legislation regarding race is also true on the equally sensitive subjects of divorce, sexuality, euthanasia and capital punishment.

However, say MPs, such legislation gives signals to society in terms of helping to shape public opinion and practice.

Another recurring theme is the increasing complexity of those moral issues brought about by advancement in medical science.

Since the introduction of the 1967 Abortion Act, for instance, medical understanding has improved the viability of life – from before the cradle to the grave. We have the technology and knowledge to be able to create life in a test tube and to sustain life for longer. By the same token in 1990 the Human Fertilisation and Embryology Act legislated for medical techniques – in terms of work with human embryos – which were if not unimaginable then technically impossible at the time the Abortion Act was put on the statute book.

Since then genetic engineering has gained more public prominence through the cloning of Dolly the Sheep in 1997 and Hollywood films such as the 1998 *Gattaca*. Against such an on-rushing tide of technology MPs, most of whom are not experts in these matters, have to make decisions that will shape what they and their fellow citizens are allowed to do. All the while many of them recognise that just because a thing is technically possible it does not make it morally right.

Similarly just because something is legal doesn't, for many MPs, mean that it's morally acceptable. Abortion, for example, is legal but there are MPs who find it morally indefensible.

In June 1998 MPs voted by a majority of 207 to lower the age of homosexual consent to 16 under an amendment to the Crime and Disorder Bill. The result of that vote has done nothing to persuade opponents that homosexual acts are morally permissible.

Of the MPs featured in the series who voted, those in favour outnumbered those against by just one vote. Typically those who voted against the bill did so because they believe all homosexual acts are wrong whatever the age of the participants. While those who voted in favour did so on the grounds of equality and human rights.

ABORTION
Abortion is without doubt the single most difficult area in which MPs are called upon to exercise conscience. It epitomises the struggle of individual conscience in the absence of any unified Christian perspective. MPs readily admit the sensitive and emotional nature of the issue. They are well aware that abortion is no mere academic issue but is literally a flesh-and-blood matter of life and death.

Through correspondence, research and constituency surgeries they know that behind each unwanted pregnancy there is heartache and many agonising nights of wondering what to do. It is a subject no MP takes lightly.

Some Christian MPs are stridently anti-abortion. Ann Winterton, for example, is chair of the All Party Parliamentary Pro-Life Group, to which some other interviewees belong. Other MPs – no less Christian – take a different view. Typically they believe the current provision – termination up to 18 weeks with the consent of two doctors who consider the health of the mother to be in danger – to be about right. Any tightening up, they argue, should come in the application rather than by reducing the time limit in which termination is allowed.

There is general agreement on three areas: all abortion is regrettable; there should be no abortion on demand; a return to back-street abortion would be intolerable. Even given this amount of common ground Christians can find themselves in opposing lobbies. A male MP, for example, saying he is in favour of limited abortion does not see his stance as less Christian than an MP mother who abhors the idea of killing life in the womb. And neither is more Christian than those who confess to being somewhere in the middle.

PUBLIC OPINION
As if wrestling with the facts and philosophies surrounding moral issues were not enough MPs are also subjected to another mighty force – public opinion.

Around election time politicians, awash with the findings of the day's opinion poll, are keen to remind us that the only poll that counts is the election itself. Polling day is the ultimate expression of public opinion. While voters have been known to complain that the only time they see politicians is when they want their vote, an election is not a one-off demonstration of public opinion. It happens all the time.

MPs recognise the power of the press. They know the media can make or break a political career. They are frustrated at not always being correctly reported and that what they consider to be newsworthy is often not covered or is trivialised. They are outraged at intrusive reporting on their families. Personally, they say, 'we are fair game, but our families are not'.

A number of MPs are also part-time broadcasters or journalists. The two worlds enjoy a symbiotic relationship. Political stories fill TV schedules and newspapers pages. This is of mutual benefit. MPs get their views across to a wide audience. Journalists get their stories. MPs recognise that while they are occasionally victims of media misrepresentation, it is the price they must pay for democratic freedom of speech.

MPs also face daily inundation from professional lobbyists and pressure groups to give their attention to one cause or another. Their mail bags also contain letters of request and complaint from their constituents. Central Lobby at four o'clock, when expected and unsolicited guests meet MPs, resembles an airport lounge during delays and resounds to the chatter of two hundred voices. This is democracy at work. The people face to face with their elected representatives.

Not all opinion is expressed in such an intimate way.

Following the shooting of 16 schoolchildren and their teacher in Dunblane in 1996 public pressure was put on MPs through the media to tighten legislation regarding the licensing of gun clubs and the banning of

270

hand guns – which they subsequently did under the Firearms Arms (Amendment) (No 2) Act of 1997. After the fatal stabbing of London headmaster Philip Lawrence there was well voiced public disquiet about the carrying of dangerous knives. And prohibitive legislation was introduced in 1997 under the Knives Act. Mrs Lawrence's widow, Frances, initiated what became known as the morality debate and the teaching of good citizenship in schools became one of the widely discussed issues.

In 1997 the Labour government (whose spin doctors were keen on the prefix 'the people's') discovered an outpouring of people power when one of their backbenchers, Worcester MP Michael Foster, introduced a private member's bill to outlaw fox-hunting. In one of the biggest rallies in London since the anti-poll tax demonstration of the Thatcher era, the Countryside Alliance demonstrated its opposition to what it saw as townies misunderstanding and interfering in rural life.

Such intensive displays of public opinion are the exception, however. It is the gradual but definite shifting of values that slowly but surely shape the way MPs will react. Perhaps this is most clearly seen in the area of marriage. For years the percentage of couples marrying has fallen while the number of marriages ending in divorce has risen. One result in recent Parliaments has been the setting up of the Child Support Agency, whose primary function is to ensure the payment of maintenance. In 1996 the Conservative Government introduced the Family Law Bill with its provision for fault-free divorce after 12 months and recommendations for conciliation and increased pre-marriage counselling.

Divorce affects more than the parties involved, their children their families and their friends. Divorce has implications for government. A divorced couple need two homes instead of one. House-building puts demands on the environment. Governments have house-building and environmental policies. A divorced mother who has custody of the children needs income. If she is unemployed, she needs increased welfare benefit. If she has a job she might well need affordable child care provision. Governments have tax, social security, education and child care policies. Part of the New Deal announced by Labour in 1998 is to encourage lone parents to move out of benefits and into work. One of the contributors to this book, Frank Field, became Minister for Welfare Reform after the 1997 election. Another, Steve Webb, led the debate in December 1997 opposing proposed cuts to lone-parent benefits. Both are Christians!

MPs are under constant pressure to comply with the often conflicting views of the electorate. MPs' opinions, just like those of the people they represent, are shaped by personal experience. Those who have been through divorce, for instance, place a high value on a good marriage. It was

271

while hitch-hiking in the Soviet Union as young man that David Atkinson had his eyes opened to the persecution of Christians. A theme he now majors in as an MP. The fact that Andy Reed was adopted colours his view on abortion and the sanctity of life. Civil rights campaigner Paul Boateng was a refugee as a teenager.

It is easy for the public to think that public servants have only a public life. They don't. They had a life before parliament, they have one outside parliament and will have one after parliament. They are not immune from personal joy and heartache – nor from pressure or persuasion.

WHIPS

One way of safeguarding MPs – and getting legislation through the House in time – is the institution of the whip. Whips are responsible for getting their MPs through the correct voting lobby. There are many myths about the tactics whips employ to achieve compliance. At the time of her interview Bridget Prentice was a Labour whip and gives enlightening insight into the role, without dispelling too many myths!

Most of the time MPs follow the whip and vote as the party requires. Not all votes are straightforward. Voting on an amendment might mean voting in the No lobby in order to say yes to the amendment. With a daily mountain of mail, committee meetings, media invitations, surgeries and visiting school parties to escort around the Palace of Westminster between divisions, guidance from the whips on such occasions is particularly appreciated.

It is not always so. When MPs are under a running three-line whip, for example, they have to be available to vote at a moment's notice and are not allowed away from Westminster until late evening. (MPs abolished all-night sittings in 1994.) Whether their office is actually in the Palace or in one of the nearby government buildings makes no difference. It is seen as an inconvenience, especially by those who live within easy reach and who have young families.

DEFYING THE WHIP

All parties allow for a breadth of expression. Each party, for instance, has its share of Europhiles and Eurosceptics. No two MPs from any party will agree with each other about every single issue. Few agree with every jot and tittle of manifesto dogma. British politics is about compromise – finding the most workable solution for the greater good.

Occasionally, however, MPs find they cannot compromise. If attempts by the whips to accommodate their views, sometimes by getting an amendment included or reworded, fail, the MP is left with no option than to defy the whip or vote with the party, as Gary Streeter puts it, 'with a heavy heart.' They choose either to abstain or to vote against the party. Most MPs do not take such action lightly. The occasional personal rebellion is seen by parties as an allowable eccentricity – possibly even privately admired by those in authority as a public show of principle. Conscience is allowed to be exercised – but sparingly. Patience wears thin with those who rebel with regularity.

All but one of the 659 current MPs belong to a party. They were interviewed by a selection committee on the basis of their membership and commitment to their party. They were selected as the official candidate because of their allegiance to the party. They were elected because they represent the party. Voting with the whip is the expected expression of party loyalty. Besides MPs wouldn't be MPs if they didn't adhere in great measure with what the party stands for.

DIVIDED LOYALTIES?
While people of no faith are not strangers to personal conscience, Christians generally would claim allegiance to a higher authority. When Christian MPs face conflicts of conscience prior to voting the struggle can take on added significance. The vote becomes a test of ultimate loyalty. Put simple, will they do what God wants or what men want?

Some people might find it comforting to think that all Christian MPs vote alike on all issues – moral and partisan. But life is not that cut and dried – inside the House or out. Christian MPs don't make perfect decisions.

What they are clear on, however, is that they are 'Christian' first and 'MP' second. They recognise their relationship with God is eternal while their relationship with the electorate is transient. They use phrases such as 'the bedrock of my life' not to describe their being in Parliament but their faith in Jesus Christ.

A widely-held Westminster view is well expressed by David Wilshire; 'Anyone who translates the certainties of their Christian faith into absolute certainties about politics is going to have trouble...The best we can do is try to reason what we believe to be the Christian response and reflect on it alongside all the other pressures. I was elected primarily as a Conservative candidate, not because I am a Christian.'

In his interview Stephen Timms goes so far as to say that a candidate's Christian faith should play no part in the minds of the electorate. 'Whether or not somebody is a Christian is not particularly important in determining whether or not to vote for them at a general election,' he says. 'It should be a question of what their party policies are, how they're going to set about doing the job, and how available to their constituents they're going to be.'

The reader looking for an indication of a definitive Christian response to David Wilshire's 'other pressures' will be disappointed. MPs themselves see neither faith nor politics in black and white. Nor can they compartmentalise two of their biggest passions.

Many MPs would sympathise with Alun Michael's view; 'For me being a Christian, a member of the Labour Party and the Co-operative movement has no boundaries. I can't see where one stops and the other starts.'

MPs realise the dangers of being misunderstood by trumpeting allegiance to the will of God over the will of the party on issues such as lone-parent benefits. Jesus Christ, they acknowledge, laid down principles not policies. Jesus was God made manifest, not God-made manifesto.

When voting on moral issues Peter Pike, for one, knows exactly where his loyalties lie. 'On conscience issues I'm not answerable to my electors … nor to the Labour Party,' he says. 'I'm answerable to myself and to God.' From the opposite benches David Atkinson summarises his overall voting strategy in the Russian abbreviation of the former Soviet Union; 'CCCP – conscience, country, constituents and party'.

When Christian MPs speak of 'following conscience' the reader can reasonably translate this as 'doing what I sense God is telling me is right' or 'What I think Jesus would do in this situation'. The fact that they do not always express it in such spiritual-sounding language should not be taken as an indication of lack of Christian commitment.

DIFFERENCE?
If there is no definitive Christian voice and if Christians can have a wide range of political views, are Christian MPs markedly different from any other kind of MP?

One might also ponder whether Christian dentists or dustmen are any different from their non-Christian colleagues. For many Christians the comparison is not 'How different am I from him?' but 'How different am I from what I used to be.'

No interviewee expresses spiritual superiority over another colleague. The overwhelming view is that they don't neither want to sound nor be interpreted as Holy Joes. They know it is easy for anyone to describe themselves as a Christian. They recognise also, as Peter Lilley puts it, a responsibility in terms of personal behaviour; 'It's tempting to put your career ahead of the things you believe in . . . As a Christian I'm under a greater obligation to try to be honest and reasonable about opponents.'

For Christian MPs, as much as for the rest of us, the evidence of the genuineness of their faith is not just in what they say or do. It is what they are like and how they behave in public and in private.

FAMILY LIFE

MPs have more people to thank than their local selection panel, party hierarchy and voters. Married MPs recognise their indebtedness to their spouses and families. Quite simply they say they could not function as an MP without loyal support and encouragement. Even so the job puts stresses on family life. Typically Saturdays are taken up with constituency surgeries or fundraising events. Sunday is hardly a day of rest. For into it is crammed family worship (often MPs are guest of honour at civic services) quality family time, reading parliamentary papers and travelling back to London.

PERSONAL MORALITY

Because Christian MPs value their families so much they are particularly distressed when they hear of marriage problems among their Westminster colleagues.

Much is made in the media of MPs' failings. How do Christian MPs feel about public expectation that MPs should be above reproach?

The first overwhelming response is: 'We're only human!'

On the issue of cash for questions there is one Christian voice – MPs should not be on the take. They should not get paid twice for doing the same job. They should not misuse their position of power and influence. They should represent all of their people, not just those who can pay for extra favours.

There's also general agreement on the question of sex – Christian MPs are reluctant to cast the first stone. Yes, adultery is wrong, they agree, but it is 'regrettable' rather than unforgivable. Almost in mitigation they point to the isolation from family, loneliness, long hours working in close proximity with members of the opposite sex, the excitement of political achievements and the old adage that 'power is an aphrodisiac'. It should come as no surprise that some MPs fall. Christian MPs are not surprised. While they try to live up to Christian ideals in their own relationships they do not bay for the resignation of those who fail in theirs. As one puts it, 'Adultery is a bad thing. But to a Christian, funnily enough, it is much easier to recognise that we are all sinners.'

In the words of another, 'It is money that corrupts not personal relationships.' And the electorate, by implication, is not entitled to expect saintly behaviour from their representatives.

The pervading attitude is along the lines of 'there but for the grace of God go I!' But mixed with this understanding attitude there are those who wonder if an extra-marital affair isn't a betrayal of a fundamental requirement of a politician – trust. 'How can constituents trust a man who has cheated on his wife?' is the substance, if not the style, of the enquiry.

When it comes to the wider area of differences between an MP's private morality and public utterances, Christian MPs are generally agreed that what the public sees is what the public should get. An MP who has traded on the image of being a loyal family man in his campaign material should not be surprised if the public call for his resignation if it is later discovered he has a mistress. Gary Streeter puts it like this: 'MPs will fall short and we need to make allowances for that. MPs who make mistakes shouldn't be hounded out of office. The cardinal sin is hypocrisy. We shouldn't present ourselves as one sort of person, then say and do something very different behind the scenes. That's where people lose trust and confidence in their leaders.'

And that's why, as this series has attempted to show, Christian MPs are united in their efforts to exorcise the spirit of cynicism. They want confidence in parliamentary democracy restored. They want MPs to be trustworthy and trusted. They want, in the words of the Bible, for righteousness to exalt the nation. And they know it must begin with them.

Table of Events

29 March	The Chief Secretary to the Treasury [Jonathan Aitken] denies that he had known that a company of which he was a non-executive director had broken the Government's arms embargo by selling arms to Iran in the 1980s.
20 April	Conservative MPs David Tredinnick and Graham Riddick are suspended from the House of Commons for accepting cash for questions from a *Sunday Times* reporter in July 1994.
11 May	The Nolan Committee publishes its first report.
4 July	John Major defeats John Redwood in the election for the leadership of the Conservative Party.
28 August	James Molyneaux announces his resignation as leader of the Ulster Unionist Party.
6 September	David Trimble is elected Ulster Unionist leader.
6 November	Opposition amendment requiring MPs to disclose how much they earn from outside consultancies is passed.
4 December	David Trimble holds talks with SDLP leader John Hume.
7 December	Public fears rise after conflicting reports of possible links between BSE in cattle and Creutzfeld-Jakob disease (CJD) in humans.
8 December	Headmaster Philip Lawrence stabbed to death defending a pupil outside his London school.
11 December	Rev Martin Smyth interviewed for *Christians in the House*.
19 December	Frank Field interviewed for *Christians in the House*.

1996

9 February	The IRA announces an end to its 1994 ceasefire. At 7pm a bomb explodes in London's Docklands, resulting in two deaths and more than a hundred people injured.
15 February	Scott Report on the Arms-to-Iraq Affair is published.
21 February	Peter Luff interviewed for *Christians in the House*.
22 February	Derek Foster interviewed for *Christians in the House*.

13 March	Sixteen schoolchildren and one teacher shot dead in Dunblane.
20 March	Government admits possible link between BSE and CJD.
21 March	Five European countries ban the import of British beef. Prices at cattle markets fall and consumers boycott British beef and beef products.
28 March	Government bans beef products from cattle over 30 months old.
8 April	Tony Blair is severely criticised after his Easter article in previous day's *Sunday Telegraph* is taken to imply a link between Christianity and party allegiance.
11 April	Simon Hughes interviewed for *Christians in the House*.
24 April	Home Secretary announces month-long firearms amnesty.
7 May	Nolan Register of MPs' Interests is published.
14 May	David Amess interviewed for *Christians in the House*. Paul Tyler interviewed for *Christians in the House*.
21 May	The Prime Minister says Britain would use its veto to block EU policy initiatives until ban on British beef is lifted.
10 June	British and Irish governments hold all-party talks on Northern Ireland at Stormont Castle, Belfast. Sinn Fein is excluded having failed to call a ceasefire.
24 June	Secretary of State for Social Security Peter Lilley announces that the Government is preparing emergency legislation to restore its powers to cut off benefits for asylum seekers.
27 June	Peter Lilley interviewed for *Christians in the House*.
2 July	Michael Mates interviewed for *Christians in the House*.
4 July	Fault-free divorce after 12 months becomes possible under Family Law Act.
10 July	MPs vote themselves a 26 per cent pay increase.
24 July	Ann Winterton interviewed for *Christians in the House*.

12 August	Government launches 'demon-eyes' poster campaign, in which Tony Blair is depicted with demon eyes.
27 August	Paul Boateng interviewed for *Christians in the House*.
11 September	Brian Mawhinney interviewed for *Christians in the House*.
16 September	Roderick Wright, Catholic Bishop of Argyll and the Isles resigns and goes into hiding with a woman from his diocese.
26 September	Ann Widdecombe interviewed for *Christians in the House*.
16 October	Cullen Report on the murders at Dunblane is published.
22 October	Stephen Timms interviewed for *Christians in the House*.
23 October	Frances Lawrence, widow of murdered headmaster Stephen Lawrence, launches personal manifesto on rights and responsibilities of good citizenship. MPs are quick to align themselves to this morality debate.
24 October	Alan Beith interviewed for *Christians in the House*.
29 October	Andrew Rowe interviewed for *Christians in the House*.
30 October	John Gummer interviewed for *Christians in the House*.
31 October	Nicholas Winterton interviewed for *Christians in the House*.
13 November	John Battle interviewed for *Christians in the House*.
	Jim Wallace interviewed for *Christians in the House*.
18 November	A House of Commons motion to impose a total ban on handguns is defeated by 25 votes.
5 December	Peter Pike interviewed for *Christians in the House*
11 December	David Willetts resigns as Paymaster-General after a report by the House of Commons committee on standards and privileges says he had "dissembled" when giving evidence on the cash for questions issue.

| 12 December | Andrew Welsh interviewed for *Christians in the House.* |
| 17 December | Gary Streeter interviewed for *Christians in the House.* |

1997

16 January	The Government becomes a minority administration.
28 January	Alun Michael interviewed for *Christians in the House.* Iuaen Wyn Jones interviewed for *Christians in the House.*
5 February	National Lottery mid-week draw is introduced.
9 February	IRA announces end of ceasefire.
19 March	Sale and possession of combat knives is restricted under the Knives Act.
21 March	The Education Act abolishes the assisted-places scheme for secondary schools.
26 March	Tim Smith resigns as a candidate in the General Election having previously admitted receiving undeclared payments from businessman Mohamed Al Fayed. Neil Hamilton resists pressure to stand down over cash for questions affair.
6 April	BBC correspondent, Martin Bell stands as anti-sleaze candidate in Tatton against Neil Hamilton.
8 April	A report, *Unemployment and the Future of Work*, is published by a working party representing 11 Christian denominations.
16 April	Prime Minister John Major appeals for support for his 'wait and see' policy on a single European currency.
1 May	The Labour Party gains 44.4per cent of the vote in the general election and has a majority of 179.
2 May	Mo Mowlam is appointed Secretary of State for Northern Ireland and visits Belfast.
16 May	Prime Minister Tony Blair makes his first visit to Northern Ireland and says that Government officials are prepared to hold talks with Sinn Fein.
19 May	Health Secretary Frank Dobson announces a ban on the sponsoring of sport by the tobacco industry as part of the Government's drive to reduce smoking.
20 May	Minister for Welfare Reform Frank Field announces welfare to work scheme.

281

21 May	Talks are held between Sinn Fein and Government officials in Belfast.
2 June	The Prime Minister, outlines plans to help the unemployed find work and says that people who decline help could lose up to 40per cent of their benefits. Chris Smith, the National Heritage Secretary orders the directors of Camelot, the National Lottery operator, to forgo their large pay rises and bonuses.
3 June	Worcester MP Michael Foster launches private member's bill to ban fox-hunting.
10 June	Peter Lilley withdraws after the first round of the election for the leadership of the Conservative Party.
19 June	William Hague is elected Conservative Party leader.
25 June	The Prime Minister announces talks on the future of Northern Ireland to commence in September 1997 and conclude in May 1998.
2 July	Secretary of State for Social Security Harriet Harman announces Government's New Deal for lone parents. The plan is to move half a million lone parents off benefits and into work.
3 July	Report published by the Parliamentary Commissioner for Standards finds five Conservative MPs to have accepted cash from businessman Mohammed Al Fayed for furthering his interests.
8 July	Bridget Prentice interviewed for *Christians in the House*.
10 July	Countryside Alliance holds mass anti-hunting ban rally in central London.
19 July	The IRA announces a restoration of its 1994 ceasefire from 12 noon on the 20 July.
22 July	Government White Paper sets out proposals for an elected Welsh Assembly.
23 July	Education and Employment Secretary David Blunkett announces scheme to replace student grants with increased student loans and a means-tested parental contribution toward tuition fees. ·

24 July	Government announces proposals for a Scottish Parliament.
27 August	David Atkinson interviewed for *Christians in the House*.
29 August	Mo Mowlam announces her intention to invite Sinn Fein to enter peace talks process.
10 September	Tony Colman interviewed for *Christians in the House*.
11 September	Scotland votes overwhelmingly for a Scottish Parliament.
7 September	Peter Robinson interviewed for *Christians in the House*.
18 September	Electors in Wales vote in favour of a Welsh Assembly.
24 September	Gillian Shephard interviewed for *Christians in the House*.
4 November	Colin Breed interviewed for *Christians in the House*.
6 November	Caroline Spelman interviewed for *Christians in the House*.
7 November	Minister for Public Health Tessa Jowell under fire after Government announces exemption for motor racing industry from ban on tobacco advertising. Ms Jowell's husband resigned his position as non-executive director of a Formula One company shortly after Ms Jowell's appointment in May.
8 November	Prime Minister under pressure to reveal whether the Labour Party received a £1 million donation from motor racing boss Bernie Ecclestone.
12 November	Ken Maginnis interviewed for *Christians in the House*.
18 November	Joan Humble interviewed for *Christians in the House*.
19 November	Martyn Jones interviewed for *Christians in the House*.
27 November	Handguns banned under the Firearms Amendment (No2) Act.
1 December	Prime Minister appoints Lord Jenkins as chair of the Commission on Voting Systems to investigate viable alternatives to the first-past-the-post system.

10 December	Forty-seven Labour backbenchers vote against Government plans to cut lone–parent benefit.
11 December	Chris Smith interviewed for *Christians in the House*.

1998

20 January	Andy Reed interviewed for *Christians in the House*.
21 January	Ruth Kelly interviewed for *Christians in the House*.
20 February	Tessa Jowell interviewed for *Christians in the House*.
4 March	David Wilshire interviewed for *Christians in the House*.
22 May	People of Northern Ireland vote by more than 70 per cent to accept Good Friday Agreement.
9 June	Steve Webb interviewed for *Christians in the House*. Desmond Swayne interviewed for *Christians in the House*.
10 June	Jeffrey Donaldson interviewed for *Christians in the House*.
16 June	David Drew interviewed for *Christians in the House*.
18 June	Government announces National Minimum Wage of £3.60 to commence in April 1999.
22 June	MPs vote by a 207 majority to lower the age of homosexual consent to 16.
25 June	Elections to the Northern Ireland Assembly.
1 July	David Trimble is elected First Minister of Northern Ireland Assembly. Seamus Mallon becomes Deputy First Minister.
5 July	*The Observer* prints allegations that some Government advisers were involved in cash-for-access schemes between political lobbyists and Labour MPs.
7 July	Michael Foster interviewed for *Christians in the House*.
22 July	House of Lords votes against Government plans to reduce the age of homosexual consent to 16 by a majority of 168.
27 July	Stuart Bell interviewed for *Christians in the House*. Legg Report into Arms-to-Africa affair accuses

	Foreign Office ministers and officials of playing down a UN ban on arms exports to Sierra Leone. Ministers were cleared of colluding with arms exporter Sandline International to defy the sanction.
30 July	Seamus Mallon interviewed for *Christians in the House*.
15 August	The Real IRA detonates a bomb in Omagh, Co Tyrone killing 28 Saturday shoppers and injuring hundreds more.
2 September	Parliament reconvenes to introduce new anti-terrorist legislation.
9 September	The Real IRA announces ceasefire. Renfrewshire MP Tommy Graham is expelled from the Labour Party over allegations of sleaze.
14 September	Northern Ireland Assembly meets in inaugural session.